THIS IS NOT A GRAIL ROMANCE

THIS IS NOT A GRAIL ROMANCE

UNDERSTANDING
HISTORIA PEREDUR VAB EFRAWC

NATALIA I. PETROVSKAIA

UNIVERSITY OF WALES PRESS
2023

© Natalia I. Petrovskaia, 2023

All rights reserved. No part of this book may be reproduced in any material form (including photocopying or storing it in any medium by electronic means and whether or not transiently or incidentally to some other use of this publication) without the written permission of the copyright owner except in accordance with the provisions of the Copyright, Designs and Patents Act. Applications for the copyright owner's written permission to reproduce any part of this publication should be addressed to the University of Wales Press, University Registry, King Edward VII Avenue, Cardiff CF10 3NS.

www.uwp.co.uk

British Library Cataloguing-in-Publication Data
A catalogue record for this book is available from the British Library.

ISBN 978-1-83772-036-1
eISBN 978-1-83772-037-8

The right of Natalia I. Petrovskaia to be identified as author of this work has been asserted in accordance with sections 77 and 79 of the Copyright, Designs and Patents Act 1988.

The University of Wales Press gratefully acknowledges the funding support of the Maartje Draak Fund from the Royal Netherlands Academy of Arts and Sciences, of the Utrecht University Institute for Cultural Inquiry, and of the Books Council of Wales, in publication of this book.

Typeset by Marie Doherty
Printed by CPI Antony Rowe, Melksham, United Kingdom

Contents

Acknowledgements — vii
List of Tables and Figures — ix
Abbreviations — xi

Introduction — 1

1 The Structure of the Narrative — 15
2 The Geography and Landscapes of *Peredur* — 59
3 Historical Context and the Empress — 83
4 Literary Context: *Peredur* and Some Lost Tales — 97
5 *Peredur* and Welsh Law — 115
6 The Witches of Gloucester and Other Problematic Characters — 137

Conclusion — 153

Bibliography — 157
Index — 177

Acknowledgements

I began thinking of *Peredur* again after reading Prof. Paul Russell's 'Three Notes on *Canu Urien*', in 2020. This led to the publication of my 'Peredur and the Problem of Inappropriate Questions' in the *Journal of the International Arthurian Society* in 2021, which in turn led me to revisit some of my other thoughts on Peredur and generated this book. I would like to thank the editors of the *Journal of the International Arthurian Society* and De Gruyter for permission to reprint a revised version of that article as Chapter 5 of this book. I am enormously grateful to Prof. Paul Russell for his comments on early drafts of both the article and the book and to Prof. Peter Schrijver for his comments on the structural analysis presented in Chapter 1. I would also like to thank the anonymous reviewer who read the book for the University of Wales Press for the enormously helpful suggestions and comments, and also Llion Wigley, Dafydd Jones and all the team at the press whose patient and meticulous work has turned this text into a published volume.

The publication of the book was made possible through the generosity of the Maartje Draak Fund from the Royal Netherlands Academy of Arts and Sciences, of the Utrecht University Institute for Cultural Inquiry, and of the Books Council of Wales.

List of Tables and Figures

Table 1	Correspondence for episodic structure of *Peredur*	17
Table 2	Occurrence of 'Constantinople' terms in medieval Welsh manuscripts	90
Table 3	Comparison of poisoned apple episodes	104
Figure 1	Fractal structure of *Peredur* (Short Version), shown as a Sierpiński gasket	26

ABBREVIATIONS

DIAS Dublin Institute for Advanced Studies
DMF *Dictionnaire du Moyen Français (1330–1500)*, *www.atilf.fr/dmf*
GPC *Geiriadur Prifysgol Cymru*, *https://geiriadur.ac.uk/gpc/gpc.html*
NLW National Library of Wales
RB Red Book of Hergest (Oxford, Jesus College, MS 111, *c*.1382×1400)
TYP[2] Rachel Bromwich (ed.), *Trioedd Ynys Prydein*, 2nd edn (Cardiff: University of Wales Press, 1978)

Introduction

Ceci n'est pas une pipe, declares René Magritte's famous 1929 painting of a pipe. The curved shape of the pipe probably evokes in many viewers childhood memories of illustrated editions of Sir Arthur Conan Doyle's Sherlock Holmes books.[1] Yet if one reads the books carefully, Holmes, in the original, does not have the trademark pipe either. Memory, or in this case, cultural memory enriched by the accumulation of later tradition, has a propensity for playing tricks.

The title of this book takes inspiration from Magritte's painting and from Michel Foucault's essay discussing that painting.[2] The impossibility of resolving a contradiction that does not have the key components requiring it to be a contradiction, such as two separate contradictory statements, or even a single whole statement that contradicts itself internally, which Foucault brings forward in his discussion of Magritte's painting, is precisely the impossibility of the medieval Welsh text *Historia Peredur vab Efrawc* (henceforth, *Peredur*).[3] This text presents the hero and much of the plotline of what in other vernacular European versions is the Grail romance.[4] It even has the scene that is generally referred to as 'the Grail procession'.[5] There is, however, no Grail in this text. Instead, the procession presents the reader with the usual spear and, instead of the Grail, a human head.[6]

The exact relationship of this text with the rest of the Grail romance tradition has crystallised into a very specific debate aimed at establishing its relationship with the earliest Grail romance proper, Chrétien de Troyes's *Le conte du graal*, also known as *Perceval* (and, henceforth, so referred to in this book), finished but not completed around 1190–1.[7] Whether the Welsh text is based on this or reflects traces of some earlier text that also informed the French composition, was a matter of heated debate for the better part of the twentieth and well into the twenty-first century, and is an extension of the difficulties of dating the Welsh text itself.[8] The pendulum continues to swing (and this book intends to give it another gentle nudge), but it seems to show a general predilection for the view that *Peredur*, at least in the form in which it now survives, is an adaptation of *Perceval*. Nevertheless, increasing numbers of authoritative voices have expressed concerns in recent years that reading the Welsh text in light of the French text is liable to lead scholarly enquiry into various and unenviable states of impasse.[9] We therefore find ourselves in the position of a hypothetical viewer of Magritte's painting who has never seen a pipe, and is looking at the painting through blurred spectacles, with Foucault whispering loudly 'ceci n'est pas une pipe'. We have a Grail romance that is not a Grail romance. It is also – a point to which we will return – not a romance.[10]

While it will be argued below, following Ian Lovecy's suggestion, that *Peredur* should not be taken as a single story any more than an episodic television or film series of the twentieth century should be, for the purposes of this introduction, and following scholarly convention, a brief outline of the surviving 'whole' is in order, to provide a framework for the following discussion.[11] It will be dealt with in a more thorough manner in Chapter 1. The plot of *Peredur*, insofar as it can be characterised as a single plot, as it has been hitherto, is similar in many ways to that of *Perceval*. Peredur is brought up in ignorance of knighthood, until one day he encounters three knights. Deciding to be like them, he journeys to Arthur's court. There, after avenging an insult to the Queen – which in the Welsh text follows the specifics of the Welsh legal tradition – he leaves because of another insult. This is followed by visits to two uncles and a magic castle. In the castle, Peredur witnesses mysterious objects being brought in (this is an element of the Grail legend). This, in turn, is followed by more adventures, one of which involves his meeting and living for fourteen years with the Empress of Constantinople, whom he marries.[12] A short early version of the story, for which we have a surviving manuscript witness (discussed in the context of the text's manuscript tradition) ends here with the words: 'Ac y velly y tervyna kynnyd paredur ap Efrawc' ('And so ends the *kynnyd* of Peredur ab Efrawg').[13] This has been read previously as a suggestion that the marriage wraps up the narrative. For the purposes of our structural analysis, the section that follows this part of the text in the longer versions in the White Book and Red Book will be referred to as the 'Continuation'.[14] This designation is justified by the fact that even for the longer version of the tale preserved in these manuscripts, the marriage is usually regarded as an ending for a section of the tale.[15] The narrative that follows this episode in the longer versions of *Peredur* attempts to explain the preceding episodes but confuses some details with those of the French romance.[16]

Typically for native medieval Welsh prose texts, *Peredur* appears to have been composed at an indefinite time before the creation of its earliest surviving manuscript witness, and its exact date of composition has therefore been a subject of debate.[17] It is preserved in four codices, ranging from the second part of the thirteenth century to the end of the fourteenth century.[18] The medieval witnesses[19] to the tale are:

- NLW, Peniarth 7 (s. xiii[2]), frag.;
- NLW, Peniarth 14ii (s. xiv[1]), frag.;
- NLW, Peniarth 4–5, 'White Book of Rhydderch' (*c*.1350); and
- Jesus College, Oxford, MS 111 'Red Book of Hergest' (*c*.1382×1400).

These four manuscripts preserve what appear to be two different versions of the tale, possibly representing different stages in its development.[20] According to Thomas Charles-Edwards, this development is characterised by a process of growth: from short (Peniarth 7) to long versions (White Book and Red Book), with any correspondence between relative dates of the manuscript and of the versions due to chance.[21] The fragmentary nature of the Peniarth 14 text, which breaks off before the conclusion of the short version, makes it impossible to determine its length.

The two earliest manuscripts are fragmentary, containing incomplete copies of the tale: Peniarth 7 has lost the beginning of the tale as a result of damage to the manuscript, as well as a folio in the middle of the tale, resulting in a gap in the text.[22] It contains what has been generally accepted to be a complete Short Version of *Peredur*, which concludes with the hero's marriage to the Empress of Constantinople and includes the concluding phrase already quoted. Peniarth 14 lacks the end of that tale, also due to loss, and the text preserved in this manuscript is interrupted soon after Peredur leaves his first uncle's house, and it contains neither the procession nor any subsequent episodes. The White Book and the Red Book contain two examples of the longest, expanded version of the tale, continuing the narrative on lines corresponding to those of Chrétien's text. I will argue in the following chapter that this 'Continuation' mimics the incomplete nature of the French narrative (and also mirrors the French 'Continuations').[23]

The survival of multiple different versions, a lack of certainty regarding the date of composition (and relationship with the French text), as well as the lack of a Grail, make for a difficult starting point for a discussion of *Peredur*. The text is also difficult because it escapes categorisation. Elements of its plot, its main character and some of its episodes link it irrevocably with the literary family of Grail romances, but it is not one of them. It is also, and this must be re-emphasised, not a 'romance'. In most early discussions, *Peredur* has been categorised as one of the three Welsh 'romances' (the other two being *Iarlles y Ffynnanwn* ('Lady of the Fountain'), also known by the name of its protagonist as *Owein*; and *Ystoria Gereint vab Erbin*).[24] None of the three are 'romances' – a generic designation borrowed from the medieval Francophone literary tradition – and they do not, despite appearances, belong together in a group.[25] The debate regarding the exact nature of their relationship with the French equivalents, under the misleading label *Mabinogionfrage*, raged for the better part of the twentieth century.[26] *Peredur* is not devoid of Continental influences, because it borrows some descriptions of its episodes, particularly in the later part of the tale, from Chrétien's romance. However, it is also not a translation of Chrétien's romance, because it contains a large number of episodes and narrative elements that are absent in the French text (and, indeed, in any other version of the Perceval/Grail story). It is, as will be argued further here, not even a single text, for the earliest manuscript preserves a shorter complete version of the narrative that is expanded and added to in the later versions (with some contradictions).[27] It is a fascinating text that is both difficult to understand and difficult to discuss.

By the fifteenth century, the name of Peredur, even in Wales, had become associated with the Grail legend proper, with all of its religious connotations as imported from the Continent, particularly in *Y Seint Greal*, the Welsh translation of the *Queste del Saint Graal* and *Perlesvaus*.[28] The triad relating to Grail heroes preserved in National Library of Wales (NLW), MS Peniarth 50 (Glamorgan, s. xv[med.]) names Peredur alongside heroes who had never formed part of the native Welsh tradition: Lancelot, Galahad and Bort:[29]

Tri Marchawc o Lys Arthur a enillawd y Greal, ac eu duc y Nef:

> Galaad vab Lawnslot y Lac,
> a Pheredur vab Efrawc Iarll,
> a Bort vab Brenhin Bort.

A'(r) ddeu gyntaf oeddynt wery o gyrff. A'(r) trydydd oedd ddiweir, am na wnaeth pechawt knawdawl ont unweith. A hynny drwy brovedigaeth yn yr amser y ennillawd ef ... verch Brenyn Brangor, yr honn a vv Ymherodres yn Constinobyl, o'r honn y deuth y Genedlaeth vwyaf or byt; ac o'r genedlaeth Joseph o Arimathia y hanoedynt yll tri, ac o lin David brofwyt, mal y tystolaetha *Ystorya y Greal*.

Three knights of Arthur's Court who won the Graal, and it brought them to Heaven:

> Galaad son of Lawnslot of the Lake,
> and Peredur son of Earl Efrawg,
> and Bort son of King Bort.

And the two first were virgin of body. And the third was chaste, for only once had he committed bodily sin; and that, through temptation, at the time when he won ... daughter of King Brangor, who was empress in Constantinople, and from whom was descended the greatest race in the world. All three were sprung of the race of Joseph of Arimathea, and of the lineage of Prophet David, as the History of the Grail testifies.

The medieval Welsh triads are a notoriously difficult source to interpret as we have no definite knowledge of their use.[30] The received opinion is that they form an index to a broader and now mostly lost literary and poetic tradition, originally functioning as mnemonic devices, referring to traditions and narratives known to contemporaries – although by the time this triad was composed, it is possible that they had acquired a more antiquarian veneer, providing more than an index to narratives.[31] The particular text quoted here, with its references to chastity, Joseph of Arimathea and the *Ystorya y Greal*, is illustrative of the process of assimilation of *Peredur* into the imported Grail tradition, for it is attested in a multilingual manuscript and the triad appears to be the redactor's work.[32] Peniarth 50 is famously multilingual (containing texts in Middle English and Latin alongside those in Welsh) and was probably produced in a monastery that was Cistercian, and thus belonging to the order that appears to have been exceptionally active in literary transmission and translation in Wales.[33] As Rachel Bromwich notes, this triad is based on

Y Seint Greal.[34] The reference to the Empress of *Constinobyl* is interesting in light of *Peredur*, for an empress associated with a similarly named location – conventionally translated as 'Constantinople' – appears in that tale (and will be discussed further in Chapter 3). At this stage, on the evidence of the Welsh *Y Seint Greal* and the triad quoted earlier, we can say with some confidence that the association of Peredur's story with the Grail is not a product of modern confusion, but rather represents a stage in the development of medieval Welsh literary tradition under the influence of translated and imported material. Just how much this process was one of conscious reconciliation of different and contradictory traditions, and how early this process began (in other words, whether the texts of *Peredur*, as we have them, already represent an early stage in that process) remains to be determined.

The main objective of *This is Not a Grail Romance* is to examine some of the most striking and unique features of *Peredur* in the context of the society and culture that transmitted and copied it. The purpose of this book, therefore, is not to provide a complete companion to *Peredur*, nor is it to answer all the questions surrounding this difficult text. Rather, it takes its cue from Brynley F. Roberts's description of the earliest version of the text as 'part of a body of material with its own cultural cross-referencing, often unstated and understood'.[35] The present book represents a series of consistent attempts to reconstruct some of these cultural cross-references. In some cases, the suggestions are extremely tentative, as with the reconstruction of the hypothetical lost story of the apples at Arthur's court (Chapter 4), while in other cases, such as that of Peredur's questions (Chapter 5), they are offered with a greater degree of confidence.[36] In all cases, the contextual reading is offered here as a possibility and is intended primarily to question our implicit assumptions regarding the tale, most of which can be traced to a tradition of English translations of the text now almost two centuries old.[37] The primary objective of this book is not to disprove previous readings of and theories about this text, but rather to offer a series of alternative interpretations in order to promote further engagement. The analysis presented here is not intended as the final word on the subject, but rather as a contribution to an ongoing conversation.

The starting point for most arguments made in this book is that the text was supposed to make sense, at least to the medieval audience. That the text was not written as a work Dadaist *avant la lettre* is the axiom on which most of the reasoning here is based. Allowance is made for the possibility that certain aspects of the narrative might have been altered in transmission, and that some of the cultural references may be largely irrecoverable as a result. Scribes and redactors are human, and therefore fallible. However, human error is never the default assumption. Had it been so, we might have dismissed *Peredur* as a strange text that makes no sense and left it at that. Instead, this book aims to uncover, where possible, the cultural, social, political, economic and literary contexts that the medieval audiences of the text would have had knowledge of, which would make sense of the seemingly strange aspects of the surviving tale. In some cases, the precise context might be irrecoverable to the modern reader, and for those cases, suggestions are made as to where the gaps in our knowledge might lie. The emphasis in *This is Not a Grail Romance* lies heavily on potential contemporary references in the text.

The book was not initially conceived as a single project. It stems, rather, from several distinct attempts to make sense of individual aspects of the text, and attempts to place these aspects in their proper context. I first became interested in this text as a starry-eyed undergraduate, writing my first dissertation under the supervision of Prof. Paul Russell in the early years of the twenty-first century. *Peredur* has since become a text to which I return with fresh enthusiasm between other projects, projects that engage primarily with medieval conceptions of geography and spatiality. Eventually, over the years, a distinct pattern in my interpretation of this text has begun to emerge. *This is Not a Grail Romance* presents a systematic argument based on that pattern.

Notes

1 For a discussion of the iconography of Sir Arthur Conan Doyle's Sherlock Holmes, see, for example, Christophe Gelly, 'Sir Arthur Conan Doyle's Sherlock Holmes Stories: Crime and Mystery from the Text to the Illustrations', *Cahiers victoriens et édouardiens*, 73 (2011), 93–106.

2 Michel Foucault, *Ceci n'est pas une pipe* (Montpellier: Fata Morgana, [1973] 2010); Michel Foucault, trans. by R. Howard, 'Ceci n'est pas une pipe', *October*, 1 (1976), 6–21.

3 Foucault, *Ceci n'est pas une pipe*, pp. 11–14; Foucault, 'Ceci n'est pas une pipe', 8–9. For an edition of the *Historia Peredur*, see Glenys Witchard Goetinck (ed.), *Historia Peredur vab Efrawc* (Cardiff: University of Wales Press, 1976). All references to the text in the present study are to this edition, unless otherwise noted. The most recent translation of the text is in S. Davies (trans.), *The Mabinogion* (Oxford: Oxford University Press, 2007), pp. 65–102. All references to the translation of *Historia Peredur* in the present discussion are

to this translation, unless otherwise noted. Other editions of the text include, for the text preserved in the White Book of Rhydderch, Peter Wynn Thomas (ed.), *Peredur: Golygiad Lleiafol* (Cardiff: Cardiff University, 2000), circulating in digital form only; I am grateful to the University of Wales Press's anonymous reviewer for acquainting me with the existence of this edition. An edition of the National Library of Wales manuscripts Peniarth 7 and Peniarth 14 based on a transcription slightly different from that included in Goetinck's edition, provided alongside an English translation, is available in Anthony M. Vitt, '*Peredur vab Efrawc*: Edited Texts and Translations of the MSS Peniarth 7 and 14 Versions' (MPhil thesis, University of Aberystwyth, 2010), pp. 136–7. Previous translations of the text include those published in Jeoffrey Gantz (trans.), *The Mabinogion* (Harmondsworth and New York: Penguin, 1976); and Gwyn Jones and Thomas Jones (trans.), *The Mabinogion* (London: Everyman, [1949] 1993). Previous volumes dedicated to this text are Glenys Goetinck, *Peredur: a Study of Welsh Tradition in the Grail Legends* (Cardiff: University of Wales Press, 1975); and the essays in Sioned Davies and Peter Wynn Thomas (eds), *Canhwyll Marchogyon: Cyd-destunoli Peredur* (Cardiff: University of Wales Press, 2000). See also a review of the latter in Paul Russell, 'Texts in Contexts: Recent Work on the *Mabinogi*', *Cambrian Medieval Celtic Studies*, 45 (2003), 59–72. I use the spelling 'Efrawc' throughout, following Goetinck's edition, for consistency's sake, unless quoting from secondary sources that use a different spelling.

4 The relationship of this text to the grail romance tradition has been the subject of many studies, references are provided; see p. 9, n. 8 of this book. For a general discussion of the European grail romance tradition, see, for instance, Richard Barber, *The Holy Grail: Imagination and Belief* (Cambridge MA: Harvard University Press, 2004).

5 Goetinck (ed.), *Historia Peredur*, p. 20; Davies (trans.), *Mabinogion*, p. 73. For a comparison between the French and Welsh 'Grail' processions, see, for instance, Jean Marx, *La légende arthurienne et le graal* (Paris: Presses universitaires de France, 1952), p. 204 n. 3, p. 383; see also the discussion in Chapter 4, which contains further references.

6 Goetinck (ed.), *Historia Peredur*, p. 20; Davies (trans.), *Mabinogion*, p. 73. This element has been much discussed; for references, see notes to Chapter 5.

7 The French text has been edited multiple times. See, for example, Chrétien de Troyes, *The Story of the Grail (Li Contes del Graal) or Perceval*, ed. by R. T. Pickens, trans. by W. W. Kibler (New York and London: Garland, 1990); Chrétien de Troyes, *Le Roman de Perceval ou Le Conte du Graal*, ed. by K. Busby (Tübingen: Max Niemeyer Verlag, 1993); Chrétien de Troyes, *Le Conte du Graal*, ed. by C. Méla, in *Chrétien de Troyes. Romans* (Paris: Livre de Poche, 1994). The latter edition is referred to throughout the present book. The

INTRODUCTION

translation used here is *Chrétien de Troyes: Arthurian Romances*, trans. by W. K. Kibler (London: Penguin Books, 1991).

8   For discussions on the possible relationship between the Welsh and French versions of the text, see Ian C. Lovecy, '*Historia Peredur ab Efrawg*', in Rachel Bromwich, A. O. H. Jarman and Brynley F. Roberts (eds), *Arthur of the Welsh: the Arthurian Legend in Medieval Welsh Literature* (Cardiff: University of Wales Press, 1991), pp. 171–82; Michelle Szkilnik, 'Medieval Translations and Adaptations of Chrétien's Works', in Norris J. Lacy and Joan T. Grimbert (eds), *A Companion to Chrétien de Troyes*, Arthurian Studies LXIII (Cambridge: Brewer, 2005), pp. 202–13 (pp. 207–8); Idris Llewelyn Foster, '*Gereint, Owein, and Peredur*', in R. S. Loomis (ed.), *Arthurian Literature in the Middle Ages: a Collaborative History* (Oxford: Clarendon Press, 1959), pp. 192–205 (pp. 199–204); Susan Aronstein, 'Becoming Welsh: Counter-Colonialism and the Negotiation of Native Identity in *Peredur vab Efrawc*', *Exemplaria*, 17 (2005), 135–68 (158–9). For a more general discussion of the 'Welsh romances', see Ceridwen Lloyd-Morgan, 'Medieval Welsh Tales or Romances? Problems of Genre and Terminology', *Cambrian Medieval Celtic Studies*, 47 (2004), 41–58. Further discussions are referred to throughout this book.

9   For instance, Ceridwen Lloyd-Morgan, 'Narrative Structure in *Peredur*', *Zeitschrift für celtische Philologie*, 38 (1981), 187–231 (187). John K. Bollard, 'Theme and Meaning in *Peredur*', *Arthuriana*, 10 (2000), 73–92, that the recent tendency to evaluate these texts in their own cultural context has been beneficial (73).

10 See p. 4 and p. 11, n. 25 of this book.

11 Lovecy, '*Historia Peredur*', p. 177. For an analysis of the structure, see Chapter 1. For a summary of the tale, see also Brynley F. Roberts, '*Peredur Son of Efrawg*: A Text in Transition', *Arthuriana*, 10 (2000), 57–72 (60–2).

12 For more on the Empress of Constantinople in this narrative, see Glenys Goetinck, 'The Female Characters in *Peredur*', *Transactions of the Honourable Society of Cymmrodorion*, (1966), 378–86; Natalia I. Petrovskaia, 'Dating *Peredur*: New Light on Old Problems', *Proceedings of the Harvard Celtic Colloquium*, 29 (2009), 223–43; and Chapter 3.

13 Goetinck (ed.), *Historia Peredur*, p. 181; I have expanded the abbreviation. Translation from Lloyd-Morgan, 'Migrating Narratives: Peredur, Owain and Geraint', in Helen Fulton (ed.), *A Companion to Arthurian Literature* (Oxford and Malden: Wiley-Blackwell, 2009), pp. 128–56 (p. 130); as Lloyd-Morgan points out, *kynnyd* can be translated as both 'progress' and 'reign following conquest'. For a brief overview and further references, see Lloyd-Morgan, '*Historia Peredur ab Efrawc*', in Ceridwen Lloyd-Morgan and Erich Poppe (eds), *Arthur in the Celtic Languages: the Arthurian Legend in Celtic Literatures and Traditions*, Arthurian Literature in the Middle Ages 9 (Cardiff: University of Wales Press, 2019) pp. 145–57, p. 146.

14 As Lloyd-Morgan points out, this section of the text is 'detachable'; Lloyd-Morgan, '*Historia Peredur*', p. 153.
15 See, for example, Roberts, '*Peredur Son of Efrawg*', 60–2; Sioned Davies, 'Cynnyd Peredur vab Efrawc', in Sioned Davies and Peter Wynn Thomas (eds), *Canhwyll Marchogyon*, pp. 65–90 (pp. 68 and 70–1); and Aronstein, 'Becoming Welsh', p. 139.
16 Goetinck, *Peredur*, p. 80. See detailed discussion on pp. 36–41 of this book.
17 Goetinck suggests *c.*1100, possibly as late as 1137; Goetinck, *Peredur*, p. 36. See also S. Rodway, 'The Where, Who, When and Why of Medieval Welsh Prose Tales: Some Methodological Considerations', *Studia Celtica*, 41 (2007), 47–89 (73).
18 Lloyd-Morgan, '*Historia Peredur*', p. 145–6. Compare, for instance, the situation of the Four Branches of the Mabinogi, summarised in Simon Rodway, 'The Mabinogi and the Shadow of Celtic Mythology', *Studia Celtica*, 52 (2018), 67–85 (67–8). For more extensive treatments, see Thomas Charles-Edwards, 'The Textual Tradition of Medieval Welsh Prose Tales and the Problem of Dating', in B. Maier and S. Zimmer (eds), *150 Jahre 'Mabinogion' – deutsch-walisische Kulturbeziehungen* (Tübingen: Max Niemeyer, 2001), pp. 23–39; Rodway, 'The Where, Who, When and Why'; E. P. Hamp, 'Mabinogi and Archaism', *Celtica*, 23 (1999), 96–110; J. Hemming, 'Ancient tradition or Authorial Invention? The "mythological" Names in the Four Branches', in J. F. Nagy (ed.), *Myth in Celtic Literatures* (Dublin: Four Courts Press, 2007), pp. 83–104.
19 For dates, see Daniel Huws, *Medieval Welsh Manuscripts* (Aberystwyth: University of Wales Press and National Library of Wales, 2000), pp. 58–60; the date that I give for Peniarth 14 is for the section containing *Peredur* only; according to Huws, the date of the rest of the manuscript is s. xiii²; Huws, *Medieval Welsh Manuscripts*, p. 58; see also Daniel Huws, 'Y Pedair Llawsgrif Canoloesol', in Davies and Wynn Thomas (eds), *Canhwyll Marchogyon*, pp. 1–9. For a list of later manuscripts containing the text, all of them derived from these, see Goetinck (ed.), *Historia Peredur*, p. ix. Goetinck's edition presents the texts of the first three manuscripts, but not that of the Red Book. For the text of the Red Book version, see John Rhŷs and J. Gwenogvryn Evans (eds), *Text of the Mabinogion and Other Welsh Tales from the Red Book of Hergest* (Oxford: Clarendon Press, 1887); or Kuno Meyer (ed.), *Peredur ab Efrawc* (Leipzig: S. Hirzel, 1887). A transcription is also available online, alongside a transcription of Peniarth 4 (White Book): Diana Luft, Peter Wynn Thomas and D. Mark Smith (eds), *Rhyddiaith Gymraeg 1300–1425* (2013), *www.rhyddiaithganoloesol.caerdydd.ac.uk* (last accessed 23 January 2023) .
20 The overview of the different versions of *Peredur* is adapted from the account that I provided in my '*Peredur* and the Problem of Inappropriate Questions', *Journal of the International Arthurian Society*, 9 (2021), 3–23, *https://*

INTRODUCTION

    doi.org/10.1515/jias-2021-0002 (last accessed 18 July 2022). For a summary and details of the manuscript tradition, see Lloyd-Morgan, '*Historia Peredur*', pp. 145–7. For detailed discussions of the manuscripts, see Daniel Huws, 'Y Pedair Llawysgrif', and Peter Wynn Thomas, 'Cydberthynas y pedair fersiwn canoloesol', in *Canhwyll Marchogyon*, pp. 10–49.

21 See Charles-Edwards, 'The Textual Tradition', pp. 24, 28. For a different view, see the discussion in Roberts, '*Peredur Son of Efrawg*', 60.

22 See also p. 35 of this book.

23 See p. 36 of this book. For recent overviews of the French Continuations of Chrétien's romance, see, for example, Matilda Tomaryn Bruckner, *Chrétien Continued: A Study of the* Conte du Graal *and its Verse Continuations* (Oxford: Oxford University Press, 2009); and Thomas Hinton, *The* Conte du Graal *Cycle: Chrétien de Troyes's* Perceval, *the Continuations, and French Arthurian Romance* (Cambridge: D. S. Brewer, 2012).

24 For the texts, see Robert Leith Thomson (ed.), *Owein, or, Chwedyl Iarlles y Ffynnawn* (Dublin: DIAS, 1968); and Robert Leith Thomson (ed.), *Ystoria Gereint uab Erbin* (Dublin: DIAS, 1997); for a discussion of the application of the term 'romance' to these texts, see Brynley F. Roberts, 'The Idea of a Welsh Romance', in *Studies on Middle Welsh Literature* (Lewiston NY: Edwin Mellen Press, 1992), pp. 133–46; R. Middleton, '*Chwedl Gereint ab Erbin*', in Rachel Bromwich, A. O. H. Jarman and Brynley F. Roberts (eds), *Arthur of the Welsh* (Cardiff: University of Wales Press, 1991), pp. 150–1; and Lloyd-Morgan, 'Medieval Welsh Tales or Romances?'.

25 This subject has been discussed extensively. See, for instance, Roberts, '*Peredur Son of Efrawg*', 58–9; Davies (trans.), *Mabinogion*, p. xi; Kirsten Lee Over, 'Transcultural Change: Romance to *rhamant*', in Helen Fulton (ed.), *Medieval Celtic Literature and Society Medieval Celtic Literature and Society* (Dublin and Portland OR: Four Courts Press, 2005), pp. 183–204; and most recently Ceridwen Lloyd-Morgan and Erich Poppe, 'The First Adaptations from French: History and Context of a Debate', in Lloyd-Morgan and Poppe (eds), *Arthur in the Celtic Languages*, pp. 97–101 (esp. pp. 113–14).

26 For a brief overview and further references, see Roberts, '*Peredur Son of Efrawg*', 58–9; Lloyd-Morgan and Poppe, 'The First Adaptations from French', pp. 111–12 and notes on p. 115. An earlier, in-depth discussion can be found in Doris Edel, 'The "Mabinogionfrage": Arthurian Literature between Orality and Literacy', in Hildegard L. C. Tristram (ed.), *(Re)Oralisierung* (Tübingen: Gunter Narr, 1996), pp. 311–33.

27 See Chapter 1 of this book.

28 For the text, see Thomas Jones (ed.), *Ystoryaeu Seint Greal, Rhan I: Y Keis* (Cardiff: Gwasg Prifysgol Cymru, 1992) and the earlier edition Robert Williams (ed.), *Y Seint Greal: Selections from the Hengwrt MSS*, vol. 1 (London: Richards, 1876); for discussions, see, for instance, Ceridwen Lloyd-Morgan,

'*Y Seint Greal*', in Lloyd-Morgan and Poppe (eds), *Arthur in the Celtic Languages*, pp. 129–37; Ceridwen Lloyd-Morgan, 'A study of *Y Seint Greal* in relation to *La Queste del Saint Graal* and *Perlesvaus*' (unpublished PhD thesis, University of Oxford, 1978); Ceridwen Lloyd-Morgan, 'Perceval in Wales: Late Medieval Welsh Grail Traditions', in Alison Adams, Armel H. Diverres and Karen Stern (eds), *The Changing Face of Arthurian Romance: Essays on Arthurian Prose Romance in Memory of Cedric E. Pickford* (Cambridge: Boydell Press, 1986), pp. 78–91; Erich Poppe, 'Ystoryaeu Seint Greal', in R. Rouse, S. Echard, H. Fulton, G. Rector and J.A. Fay (eds), *The Encyclopedia of Medieval Literature in Britain* (Wiley Online Library 2017), *https://doi.org/10.1002/9781118396957.wbemlb436* (last accessed 7 July 2021); and Claudia Zimmermann, 'Between me and God! Interjections in the Middle Welsh *Ystoryaeu Seint Graal* "Stories of the Holy Grail" and their French Source Texts', in Axel Harlos and Neele Harlos (eds), *Adapting Texts and Styles in a Celtic Context: Interdisciplinary Perspectives on Processes of Literary Transfer in the Middle Ages: Studies in Honour of Erich Poppe* (Münster: Nodus Publikationen, 2016), pp. 185–94.

29 The quotation and translation are from Rachel Bromwich (ed.), *Trioedd Ynys Prydein*, 2nd edn (Cardiff: University of Wales Press, 1978), p. 212 (triad 86); this volume is henceforth referred to as *TYP*[2]. For Peniarth 50, see *TYP*[2], pp. xxxi–xxxiv; Daniel Huws, *Medieval Welsh Manuscripts* (Cardiff: University of Wales Press, 2000), pp. 17, 61; Helen Fulton, 'The Geography of Welsh Literary Production in Late Medieval Glamorgan', *Journal of Medieval History*, 41 (2015), 325–40; William Marx, 'Middle English Texts and Welsh Contexts', in Ruth Kennedy and Simon Meecham-Jones (eds), *Authority and Subjugation in Writing of Medieval Wales* (Basingstoke: Palgrave Macmillan, 2008), pp. 13–26 (pp. 17–23).

30 The best and most authoritative discussion of the triads remains *TYP*[2].

31 *TYP*[2] 'Introduction'. See, however, the comments on this point in Aled Llion Jones, *Darogan: Prophecy, Lament and Absent Heroes in Medieval Welsh Literature* (Cardiff: University of Wales Press, 2013), p. 91. The mnemonic qualities of triadic structures are discussed on pp. 32–5 of this book.

32 *TYP*[2], p. 213.

33 See William Marx, 'Middle English Texts and Welsh Contexts', p. 18; Natalia I. Petrovskaia, 'Les Cisterciens transmetteurs de littérature vernaculaire. Le cas gallois', in Anne-Marie Turcan-Verkerk, Dominique Stutzmann, Thomas Falmagne and Pierre Gandil (eds), *Les Cisterciens et la transmission des textes (XIIe–XVIIIe siècles)* (Turnhout: Brepols, 2018), pp. 355–79. Peniarth 50 is discussed in depth in Aled Llion Jones, *Darogan*, esp. Chapter 3, pp. 128–32.

34 *TYP*[2], p. 213.

35 Roberts, '*Peredur Son of Efrawg*', 52.

INTRODUCTION

36 Chapter 5 presents a discussion of the legal context of the procession scene in *Peredur*. It was published originally as the *Journal of the International Arthurian Society* prize essay in the *Journal of the International Arthurian Society* 2021 issue. The essay is reprinted here as it was published with only a few minor alterations designed to bring it further into line with the rest of the book. Some of these are purely cosmetic (e.g., referencing), others include additions of cross-references to other chapters and relevant examples, as well as references to secondary literature cited elsewhere in the book. The main alteration in the text of the argument itself consists of the incorporation of this book's analysis of the episodic structure of *Peredur*.

37 The reference is to Lady Charlotte Guest's mid-nineteenth-century translation. For a discussion of her translations of medieval Welsh prose texts and their influence on later scholarship, see, for instance, Rachel Bromwich, 'The Mabinogion and Lady Charlotte Guest', *Transactions of the Honourable Society of Cymmrodorion 1986*, (1986), 127–41; Donna R. White, 'The Crimes of Lady Charlotte Guest', *Proceedings of the Harvard Celtic Colloquium*, 15 (1995), 242–9; Davies (trans.), *Mabinogion*, pp. xxvii–xix; Sioned Davies, 'A Charming Guest: Translating the Mabinogion', *Studia Celtica*, 38 (2004), 157–78; and most recently, Krista Kapphahn, 'Celtic Heroines: The Contributions of Women Scholars to Arthurian Studies in the Celtic Languages', *Journal of the International Arthurian Society*, 7 (2019), 120–39 (122–3).

1

THE STRUCTURE OF THE NARRATIVE

The structure of *Peredur* has been the subject of much discussion.[1] A particular challenge appears to be posed by the perceived lack of unity in what is generally treated as a single narrative.[2] To quote Ceridwen Lloyd-Morgan, 'In many cases the framework suggested is based largely on a hypothetical evolution of the text, or else is not immediately apparent in the tale as we have it, but can be understood only in terms of a slowly and painfully excavated or reconstructed "deep structure"'.[3] The model proposed in this chapter has the advantage of working exclusively with the text in the form in which it survives, and which presumably was meant to make sense to a medieval audience.[4] The only precondition is taking the basic structure of the Long Version as 'Short Version + Continuation' and putting the latter aside for the purposes of the initial analysis because its structure has different origins.

The present approach follows the lines of argument laid out by Lloyd-Morgan in the article quoted, as her proposed solution seems to be the most promising: 'If the material before us fails to conform to our present-day European concepts of logic and unity, perhaps instead of rejecting the text we should reject the logic and find a new one.'[5] I take this line of thought further and suggest that the problem of unity in the story of *Peredur* is as much of a problem as that of the structure of the 'romance' of *Peredur*. What we now take as a unit of the Short Version should not be taken as a unit at all, and the imposition of the idea of it as a single narrative is as anachronistic as the imposition of the label 'romance'.[6] I suggest that we should move away from Brynley F. Roberts's definition of *Peredur* as 'a single composed tale', and the idea that unity of theme or plot can be found in the various episodes, which has characterised most attempts to analyse the tale so far.[7] Roberts offers a description of the component 'episodes and sections' of the text, but given the lack of continuity between many of these, it would perhaps be wiser to take these 'episodes' as independent stories, where there was no single story arc.[8] The suggestion is not entirely new – it follows quite closely Ian Lovecy's view that '[t]he tale is made up from a number of stories connected by the identity of the hero and little else', but with the additional proviso, reviving Rudolf Thurneysen's suggestion from 1912, that we should not take *Peredur* as a single tale at all.[9] What we have instead in the Short Version, are three stories about the same character.

Thurneysen's view is worth quoting, because in a hunt for unity of the perceived single tale, it has not been as prominent as it deserves:

> Wir besitzen also tatsächlich vier kymrische Erzählungen von Peredur, von denen zwei (Ib und II) keine nähere Berühung mit französischen Texten zeigen; nur haben sie aus Teil Ia die allgemeine Situation entnommen, dass Peredur als Artus-Ritter auf Abenteuer auszieht.[10]

> We thus in fact have four Welsh tales about Peredur, of which two (Ib and II) show no close proximity with the French texts; they have only taken from Part Ia the general setting, that Peredur heads out on adventure as an Arthurian knight.

Thurneysen's four episodes are designated, somewhat confusingly, Ia, Ib, II and III. Of these, Ia–II correspond to what I call the Short Version. Sioned Davies has followed Thurneysen's division, altering his designation to I, II, III and IV (with I–III being the Short Version).[11] The following discussion – in the interest of minimising confusion and for the purpose of highlighting triadic structures – designates these Episodes I, II and III.[12] The correspondences between the three systems are laid out in Table 1. The two columns on the right give a brief summary of the episodes in question and whether equivalents are found in Chrétien's *Perceval*. A fuller summary of the text is provided below in the discussion of the structural patterning of *Peredur*.

Thurneysen's III and Davies's IV correspond to what I call the 'Welsh Continuation'. The reason why Thurneysen uses Ia and Ib in his analysis is that the manuscripts show no distinction between these episodes through any layout or rubric demarcation, but he does acknowledge that these are

Table 1: Correspondence for episodic structure of *Peredur*

This Book	Thurneysen	Davies	Summary	In French version
Episode I	Ia	I	Peredur's upbringing, arrival at Arthur's court, first series of adventures, returning to court after avenging insult to the dwarfs	Yes
Episode II	Ib	II	Adventures following encounter with Angharad Law Eurog, until return to Arthur's court and reconciliation with her	No
Episode III	II	III	Adventures following a hunt, culminating with marriage to the Empress	No
Continuation	III	IV	Adventures following arrival of the Ugly Damsel at Arthur's court, culminating with victory over witches of Gloucester	Yes (sans witches)

two distinct sections.[13] However, since Thurneysen's Ia (our I) corresponds to Chrétien's text, while Ib (our II) does not, and since it is quite possible that the various episodes originated in an oral environment and were later copied into manuscripts, manuscript layout and rubrication can provide a guide but should not bind us unduly in the analysis of the tale.

The episodic nature of the medieval Welsh prose tales in general has been remarked on by Sioned Davies, who points out that despite the survival of these tales in written form, their structure is 'inexorably linked to memorability' and to their oral history of composition, transmission and performance.[14] Davies states that the size of the episodes into which the tales are divided is manageable for oral performance, and this is usually marked in the manuscripts by layout, rubrication or decoration.[15] Lovecy has remarked that the Peniarth 7 text of *Peredur* has a 'very lively' style, which may be accounted for by an oral past.[16]

The analysis in this chapter takes the structure of *Peredur* as we now have it as a composite text, with three distinct stories, followed by a Continuation adapted from French sources.[17] This Continuation has previously been taken alongside what I call Episode I, as a badly redacted version of what originally was a single narrative (in which vengeance is seen as the central theme), with some irrelevant episodes thrown into the middle of it.[18] The present discussion aims to demonstrate that more credit is due to the Welsh redactors. The confirmed independent existence of the Short Version is used as the basis for the analysis. It will be shown that this Short Version has a patterned structure, probably linked to its origins in oral transmission or, at any rate, facilitating memorisation and oral performance. The Long Version does not have such a structure, but is instead a composite construction of Short Version + Continuation. The Continuation, it will be argued, is not only heavily influenced by the French text in terms of its plot, but also represents a replica of the French Grail romance in terms of its formal narrative patterning.[19] It will also be shown that tripartite structures and three-fold repetition are not only 'prevalent', as Davies puts it, in the Short Version, but form the key to its structure and its memorability.[20] It will be shown that the Short Version is composed of three distinct and easily recognisable narratives – these will be given the designations Episode I, Episode II and Episode III. A full summary is provided later in this chapter, outlining each episode, to demonstrate the structural patterns.

The suggestion here is that we should not read even the Short Version of *Peredur* as a single continuous narrative, and that we should expect consistency not between, but only within these episodes. The Long Version, I will argue, should also not be taken as a single text, but rather as a compilation along the lines of the loose collection of material known as the 'Welsh Charlemagne Cycle'.[21] The idea of a single narrative arc is imposed by the Continuation, which attempts to bring *Peredur* in line with the French romance. Thus, the medieval Continuation both facilitates (for later scholars) and perpetrates (by its own existence) the fallacy of subjecting the Welsh text to reading in light of Chrétien's romance.[22] The Welsh text, however, resists this treatment.

Peredur fully opens up to its audience only once the Short Version is taken on its own; and as three independent episodes, only loosely connected more or less by featuring the same main character (it may be helpful to think in terms of the original mid-twentieth-century *Doctor Who*, *Star Trek* and *James Bond* series). In particular, it will be seen that many of the perceived faults of the text are in fact not there. For instance, Sioned Davies describes the text as follows: 'The treatment tends to be uncourtly, with no interest in the characters' feelings or motives, no authorial asides or comments; rather, the emphasis throughout is on the action, with no attempt whatsoever at psychological digressions.'[23] This is correct insofar as the point about the lack of 'psychological digressions' and the 'uncourtly treatment' (this is not a courtly romance). However, emotion is shown, if not discussed at length, in the text.[24] To offer only a few examples, Cai and Gwalchmai's interactions show emotion (if mostly annoyance or irritation), the oppressed countess bursts into tears on arriving in Peredur's chamber to offer herself to him (having been pushed to it by her advisers) but only tells him about the count who stole her lands when Peredur asks her why she is crying. Peredur's own meditation on the girl of the day is so intense, in both the blood on the snow scene, and when he first sees the Empress, that he displays signs of what may be described as hyperfocus.[25] The display of emotion extends to minor characters and opponents, as the Proud One of the Clearing is extremely jealous of his lady (in a pattern highly reminiscent of *Gereint*), and the one-eyed Black Oppressor is clearly incensed when a drunk Peredur taunts him about losing his eye. The idea that the text has no interest in the internal life of the hero applies only if we assume that we are dealing with a single narrative and therefore expect consistency between what in reality are distinct narratives. In such a view, it does appear to be a sign of inconsistency when the hero first contemplates the raven and blood on the snow thinking of his love, then meets and declares his love for Angharad Law Eurog ('Angharad Golden Hand'), and then meets, falls in love with and remains for fourteen years with the Empress of Constantinople. As will be demonstrated, however, these are three separate episodes, with three separate 'Bond girls', or, rather, 'Peredur girls'.

Brynley Roberts observes that the individual episodes often begin and end at Arthur's court.[26] These can be taken not merely as episodes in a grander narrative, but also as complete semi-independent narratives, forming distinct units that can be removed, replaced and re-ordered.[27] Most importantly, there are no internal contradictions or inconsistencies within each of these units. Any inconsistencies that can be found (e.g., the seemingly ever-changing object of Peredur's affections) are to be found between these episodes, not within them. The unit argument proposed here applies primarily to the shortest, earliest version of the text, and thus to the narrative up to and including the hero's meeting with the Empress.

The Continuation in the longer version, with its references to Chrétien's French narrative, appears to function according to a different structural logic. We will return to this section of the text at a later stage.

The Short Version falls into three distinct sub-narratives, which I call Episode I, Episode II and Episode III (see Table 1).[28] Each is composed of smaller episodes, which are interconnected and will be designated with capital letters in brackets, as (A), (B) and (C). The discussion here provides detailed outlines of each episode with a commentary, as it is necessary to both convey the flow of the story and to explain the exact nature of its structure. Episode I will be examined first, followed by a structural analysis based on this annotated summary, which will provide a formal structural pattern against which the two other episodes will be read. The proposed structural pattern is based on a fractal system of triadic structures, already visible in the triadic division of the three independent episodes. A definition of fractals and an explanation of how *Peredur*'s episodic structure corresponds to a fractal model is possible only once the data is provided, and so follows the outline of Episode I.

In broad brushstrokes, Episode I might be said to correspond to the first part of Chrétien's text, in that it recounts the hero's childhood; first encounter with knights; meeting the maiden in a tent; arrival at Arthur's court; battle with the knight of the cup; and visits to the two uncles. However, the Welsh text, while less expansive in description, adds some scenes or encounters that are absent in the French version and, as will be demonstrated, form an inalienable part of the Welsh text's formal structure. A number of sub-episodes are also presented in a different order in the Welsh and French versions (these differences are noted in the summary later in this chapter). Episodes II and III are unique to the Welsh text, for Chrétien's narrative, after its equivalent of Episode I, moves directly on to what in the Welsh constitutes the Continuation, with the arrival of the Ugly Damsel.[29] It should be observed that most previous studies of the tale's structures perceive a continuity between two or more of these episodes. Ceridwen Lloyd-Morgan, for instance, describes what we call Episodes II and III as 'the Angharad Law Eurog section', but most importantly, for our purposes, adds that 'there is no reason to suppose that this section is not home-grown'.[30] There are no equivalents elsewhere in the broader Perceval/Grail tradition for Episodes II and III. Given the uniformity of structure between Episode I (the adventures in which are paralleled, though in a different order, in Chrétien's version) and Episodes II and III, I would also venture to suggest that it might be worth re-considering the currently accepted view that even the Short Version is an adaptation of the French romance. The structure seems too perfect, and the narrative logic too tight, especially in comparison with the very messy Continuation.[31]

Episode I

Episode I commences with Peredur's background, his first encounter with the knights, his mother's instructions to pray in front of churches, to take food if it is not offered freely, to run towards rather than from screams, and to make love to young women; the encounter with the maiden of the tent on the way to Arthur's court where all his mother's instructions are followed to the letter, except for running towards the screaming; arrival at Arthur's court and Cai's insult to the dwarfs.[32] Let us call this Episode I(A). Peredur arrives at Arthur's court in the midst of a crisis: a knight had caused offence to the Queen by snatching her goblet and splashing her with its contents (a legally recognised form of offence that we also find codified in contemporary Welsh law), and then rides off with the goblet. No one wishes to avenge the insult, for all are afraid of the knight. Peredur is greeted by two dwarfs as a flower of knighthood (a role that in Chrétien's version is fulfilled by a maiden, supplemented by a jester who explains her actions), and the dwarfs are hit by Cai. Cai then sends Peredur to what he assumes will be his doom to avenge the queen. Peredur duly overthrows the knight and refuses to return to Arthur's court until the insult to the dwarfs is avenged. This is reported to the court by Gwalchmai (Peniarth 7)/Owain (Red Book and White Book).[33] It is followed by two further exploits (a total of three, if we include the knight with the goblet), each time starting with 'Ac ynteu Peredur a gerdwys racdaw y ymdeith' ('Peredur went on his way').[34] These two further encounters, making up the triad, are not present in Chrétien's text, where Perceval immediately proceeds to the castle of Gornemant of Gohort (who corresponds to the first uncle).[35] The first is a very formulaic encounter with a strange knight.[36] Peredur vanquishes the knight and sends him to Arthur, and 'Peredur a gerdawd racdaw y ymdeith' ('Peredur went on his way' (again)) meeting sixteen knights and sending them to Arthur.[37] It is worth noting that there are, thus, three military encounters in close succession after Peredur leaves Arthur's court. Back in Arthur's court 'A cheryd a gafas Kei gan Arthur a'r teulu' ('Cai was reprimanded by Arthur and the retinue') (all versions), 'a goualus uu ynteu am hynny'

('And he was worried on account of that') (White Book and Red Book).[38] This glimpse into Arthur's court is part of a pattern: as we shall see, each section of Episode I concludes with a similar scene set in Arthur's court. This concludes Episode I(A).

Episode I(B) contains two of three stages of Peredur's training as knight, both at his uncles' houses (stage three is in Episode I(C) with witches to whom he is not related), followed by a third familial encounter, with a foster sister, and battle with a knight, sent back to Arthur's court. It is thus composed of three encounters with relatives (two uncles and a foster sister).[39] It begins with the phrase 'Ynteu Peredur a gychwynwys ymdeith' ('Peredur set off') and the hero's consequent arrival at a lake and the court of a lame grey-haired man who turns out to be Peredur's uncle.[40] This is the first of two uncles and the first of three stages of Peredur's military training. The uncle asks Peredur if he can fight with a sword, then has him practise against one of his two sons. He comments, 'a goreu dyn a lad a chledyf yn yr ynys hon vydy' ('You will be the best swordsman in this Island') and proposes to teach 'manners and etiquette', explicitly superseding Peredur's mother's earlier instructions (cross-reference to Episode I(A)).[41] With his uncle's permission, Peredur departs and arrives in due course at a court beyond a meadow at the far end of a forest, where he encounters his second uncle, who teaches him more swordsmanship by having him hit a sword against a pillar, breaking both sword and pillar, fitting them back together until they fail to fit back together again.[42] After this, he comments 'Yn y teyrnas goreu dyn a lad a chledyf wyt' ('You are the best swordsman in the kingdom'), but adds that while Peredur now has two-thirds of his strength, one third remains.[43] This is a foreshadowing of a tripartite structure. At this point, in other 'Grail' romances the Grail procession commences, with two young men bearing a very large spear pouring three streams of blood, followed by two young women carrying a salver with a head on it, and everyone mourning loudly.[44] With his uncle's permission (again), Peredur leaves the next day. Almost immediately he encounters a foster sister of his who is mourning the death of her husband and who accuses Peredur of causing his mother's death by his sudden departure (a cross-reference to Episode I(A) again).[45] Peredur overcomes the knight who killed his foster sister's husband, marries her off to him and sends him to Arthur's court, following the pattern established in Episode I(A). At Arthur's court, Arthur's patience is exhausted and he declares that he intends to 'a geissaf ynyalwch Ynys Prydein ymdanaw yny kaffwyf' ('search the waste lands of the Island of Britain until I find him').[46] This glimpse into Arthur's court concludes Episode I(B) in exactly the same manner as the close of Episode I(A).

Episode I(C) contains three sub-episodes with battles to defend women. Only the first of these can be technically described as a 'damsel in distress', since the second woman is married (she is the tent maiden from Episode I(A)) and the third is described as a 'large woman' and is probably not very young.[47] In Chrétien's text, the first of these damsel-in-distress episodes comes between Perceval's visit to Gornemant (the equivalent of the first uncle) and his visit to the Fisher King (the equivalent of the second uncle), while he encounters the tent maiden immediately after meeting his cousin (the equivalent of the foster sister).[48] This tidy triadic structure is a feature of the Welsh text only. In the Welsh version, Episode I(C) commences with the now familiar connective formula 'Ynteu Peredur a gerdwys racdaw ymdeith' ('Meanwhile Peredur went on his way').[49] He crosses a pathless forest and arrives at an ivy-covered fortress belonging to a beautiful countess who had been deprived of her possessions by a cruel neighbouring count. The lady is described as 'Yn y gwelit y chnawt trwyddaw, gwynach oed no blawt y crissant gwynhaf; y gwallt hitheu a'e dwyael, duach oedynt no'r muchyd; deu vann gochyon vychein yn y grudyeu, cochach oedynt no'r dim cochaf' ('where her flesh could be seen through it [the tattered silk dress], it was whiter than the flowers of the whitest crystal; her hair and her eyebrows were blacker than jet; two tiny red spots in her cheeks, redder than the reddest thing').[50] It is worth remembering this description, as it matches the subject of Peredur's reverie later in Episode I when he is contemplating the raven and the blood on the snow.[51] This is also the same character who in the French version becomes the object of the hero's affections, although there she is described as blonde and given the name Blancheflor.[52] The young woman and her court survive on sustenance shared by a neighbouring convent. In the evening, on the encouragement of others, she tries to offer herself to Peredur, who either misses the point (the reason for her tearful presence in his bedchamber) or gets straight to the point, by asking why she is crying and discovering that she had been deprived of her lands and needs protection.[53] The traditional interpretation of Peredur as a little naive would suggest the former reading, but there is no textual basis to read that Peredur is naive here. After three rounds of fighting on three consecutive days with the earl's *penteulu* ('chief of the household troops'), *distain* ('steward') and the earl himself, Peredur returns the countess's lands in three parts.[54] This adventure is followed by a second meeting with a distressed lady, this time the girl from the tent, the wife of the Proud One of the Clearing (first encountered in Episode I(A)). The third and final woman in need of assistance, is described as 'gwreic vawr delediw' ('large, handsome woman') whose house is the only one left in a region laid waste to by the witches of Gloucester.[55] Peredur engages one of the witches and she offers to complete his military training.[56] The subsequent training with the witches of Gloucester gives Peredur the third part of his power promised by the second uncle in Episode I(B). This is followed by an encounter with Arthur and his men who are now actively looking for him (a cross-reference to the conclusion of Episode I(B)). Peredur is found deep in thought, contemplating the sight of a raven and blood on the snow and thinking about 'y wreic uwyhaf a garei' ('the woman he loves best').[57] This has to be the first countess in distress (the girl who had tearfully offered herself to him), as she was described in exactly those terms.[58] A number of messengers are sent to Peredur to negotiate, but are unsuccessful as they interrupt his reverie. This is a triplet: starting with a single squire, followed by twenty-four knights, and then followed by Cai.[59] Cai, thrown from his horse ignominiously, is punished for his discourtesy to the dwarfs (a cross-reference to Episode I(A)), removing the only obstacle that stood in Peredur's way to joining Arthur's court. Gwalchmai points this out to Peredur and leads him back. The phrase 'ac ymhoelut a orugant parth a Chaer Llion' ('And they returned to Caerllion') concludes Episode I.[60]

This overview shows a complicated pattern in the episode structure that is best described as fractal.[61] In mathematical theory, fractal objects are objects that are scale-symmetric and self-similar; that is, the pattern is repeated at any scale, no matter how far one might zoom in on the micro-structure: the pattern repeats each time on a smaller scale, *ad infinitum*.[62] The most familiar naturally occurring fractal structure is the snowflake. The Romanesco broccoli is another example. Here, this is a self-replicating triadic patten found at every narrative level: a triadic structure within each triadic structure within each of the three separate independent episodes.[63] While the narrative structure of Episode I is not a perfect fractal, because it involves a non-symmetrical system of cross-references between sections A, B and C, the repetition of triadic structures on multiple levels of the narrative represents a fractal pattern; indeed, the cross-references do not disturb the scale-symmetric repeating triadic structure.[64] The structure of Episodes I to III can be visually represented as a Sierpiński gasket with its repetitive pattern of triangles.[65] Evidence for the applicability of this concept to the analysis of medieval works is provided by surviving visual representations of what we now term a Sierpiński gasket of the twelfth century, in the mosaic stone floor of the cathedral in Anagni (Italy) dated to 1104.[66]

Figure 1 represents a diagrammatic analysis of the fractal structure of the Short Version of *Peredur* (up to the concluding phrase of the Empress episode). The diagram shows the narrative structures of *Peredur* mapped onto a Sierpiński gasket. The fractal structure in the diagram has been labelled only down to one level beyond the A-B-C sub-episode structure, but some of the further substrata of triads are highlighted in the annotated outline of Episodes II and III. The point that the figure is intended to illustrate is that *Peredur* is composed of triadic structures at every level: three episodes, each of which contains either three sub-episodes or triadic repetitive structures, some of which can be further sub-divided into threes. Cross-references and the recurrences of characters or themes from, for instance sub-episode A somewhere in sub-episode B or C, provide internal unity to the narrative that does not, however, disturb or disrupt this structure.[67] If the objection is raised that the triadic structures I have already outlined in my analysis of the plot of Episode I, and later of Episode II and III, do not map perfectly onto a Sierpiński gasket and do not represent a perfect fractal, then in response it must be made clear that mathematically perfect fractals are merely an approximation of what is found in nature and I do not suggest that medieval Welsh authors had set out to deliberately compose a fractal system.[68] *Peredur* in this analysis represents a natural occurrence, and the fractal model (and by extension Figure 1) represents no more and no less than an idealised model intended to aid the analysis of this real-world object, not to map it perfectly point by point. In Ian Stewart's words, 'A map must be simpler than the territory'.[69]

The analytical model proposed here does not imply that medieval Welsh authors, compilers or audiences thought of their compositions in terms of fractals, but the scale-symmetric mathematical model does provide a useful way of analysing *Peredur* to identify patterns behind the seeming chaos. It has been pointed out that, historically, in art, fractals have been used to mimic chaotic structure (whether consciously or unconsciously), and I would like to suggest that this is the case *Peredur* – it has worked so well that the tendency in scholarly discussions has been to see only the chaos.[70] As Stewart puts it, fractals 'give scientists a powerful tool with which to understand processes and structures hitherto described merely as "irregular", "intermittent", "rough", or "complicated"', and it is exactly this that fractals provide for our understanding of the structure of *Peredur*, which I propose is best regarded as one of those 'fractal objects [that] possess a distinctive character and structure, and are not just irregular or random'.[71] Intentionality (or at least design) in the sequence of self-similar scale-symmetric triadic compositions in the case of the Welsh text might be a reasonable supposition given the well-known tradition of triads, already referred to in the Introduction.[72] The observation made here of the tendency towards three-fold structure and three-fold repetition is also not new.[73] This well-known cultural context supports the proposed theory that the three-fold structures as scale-symmetric and self-similar are thus mappable onto a recognisable fractal model.

Figure 1: Fractal structure of *Peredur* (Short Version), shown as a Sierpiński gasket

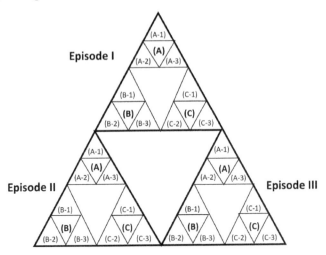

To evaluate the mnemonic quality of the fractal model of triadic structures mapped out in this text, I invite the reader to try remembering the sequence of events in *Peredur* by mapping the narrative as a sequence of three episodes, each composed of three sub-episodes (A-B-C), each involving three consecutive scenes of encounters. The narrative sequence will turn out to be easily memorisable.

Episode II

We can now continue examining the structure of the Short Version of *Peredur*, with fractals in mind. Episode II begins with seeming continuity to the previous episode: 'Ar nos gyntaf y doeth Peredur i Gaer Llion y lys Arthur, ac adoeth yd ydoed yn troi yn y gaer gwedy bwyt' ('The first night Peredur came to Caerllion to Arthur's court, he happened to be strolling in the castle after dinner').[74] The continuity, however, is merely on the surface. This can easily be a beginning of a new story, and the sentence can be replaced or removed without any violence to the plot. If we take it as a new and separate story, we will find no discontinuities or contradictions internal to it. Episode II(A) begins with Peredur's encounter with a girl named Angharad Law Eurog while on an evening stroll. The attraction is unilateral, and Peredur swears to speak to no Christian until the girl changes her mind. The following day he sets off on his adventures. He finds his first adventure in the Round Valley inhabited by non-Christian giants.[75] The giants do not let any Christian leave the valley alive.[76] The episode contains a triadic combat structure, as Peredur first battles the grey-haired man's host and kills one-third of his soldiers, then kills two of the man's sons, one by one. After each of these, the man's wife and daughter tell him to ask Peredur for mercy, and only after the third time does the giant man acquiesce (fractals again). The adventure concludes with the grey-haired man going to Arthur and paying homage to the king. This marks the beginning of Episode II(B), as Peredur sets out the next day through the wilderness until he reaches a small and poor house where he hears of a new adventure: 'bot sarff yn gorwed ar vodrwy eur, heb adel kyfanhed seith milltir o pop parth idi' ('a serpent that lay on a golden ring, leaving no dwelling standing for seven miles around').[77] There is no particular reason given for the battle with the serpent, nor any information about the ring.[78] Peredur overcomes the serpent, and, we are told, continues without speaking to any Christian (link to Episode II(A)). Episode II(B) is told very briefly and Peredur proceeds back towards Arthur's court. Here begins Episode II(C). As in Episode I(C), in Episode II(C) Peredur encounters Cai, but this time it is Cai who attacks him; however, Peredur remembers his oath not to speak to any Christians (cross-reference to Episode II(A)) and does not retaliate or speak with him. I suggest that he also knows that the oath applies, which he did not in the Round Valley of the non-Christian giants, since he recognises Cai (and since he knows that he is now in Arthur's lands). Meanwhile, a strange knight arrives at Arthur's court and proceeds to overthrow all knights until Arthur calls for his armour to battle the knight himself. The armour is intercepted and worn by Peredur, who proceeds to overthrow the knight. After conquering the knight, Peredur – now known as the Mute Knight – returns to court and is greeted by Angharad, who is now willing to love him, were he only able to speak. This carries more significance than might be immediately apparent to the modern reader: the legal connotations of status associated with disability and muteness specifically. A mute man had severe limitations socially, as he was not allowed to inherit, rule or receive insult compensation.[79] We will return to the issue of legal echoes in these episodes in Chapter 5. For now, it is important to note that this type of incidental reference combines with external contextual information available to the text's medieval audiences to enrich meaning – this book aims to show that context is paramount to understanding this text. As Peredur is not in fact mute, Angharad's words absolve him from his oath (a cross-reference to Episode II(A)) and he speaks and is finally recognised. This concludes Episode II, which is thus composed of three main sections: (A) the Round Valley and non-Christian giants; (B) the encounter with the serpent; and (C) the successful combat with the knight who had challenged Arthur's court, and reconciliation.

There are some indications in Episode II that Peredur may have travelled a long way and may have been away for a long time. I have previously argued that the Round Valley may represent crusading themes, specifically conversion of non-Christian opponents.[80] Little can be gleaned from the serpent with the ring, since there is no description in Episode II(B), and it is very brief, but the conclusion of Episode II(C) makes sense only if we assume that Peredur was away for a long time. In the first place, no one (not only Angharad) recognises Peredur, even though he had removed the armour and approached the court on foot (presumably unarmed). This lack of recognition is in sharp contrast with the pattern in Episode I where everyone seemed to know Peredur: his uncles, his foster-sister, the witches – all recognised him and gave him information relating to himself. In Episode II no one that he meets on his adventures in both (A) and (B) knows Peredur, and those who had met him previously – Arthur's men encountered in (C) – do not recognise him. Only after he speaks is he recognised: 'Ac yna y gwybuwyt mae Peredur oed ef' ('And then they realised that he was Peredur').[81] It is through the act of speech that formal recognition is enabled (a pattern seen elsewhere in medieval Welsh tales). In this case, however, an additional detail reinforces the point of recognition and the suspicion that Peredur might have been away for a long time: 'Ac yna y delis ef gedymdeithas a Gwalchmai ac ac Owein vab Vryen ac a phawb o'r teulu' ('He renewed his friendship then with Gwalchmai and with Owain son of Urien and all the retinue').[82] Presumably, there would be no need to renew a freshly made recent friendship (since he had only arrived at Arthur's court at the beginning of Episode II), but renewal would be very much in order after a long absence. One is also tempted to add that it would be more likely that Peredur would not be recognised immediately after a long absence given his age. Although there is no specific indication of his age in the text, the younger Peredur was at the outset, the more likely he would have changed sufficiently, even over a short absence, to be unrecognisable by those who met him only briefly.[83]

Episode III

Episode III commences with a hunt, on which Peredur accompanies Arthur. Peredur's dog follows and kills a stag in a 'deserted place', and Peredur continues from there. It is not stated that he is not wearing armour and is unarmed, but given that he had been hunting, it is assumed, and we will see that the point returns throughout the episode. Again, there are three main sub-episodes in the text, with in-built triadic structures on multiple levels. Episode III(A) pitches Peredur against the one-eyed Black Oppressor. Zooming in, we still see the fractal structure, for when Peredur arrives at his court he sees 'tri gweis moelgethinyon yn gware gwyddbwyll' ('three swarthy, bald young men playing *gwyddbwyll*), and three maidens on a couch.[84] The Oppressor is aggressive but agrees to spare his guest on the request of one of the maidens, until Peredur becomes intoxicated and asks him how he lost his eye. When the black-haired Oppressor prepares to fight Peredur the next day, Peredur demands that the combat be even: either both be armed (as his opponent) or both unarmed (as Peredur).[85] On losing the combat, the Oppressor agrees to explain that he had lost his eye to the Black Serpent of the Cairn, under the Mount of Mourning, which has a magic stone in its tail that magically makes gold appear for whoever holds it.[86]

When Peredur asks for directions, these prescribe three stages to the adventure, which in themselves constitute Episode III(B): the court of the Sons of the King of Suffering (Episode III(B-1)); the court of the Countess of the Feats (Episode III(B-2)); and the 300 pavilions surrounding the Mound of Mourning (Episode III(B-3)).[87] For the purpose of illustrating the fractal structure of the narrative, there are three Sons of the King of Suffering, who are killed each day by a monster and revived by their three sisters. The sub-episode of the Sons of the King of Suffering is also tripartite, for after he leaves their court following them, Peredur encounters a maiden on a mound (section 1 of 3). He falls in love with her at first sight, and she tells him to seek her in the direction of India. This does not contradict his love for Angharad Law Eurog because she belongs to a different story (Episode II, which we are treating as unrelated). The girl of the mound gives him instructions on how to kill the monster that he is hunting and a magic stone to help him. This monster is the one that kills the Sons of the King of Suffering, although the Black Oppressor had described it as *adanc llyn* ('lake monster') and the girl said that it lives in a cave.[88] The cave-monster appears to be humanoid, as it kills its opponents with a spear. Then follows what is known as the Valley of Changing Sheep (section 2 of 3): Peredur comes across a valley with a river, with white sheep on one side and black sheep on the other, and which occasionally cross sides and change colour.[89] A half-burning-half-green tree and a squire on a mound complete the picture (again, three elements). There are three paths (a further fractal) from the mound and Peredur seeks the squire's advice regarding which one takes him to the monster's cave. On arriving at his destination (section 3 of 3), Peredur uses the magic stone received from the girl on the mound to kill the monster. He meets the three Sons of the King of Suffering at the mouth of the cave (alive), who offer him their three sisters. This concludes Episode III(B-1).

In Episode III(B-2), Peredur continues his journey, still following the route marked by the Black Oppressor on the way to the serpent with the magic stone in its tail. Here, he encounters Edlym Gleddyf Goch ('Edlym Red Sword'), who demands to be his man despite their equal status, and they arrive together at the court of the Countess of the Feats.[90] The Countess turns out to have been in love with Edlym, never having met him. Peredur, who had overthrown her 300-strong retinue (three times 100 – fractal), introduces them. This concludes this stage of the journey, as he sets off the next day in Episode III(B-3) to the Mound of Mourning, where he duly encounters 300 pavilions (fractal), and Peredur challenges them in 100-pavilion groups (the third group gives in and pays him homage instead of being beaten). Peredur defeats the serpent and pays everyone with the gold he has acquired by means of the magic stone, which he had learned of from the Black Oppressor in Episode III(A).

Episode III(C) is the episode of the Empress of Constantinople, and it also has a fractal structure. Peredur arrives at a valley filled with mills and pavilions, the latter belonging to the Empress of Constantinople and her followers.[91] He stays at the house of the head miller and borrows money from him to take part in the tournament. However, on each of the first two days he is distracted by the sight of the beautiful Empress and never reaches the tournament. On the third day (fractal), the miller gives him a blow with the blunt end of an axe to wake him up and gets him to the tournament. Having been successful, he is invited by the Empress (through three successive unsuccessful embassies – fractal) to come and visit her. When he is finally convinced by a wise adviser of the Empress to visit, there is a further series of fractals: Peredur makes two peaceful visits to her pavilion, the second visit sees three men with three cups challenge him for the Empress's love, and the third visit, which marks their union, is preceded by combat against the three men.[92] The union with the Empress concludes Episode III(C) and the Short Version of the text.

As can be seen from the detailed summary, the structure of the Short Version can be described as a series of fractals. Triadic constructions are known as a mnemonic device, and the fact that the entire tale is constructed on the self-similar scale-symmetric triadic fractal pattern could be argued to point to oral origins or at least oral delivery.[93] The intricate and complex construction does not preclude memorisation, but rather aids memorisation, since all that must be remembered is the structural principle and broad outlines of the plot. That the minor detail could be interchanged and replaced is attested by the variation found between the Peniarth 7 and the White Book and Red Book versions, such as Gwalchmai/Owain leading the knights who meet Peredur in Episode I and subsequently helping him to divest the Knight of the Goblet of his armour.[94] While such variation might be argued to result from a lengthy period of oral and/or written transmission, it also maps onto Walter J. Ong's observations on memorisation in oral cultures.[95] Importantly, it also corresponds to Sioned Davies's observations on the performative qualities of medieval Welsh prose narratives.[96] While no data is available on the length of oral performances of prose tales in medieval Wales, it could be supposed, given its length, that even the Short Version of *Peredur* would take too long to recite for a single performance of any reasonable length. This argument has already been put forward by Ceridwen Lloyd-Morgan, who distinguished three sections in the Long Version, marked by the large initials in the White

Book.[97] These divisions, the first of which comes after Episode II and the second after Episode III, yield very long first and last sections.[98] By contrast, each of its three episodes as I have outlined them is sufficiently short to be suitable for individual performance. Davies has observed that if this episodic division were to be observed in oral performance, one would expect the episodes to have been equal in length.[99] However, this presupposes a common origin for the episodes as a single complex of performable segments. However, if we are to suppose that the episodes were not intended to be performed in a sequence in a series of sittings, then it would not matter that they were of different lengths. Furthermore, since there is no cross-reference between the episodes (and no need for an equivalent of 'previously, on *Peredur* …'), one might suppose that an episode could be chosen for performance based on its length and the time available. An experiment of reading Episode I (the longest episode) out loud at a moderate pace yielded a reading time of fifty-five minutes. Depending on the pace of performance (pace of reading in our case), therefore, a performance of the episode could take between forty-five minutes and an hour.[100] Although this estimate is approximate, and variation in performance speed may yield a longer performance, even a performance of slightly longer than an hour may not be considered particularly long.[101]

The fractal structure of repeating triadic patterns makes each of the three episodes of the Short Version of *Peredur* highly memorable. Once the triadic structure is understood, it becomes very easy to recite the narratives by heart. This does not correspond entirely to the mnemonic techniques inherited by the European Middle Ages from the classical rhetorical tradition, but it functions on very similar principles, in which '[t]he crucial task for recollection is the construction of the orderly grid through which one can bring to mind specific pieces of text', as Mary Carruthers describes it.[102] Carruthers' investigation concerns the memorisation involved in a specifically written literary context, while the patterns that we see in *Peredur* are particularly suitable for memorisation for oral delivery (and oral transmission). I do not mean to claim here that this represents an earlier, ossified stratum of the tale's transmission, mechanically copied into manuscript form. Brynley F. Roberts and Sioned Davies have put forward convincing arguments that the two cultures – oral and written – overlapped, and there is no need to postulate that medieval Welsh texts were no longer performed orally once a version was written down.[103] Davies also warns, however, that the exact relationship between oral tradition and the written versions of the native tales preserved in our surviving manuscripts is difficult to ascertain.[104] My suggestion here is that the Short Version of *Peredur* represents a contemporary snapshot of a living oral tradition, and its fractal structure reflects the mnemonic grid used by the storytellers of the oral tradition. The fact that it is so clearly visible in the narrative as it is preserved shows just how solid a device this structure was. The fact that the Long Version of the White Book, despite the completely different form and structure of the Continuation that these manuscripts preserve, shows little variation in Episodes I to III in respect to the Peniarth 7 version, serves to reinforce this impression. It is also striking that variation is limited to what one might describe as moveable components: in Episode I(A) the knight leading the group who Peredur mistakes for angels and who explains to the hero the nature of their armaments and later helps him divest the knight with the goblet of his armour after Peredur's victory, is Owain in one version and Gwalchmai in the other.

One of the most striking aspects of the fractal structure of *Peredur* is that it aids the recollection of individual episodes, sub-episodes and scenes in groups of three but in any order. Unlike rote memory, which relies on a strict repetition of the sequence in one order only, it makes it possible to recall any part of the narrative and to recite these in any order.[105] To understand the difference it is useful to recall the distinction between the two types of memorisation provided by Albertus Magnus (*c*.1200–80), as summarised by Carruthers:

> The distinction is clear in Albertus Magnus's commentary on Aristotle's *De memoria et reminiscentia*. Albertus says that the iteration, or rote repetition, of knowledge is not at all a task of *memorial* recollection or *memoria*. He defines reminiscence or recollection as the rational discovery (*investigatio*) of what has been set aside (*obliti*) through and by means of the memory. This process differs in nature from 'rote repetition' (*iterata scientia*). Recollection occurs consciously through association: one finds or hunts out the stored memory-impressions by using other things associated with it either through a logical connection or through habit (*consuetudo*), the sort of associations taught by the various *artes memorativa*. Rote repetition, since it is not 'found out' by any heuristic scheme, is not considered recollection or true memory (*memoria*).[106]

The distinction, elided in modern ideas of memory and memorisation, is a useful one to retain for understanding the process of memorising narratives for the purposes of flexible recollection and performance. Albertus was writing about memorisation of texts for the purposes of study and analysis, he was not reflecting on the Welsh *cyfarwyddyd* ('storytelling') traditions (nor were these traditions based on Albertus or Aristotle), but the description of the process of memorisation by associating the remembered material through logical connection as well as through habit provides an extremely useful model for understanding how self-similar triadic structures of the fractal narrative might have been memorised by a medieval Welsh *cyfarwydd* ('storyteller').[107] While Bromwich states in her discussion of the triads that there is little evidence for medieval Welsh bards having any advanced knowledge of Latin before the fourteenth century, there is sufficient evidence to the contrary to take Welsh literary productions in a broader medieval cultural context.[108] The quotation serves as a reminder that when we speak of memory and mnemonic techniques in pre-modern contexts, we are not by default dealing with rote learning, nor with a process of memorising as contemporary students at all levels do with mathematical tables, verb endings or bits of poetry.[109]

It is also particularly useful to consider these parallel medieval mnemonic traditions side by side, because the term *cyfarwyddyd*, although normally translated as 'storytelling', has strong connotations of 'learning' and 'knowledge'.[110] Particularly interesting in terms of the argument proposed here is that the term appears to be a combination of *cyf-* ('together') + *arwydd* ('sign'), suggesting the association of the profession with the ability to put signs and patterns together to construct a meaningful whole.[111] The ability to connect seemingly unrelated components (e.g., the various adventures of Peredur in this case) into a single whole using patterns invisible and inaccessible to the uninitiated is precisely what appears to be happening with the structured pattern of *Peredur*.

It is an extremely important point that, as Sioned Davies notes, 'Various classes of learned men would have been responsible for the different aspects of *cyfarwyddyd*, including the lawyers, mediciners, and bards', because triadic structures are found not only in prose (and poetic) texts that we now would designate as literary, but also in native Welsh legal and technical tracts, suggesting that triadic structures were part of the mnemonic techniques of *cyfarwyddyd*.[112] That mnemonic techniques would have survived well into the period of written transmission is a view that has already been expressed by Brynley F. Roberts: 'Orality, allied to conventional similes, metaphors, allusions, and epithets, can co-exist with fixed forms and memorizing in a culture which nevertheless may live adjacent to a literate book-based society'.[113] Roberts further observes that this is valid particularly for poetry, because of its fixed metrical forms. Based on the evidence of the distinctive fractal structure of *Peredur*'s Short Version, I would venture to suggest that the same applies to prose texts, and thus might in fact be valid for the whole *cyfarwyddyd* tradition broadly defined (including laws and, more predictably perhaps, triads themselves). The fractal structure of *Peredur* provides a mnemonic model that corroborates the general observations on the patterns of memorisation discussed by Sioned Davies with reference to the role of memory for medieval Welsh *cyfarwyddyd*.[114] Such fractal structure is to be found in other medieval Welsh prose texts. Much the same structure has been found in *Manawydan uab Lyr*, for instance (also known as the 'Third Branch of the Mabinogi'), by Ian Hughes, who does not identify it as fractal, however.[115] Further investigation of its role as a mnemonic device for oral composition is needed. Either the nature of its transmission and the surviving variant versions allow us a better glimpse into earlier stages than for the other texts, most of which survive in only the White Book and Red Book versions (later and more literary), or *Peredur* required a tighter formal structure than the other tales because of a lack of unifying plotline.[116] Confirmation of this theory would require further investigation in the frame of a larger and different project, and thus lies beyond the scope of the present study.[117] The argument presented here, combined with what has hitherto been demonstrated for the Welsh oral tradition, especially by Brynley F. Roberts and Sioned Davies, would justify such a project.

The analysis here is based entirely on the internal narrative structure. This structure is not entirely reflected in the manuscript tradition.[118] For the break between Episodes I and II, there is no indication in any of our manuscripts that a new episode begins at this stage, and the account of Peredur's evening stroll continues directly on the reference to his return to Arthur's court as continuous text in all three manuscripts. In Peniarth 7 (and in Sioned Davies's translation), what is here interpreted as an episode break falls within a single sentence, while in the White Book there is a sentence break but no coloured initials or any other indications of an episode break.[119] Whether Peniarth 7 marks a break between Episodes II and III is unknown because of the gap in the manuscript at that point.[120]

The White Book (Peniarth 4), does mark the break between Episodes II and III with a large coloured (red) initial on f. 38v.[121] The *Peredur* text in the manuscript, however, does not show any use of red to mark smaller capital letters in the Short Version before or after f. 38, where red lines are also used to decorate regular initial capitals (four in the first column and two in the second column).[122] The only use of red is in the faded, large, coloured initial *E* at the beginning of the text on f. 30r. The Continuation, after the Empress episode and the conclusion of Episode III, is also marked by a large red initial, with at least two further letters in the same section of the column (after the coloured initial) decorated in red.[123] There is no further use of red to mark sections or initials until the red initial of the following text (*Breudwyt Macsen Wledic*) on f. 45r. The rubrication pattern in the Red Book is the same as that in the White Book, with episode breaks marked between Episodes II and III but not between Episodes I and II, although the presence of red decoration on regular initials means the break between the sentence ending Episode I and that beginning Episode II is marked (but not distinguished from other sentence breaks).[124] While some conclusions may be drawn on the basis of these patterns, including that copyists or rubricators appear to have recognised some breaks in the tale, manuscript evidence represents only some reflection of oral performative culture in written witnesses, and therefore should not be taken as the exclusive guide.[125]

The fact that the manuscripts seem to be imposing a slightly different organisational system on the text, diverging from the fractal system described earlier, appears to be part of the creation of a hybrid product, with the addition of the Continuation. This part of the text belongs to a hybrid culture, as it is clearly derived from the written (at best aural) culture of the French *Perceval*. It also echoes Chrétien by beginning and then abandoning an account of the adventures of Gwalchmai. It is worth examining the Continuation a little more closely.

Initially, the Welsh text follows Chrétien closely. It commences at Arthur's court with the arrival of the Ugly Damsel, who greets everyone except the hero.[126] She then gives an account of the lance procession, but not as it stands in Episode I.[127] Instead of three streams from the lance, there is one drop of blood, there is only one lance-bearer rather than two, and the king is lame (the lame uncle was the first, not the second uncle).[128] She does not refer to the head but rather obliquely to 'other wonders' witnessed during the feast. Her home is the Castle of Pride, which in the French text is her destination, but the description is virtually identical: in both castles fame can be acquired, and 566 knights are already present.[129] Like her French counterpart, she also continues with the description of the besieged maiden.[130] Her speech evokes responses from Gwalchmai and Peredur. Gwalchmai wishes to liberate the maiden. Peredur responds to the accusation that he asked no questions of the spear: he wishes to learn its story.[131]

Before they have a chance to set out, a second visitor arrives: a knight in golden armour with a blue cross on a golden shield.[132] In French he is identified as Guinganbresil, but in Welsh he remains nameless.[133] He delivers an accusation against Gwalchmai for killing his lord, which is identical in the French version, and invites him do defend himself before his (also unnamed) king.[134] Gwalchmai accepts the challenge (as does Gauvain in the French) and refuses offers at court of different armour (also in the French). Peredur and he set out together.

At this point, the tale follows Gwalchmai, just as the French text follows Gauvain at this juncture. This is an abortive example of the narrative technique of interlace, which, to quote Frank Brandsma's description, 'consists of the alternation of narrative threads', and is frequently found in French narratives.[135] Abortive, in this case, because the Welsh narrative never returns to Gwalchmai, whereas the French does return to Gauvain at a point that will be signalled in the summary to follow in this chapter and that marks a departure of the Welsh text from the French.[136]

Gwalchmai arrives, as Gauvain does, at the castle of those whose lord he is accused of killing. His is unaware of this and is not recognised. As in the French text, in the Welsh version he is sent on by the lord whom he meets on the way (the son of the man that he is supposed to have killed) and directed to the lord's sister, who welcomes him. In the French version, Gauvain makes love to her, while in the Welsh text they talk. The difference is crucial but all the more striking because when surprised *en flagrant délit* by a vavasour in *Perceval*, the lady receives a long lecture on the fickleness of women who prefer evil to good, while in the Welsh text she is immediately and seemingly without particular provocation called *achenoges butein*, translated by Sioned Davies as 'whore'.[137] This is a striking example of verbal abuse, highly uncommon in the Welsh texts, and it seems to be responding to the action of the French version of the scene, rather than that of the Welsh. There is only one other instance of address in *Peredur* that might be interpreted as an insult, when the hero addresses one of the witches of Gloucester in Episode I(C), and the priest addressing Peredur as *truan* ('miserable wretch') later on in the Continuation itself.[138] No similar insults in forms of address are found in either *Owain* or *Gereint*.[139] The fact that the insult in this episode of *Peredur* is unique and that it better matches the situation in the French text, suggests that this is a case of adaptation.

It may be that what we have in the Welsh version is an abridged retelling that was intended to serve as a canvas for the oral narration. A storyteller could fill out the details based on the general outline available.[140] This explanation would help make sense of the otherwise oblique reference to Gwalchmai using the *gwyddbwyll* board to prevent others from entering the room. However, the question remains of how exactly did he use it? The French narrative provides a lengthy explanation wherein it is made clear that Gauvain uses the chessboard as a shield. Another similar example is to be found slightly further into the narrative, where, once the earl arrives and Gwalchmai's identity is discovered, the French narrative has Gauvain's trial postponed with the assignment given him to try and find the lance. In the Welsh version, his hosts are unable to extract revenge (because they are his hosts), but the pattern of the story must be followed, so he is given a year's respite, to return again afterwards, but in this case to accept or deny the charges. Further – and this is where the Welsh version is clearly abridging – Gwalchmai is not assigned the quest of the lance at this point, but claims to be on an unspecified quest himself: 'Neges yd wyf i yn mynet y Arthur ac i mi hun' ('I am on a quest for Arthur and myself').[141] This is probably a reference to the maiden in need of rescue, mentioned by the Ugly Damsel at the beginning of the episode. He sets off the next day, and the narrative abandons this story for good, returning to Gwalchmai only at the conclusion.

Peredur, meanwhile, proceeds on his journey. At this point, the Welsh narrative begins to diverge progressively from the French.[142] The French version tells its readers that Perceval had wandered for five years, forgetting God. The Welsh version, that Peredur had wandered (for an unspecified amount of time that is later found to be one year).[143] On Good Friday, Perceval meets knights and ladies afoot who admonish him fairly gently for riding, while Peredur meets a priest, who begins by calling him a *truan* ('miserable wretch').[144] Peredur travels on and ends up staying with the same priest later. It is worth pointing out that the Welsh Continuation appears to be uncomfortable not only with the material but also with description. Perceval stays at a hermitage. Peredur stays at a *caer uoel* ('fort with no towers') where the priest lives.[145] One assumes that a hermitage is meant, but the Welsh redactor is either having difficulty finding an appropriate term, or is presenting Peredur's view, with assumption that Peredur would not recognise a hermitage if he saw one.[146] Whereas the French narrative has the religious explain the Grail procession to Perceval, no such explanation or mention of the procession is made in the Welsh text. Instead, Peredur asks of the Fortress of Wonders and receives information about a castle where he may find further directions. Chrétien's narrative at this point switches back to Gauvain and never returns to Perceval.

The remainder of the Welsh Continuation, which follows Peredur's adventures, is thus independent of Chrétien, but does share some elements with his continuations, and in particular it has been argued that it was dependent on the *Second Continuation* (*c*.1200) for its sequence of adventures at the Fortress of Wonders: the adventures of the chess/*gwyddbwyll* board, the magic stag, and the warrior under a slab.[147] Claude Luttrell has pointed out the nearly identical nature of the episodes in *Peredur* and the *Second Continuation*, and suggested that taken alongside parallels between *Peredur* and Chrétien and *Peredur* and the *Lancelot* (s. XIII[1]), this means that the Welsh text uses the French sources.[148] As far as the *Peredur* Continuation is concerned, this seems to be a valid argument, because the sequence only makes sense in light of the French text. The single adventure that Peredur has before arriving at the Fortress of Wonders, where he is imprisoned by a king and temporarily released by the king's daughter to participate anonymously in a contest, has, as Luttrell points out, a close parallel in *Lancelot*.[149]

It is worth dwelling for a moment on the sequence found in the Fortress of Wonders episode. Luttrell's argument runs that because the Welsh author uses Chrétien, and because there are similarities with other French texts, the sections that are paralleled with other French texts must be adapted from them by the Welsh. However, it does not seem to me to be self-evident that if the Welsh author or redactor of the Continuation used one French source that it would necessarily follow that he must have used exclusively French sources, selecting individual episodes from them for adaptation. It is not impossible, but it is not self-evident.

The structure of the Fortress of Wonders sequence is suspiciously tripartite and may merit further investigation. Once Peredur enters the fortress he sees a *gwyddbwyll* board with pieces playing themselves, and once one side wins, the pieces cheer. In annoyance, he throws the board out of the window and a black-haired damsel arrives to chastise him and give him a task to retrieve the board: to fight the black-haired man in the

Fortress of Yspidinongyl, who oppressed the Empress's land.[150] Sir John Rhŷs had argued on the basis of the similarity between this name and a personal name found in Sir Thomas Malory's *Morte Darthur* (and some of Malory's sources), Espinogre, ultimately derived from Ysbaddaden chief giant, the main antagonist in the native Welsh Arthurian narrative *Culhwch ac Olwen*, that the *Peredur* reference, too, is derived from Welsh sources, but in this case via the French.[151] The second of three challenges faced by Peredur is assigned to him on completion of this: to kill a stag with a horn in its forehead (one wonders if this is a unicorn).[152] He kills it with the help of the Empress's small dog, and beheads it, only to be upbraided by a lady. As recompense, she assigns him his third labour: to challenge a man under a slab. There is another tripartite element here, as she tells him to ask for the man three times.[153] The battle with the man (black-haired also) concludes this sequence.

It will be seen that while there is a tripartite structure here, and that there is at least one hint of further in-built three-fold repetition, it is not as intricate as the fractal pattern found in Episodes I to III. In light of this, it seems reasonable to accept Luttrell's conclusion that this is borrowed from the *Second Continuation*. However, I would venture to suggest that the traces of a triadic structure in the episode, combined with Sor John Rhŷs's suggestion regarding *Ysbidinongyl*, point (albeit tentatively) to the possibility that in origin this episode may have come from an oral Welsh tradition, shared with Episodes I to III, and made its way back to Wales via the French texts.

Thereafter, the narrative is brought to an abrupt conclusion, which is unparalleled in the Grail tradition because it attempts to link the Continuation back to the elements that are unique to the Welsh Episode I. Peredur travels along a mountain to a river valley, where he finds a fortress in which a grey-haired lame man, Gwalchmai, and a yellow-haired youth await him (note that we have three characters here).[154] We are never told how Gwalchmai came to be there. The youth explains to Peredur that in the procession in Episode I he had carried the head of his cousin (but the details of the procession are blurred now, as the lad says he brought the head and the lance).[155] He tells the hero that it is he who is prophesied to avenge the cousin against the witches of Gloucester, and Peredur, Gwalchmai and Arthur complete this mission. The Continuation closes with the words 'Ac velly y treythir o Gaer yr Ynryfedodeu' ('And that is what is told of the Fortress of Wonders').[156] The conclusion suggests that it hereby closes only this part of the *Peredur* story, thus confirming the idea of the episodic nature of the narrative and the semi-independent nature of the Continuation.[157]

Although this conclusion is unparalleled in the Grail tradition, it does share certain similarities with the redactorial interventions in the Welsh compilations of translated material concerning Charlemagne, known as the Charlemagne Cycle. The Welsh Charlemagne Cycle is a loose collection of translated texts concerning Charlemagne, using a translation of the Pseudo-Turpin Chronicle as a framework. It survives in a large number of manuscripts (not always in the same sequence of texts) and appears to have taken shape towards the end of the thirteenth century and includes *Cân Rolant* ('Song of Roland'), *Pererindod Siarlymaen* ('Pilgrimage of Charlemagne'), the *Cronicl Turpin* ('Pseudo-Turpin Chronicle') and *Rhamant Otuel* ('Romance of Otuel').[158] The Welsh Charlemagne Cycle introduced transitional passages to link the different texts composing the cycle together.[159] Although no transitional passage is introduced at the beginning of the Continuation, the addition of the explanation at the end, linking the Continuation to Episode I seems to represent the same approach to compilation of originally separate narratives as the one we see in the use of the *Cronicl Turpin* to frame the collection of disparate texts in the Welsh Charlemagne Cycle.

This similarity yields some additional support to the proposed reading of what we now term *Peredur* as a combination of four distinct units: Episodes I, II, III and the Continuation, brought together as a loose collection of tales with the same hero. The relationship that each one of these component narratives has to Chrétien's text and the Continental tradition is therefore distinct and should be treated separately. Thus, although Luttrell's view that the Continuation is dependent on French narratives is accepted here, his arguments for the other Episodes of *Peredur* cannot be. Nevertheless, some of the reasoning that he puts forward in support of his thesis that all episodes of *Peredur* constitute adaptations of French sources deserves some comment.

Luttrell also compares the *Lancelot* sequence, where the hero is released from captivity to fight, with the Empress episode (in Episode III) of *Peredur*, but I am inclined to see the similarities – the hero mesmerised by the sight of beauty, and the subsequent awakening by being hit – as a *topos* that may indeed be a borrowing (possibly from a common source – *Lancelot* borrows its episode from Chrétien's *Chevalier de la charette*) but does not prove that the entire episode was borrowed.[160] Similarly, he suggests that *Peredur* borrowed its account of the hero's combat with the knights of the Countess of the Feats (Episode II) from a lost Anglo-Norman French source, as the pattern is attested in a surviving German text from c.1200. This is not impossible, but it requires too many presuppositions. Furthermore, the episode is not identical to *Peredur*'s, as there is no simultaneous combat against 300 knights, but rather combat against knights one by one after touching their shields, in order to sit by the Countess. In the case of the correspondences he finds in the sections that we designate here as Episodes II and III, Luttrell acknowledges that the Welsh redactor's use of French sources is combinatory, not straightforward, and different in each case.[161] While it is possible to read each instance of correspondence between French sources and Welsh narrative as the use of the former by the latter, the resulting picture is of a singularly well-read but spectacularly incompetent redactor. In particular, the logic of the main argument appears somewhat biased: 'La dépendance du conte gallois vis-à-vis du roman de Chrétien, et non pas dans l'autre sens, se révèle par le fait que l'*Historia Peredur* laisse voir des reflets d'autres sources françaises' ('The dependence of the Welsh tale on Chrétien's romance, and not in the other direction, is shown by the fact that the *Historia Peredur* shows reflections of other French sources').[162] It is unclear to me why the theory that a hypothetical single redactor of *Peredur* used multiple different, very recent sources (some of which date to c.1200, and the earliest surviving manuscript of *Peredur*, which cannot have been the first, dates to the second half of the thirteenth century), most of which are extremely long texts, to extract particular scenes, is more acceptable than the theory that these French texts might ultimately have drawn on the same tradition as the redactor of *Peredur*. Occam's razor seems to suggest the latter.[163] Research on other elements of the Grail legend, such as the association of the Fisher King with Bran, described later, has provided ample evidence for the wider circulation of themes and elements that various medieval authors drew on.[164] As far as the Welsh Continuation, and it alone, is concerned, the view upheld here is that Luttrell's conclusions hold.

Hitherto, analyses of the structure of *Peredur* as a multi-episode tale (whether in its short or long versions) have tacitly assumed that the narrative whole would be experienced as a single unit, whether through reading or consecutive sessions of oral performance. The inclusion of the Continuation in the Long Version preserved in the White Book and the Red Book has facilitated this perception of *Peredur* as a single tale, because it constituted an addition based on a combination of elements derived from the French tradition, from both Chrétien's text and its own various continuations.[165] Rather than taking this as an incompetent redactor's attempt at editing the text into a single tale, it might be useful to see this as an antiquarian exercise of the type that we see medieval Welsh compilers and scribes engage in for other texts, including in particular the Welsh Charlemagne Cycle.[166] One might also be tempted to see the Welsh Continuation less in terms of a conclusion to the story and more in terms of a sequel, or perhaps even as a spin-off about a favourite character, of the type proliferating in modern television.[167]

Recent research has shown that this Continuation is an addition made to the longer version, and that the Short Version preserved in Peniarth 7 represents an earlier stage of development. The notion of consecutive consumption of a narrative common to modern readers or audiences does not necessarily have to be shared by medieval audiences and is heavily reliant on reading culture. Taking oral creation, transmission and performance as the base assumption helps to see *Peredur* not as a single text but as a combination of independent narratives. The discussion in this chapter has built on this and followed the division of the text proposed by Thurneysen and later elaborated by Davies, and has shown that the three episodes of the Short Version are unconnected to each other and can be perceived and performed as separate narratives. The analysis of these episodes' narrative structures has yielded a new structural model, based on the geometrical concept of the fractal. The scale-symmetric self-similar repetitive pattern observed in this analysis supplements previous research on the oral composition techniques of medieval Welsh narratives and shows that the triad served as a much more fundamental mnemonic tool than had been previously supposed. The regularity of the pattern suggests that the currently accepted view that *Peredur* is, by modern standards, a confused and chaotic narrative should be abandoned. Benoît M. Mandelbrot's fractal theory can help re-evaluate it in exactly the same way that it did the mathematical 'gallery of monsters', including Brownian motion and the Cantor set.[168] This structural regularity is, unsurprisingly, a feature only of the Short Version Episodes I to III.

Having shown that *Peredur* as a narrative complex is not the monster it has been previously taken for, we may allow Peredur the hero to set out on his series of journeys. The following chapter examines the imaginary geography of Episodes I to III. It will be shown that the three narratives take place in locations that are differently marked and may correspond to imaginary representations of different parts of the world, thus reinforcing the independent nature of the three episodes shown in this present chapter.

Notes

1. For previous discussions, see, for instance, Lloyd-Morgan, 'Narrative Structure in *Peredur*'; and most recently Lloyd-Morgan, '*Historia Peredur*', pp. 150–4, including an overview of previous studies. For a detailed analysis of further earlier discussions of the story's structure, with summaries of the story elements, see Goetinck, *Peredur*, pp. 18–20. See also the outlines of the tale provided in Brynley F. Roberts, 'Tales and Romances', in Brynley F. Roberts, *Studies on Middle Welsh Literature* (Lampeter: Edwin Mellen Press, 1992), pp. 41–79 (p. 60); Bollard, 'Theme and Meaning', 75–7; and Helmut Birkhan, 'The Unholy Grail in Britain: A Remarkable Example of Secondary Paganisation', in Susanne Friede (ed.), *Autour du graal: Questions d'approche(s)* (Paris: Classiques Garnier, 2020), pp. 117–41 (pp. 126–31).
2. An excellent overview of some of the problems encountered by previous scholarship is to be found in Lloyd-Morgan, 'Narrative Structure in *Peredur*', 188–9.
3. Lloyd-Morgan, 'Narrative Structure in *Peredur*', 188.
4. For an argument in favour of reading medieval texts in the form in which they have come down to us, see R. M. Jones, 'Narrative Structure in Medieval Welsh Prose Tales', in Ellis D. Evans, John G. Griffith and E. M. Jope (eds), *Proceedings of the Seventh International Congress of Celtic Studies* (Oxford: D. E. Evans: Distributed by Oxbow Books, 1986), pp. 171–98 (pp. 175, 177).
5. Lloyd-Morgan, 'Narrative Structure in *Peredur*', 191. See also subsequent discussion in Bollard, 'Theme and Meaning', 73–4 and the earlier observations in R. M. Jones, 'Narrative Structure in Medieval Welsh Prose Tales'.
6. For references to discussions, see n. 24 and 25 in the Introduction.
7. Roberts, '*Peredur Son of Efrawg*', 60; Lovecy, '*Historia Peredur*', pp. 174–5; Lloyd-Morgan, '*Historia Peredur*', pp. 150–3.
8. For summaries of the episodes of *Peredur*, see Roberts, '*Peredur Son of Efrawg*', 60–2. Cf. Ned Sturzer's observation that medieval Welsh narratives 'were composed by stringing together unrelated episodes'; Sturzer, 'Inconsistencies and Infelicities in the Welsh Tales: Their Implications', *Studia Celtica*, 37 (2013), 127–42 at 131. The argument that I propose here, however, is that there is a much more formal aspect to the organisation of *Peredur* than a mere 'stringing together' of 'unrelated episodes'. This is in line with M. R. Jones's observations that in medieval Welsh tales, triadic structures as more than 'a merely stylistic device'; 'Narrative Structure in Medieval Welsh Prose Tales', p. 182. Compare also Ian Hughes's discussion of what appears to be a very similar structure in the Third Branch of the Mabinogi (also known as

Manawydan) in Ian Hughes, 'Tripartite Structure in *Manawydan Uab Llyr*', in Mícheál Ó Flaithearta (ed.), *Proceedings of the Seventh Symposium of Societas Celtologica Nordica* (Uppsala: Uppsala Universitet, 2007), pp. 99–109. I am currently in the process of writing a more general discussion addressing the topology of medieval Welsh prose tales in general.

9 Lovecy, '*Historia Peredur*', p. 180. Rudolf Thurneysen, review of Mary Rh. Williams, *Essai sur la composition du roman gallois de Peredur* (Paris, Champion, 1909), published in *Zeitschrift für celtische Philologie*, 8 (1912), 185–9. See also the discussion in Foster, '*Gereint, Owein,* and *Peredur*', pp. 200–1; and Goetinck, *Peredur*, pp. 18–19. Goetinck's argument that '*Peredur* is not suited to the tripartite mould' (Goetinck, *Peredur*, p. 11) will be shown below to be unnecessarily defeatist. The text is consummately triadic in structure.

10 Thurneysen, review of M. Williams, *Essai*, 186. For a helpful tabular summary of Thurneysen's structure analysis and a discussion of alternative structural analyses from the same period, see Lovecy, '*Historia Peredur*', pp. 172–3.

11 Davies, *Crefft y Cyfarwydd* (Cardiff: University of Wales Press, 1995), pp. 88, 90–1.

12 That *Historia Peredur* has a triadic structure has been observed by Ceridwen Lloyd-Morgan, 'Triadic Structures in the Four Branches of the *Mabinogi*', *Shadow*, 5 (1988), 3–11, at 4, although she appears to take the whole surviving text as triadic (thus recognising breaks between Episodes II and III, and between Episode III and the Continuation), Lloyd-Morgan, 'Triadic Structures', 10 n. 4. I keep the term 'episode' here for the sake of convenience, although my argument is that we are dealing with separate stories about the same character.

13 Rudolf Thurneysen, review of M. Williams, *Essai*, p. 186. See pp. 35–6 of this book.

14 Davies (trans.), *Mabinogion*, p. xv. Cf. also M. R. Jones's remarks on the differences in audience perceptions of the structure in medieval texts; 'Narrative Structure in Medieval Welsh Prose Tales', p. 184.

15 Davies (trans.), *Mabinogion*, p. xv; Sioned Davies, 'Written Text as Performance: The Implications for Middle Welsh Prose Narratives', in Huw Pryce (ed.), *Literacy in Medieval Celtic Societies* (Cambridge: Cambridge University Press, 1998), pp. 133–48; Sioned Davies, 'Performing *Culhwch ac Olwen*', in Ceridwen Lloyd-Morgan (ed.), *Arthurian Literature XXI: Celtic Arthurian Material* (Cambridge: Boydell & Brewer, 2012) pp. 29–52 (pp. 50–1). See also the remarks in Lloyd-Morgan, 'Narrative Structure in *Peredur*', 197; and Lloyd-Morgan, 'Triadic Structures', p. 4. See pp. 31–2 of this book.

16 Lovecy, '*Historia Peredur*', p. 172.

17 This view thus proposes a third alternative to the two approaches summarised by Lovecy, which constitute 'attempts to find narrative unity' on the one hand and suggestions of 'narrative *dis*unity resulting from the failure of successive

redactors to understand the myth which underlies the story'; Lovecy, '*Historia Peredur*', p. 173, emphasis Lovecy's. The view expressed in the present chapter is that there is no 'narrative unity', and no redactor tried imposing any, successfully or otherwise.

18 See overviews of previous scholarship in Foster, '*Gereint, Owein*, and *Peredur*', pp. 201–3; Lovecy, '*Historia Peredur*', pp. 173–5; and most recently Lloyd-Morgan, '*Historia Peredur*', pp. 150–4.

19 For previous discussions of the dependence of the Welsh Continuation on the French tradition, see Lovecy, '*Historia Peredur*', pp. 178–9; and Lloyd-Morgan, '*Historia Peredur*', pp. 147–50.

20 Davies (trans.), *Mabinogion*, p. xvi.

21 See p. 41 of this book.

22 For discussions of this fallacy see references in n. 9 in the Introduction.

23 Davies (trans.), *Mabinogion*, p. xxiv.

24 For more on emotions in medieval Welsh 'romances', see, for instance, Helen Fulton, 'Gender and Jealousy in *Gereint uab Erbin* and *Le Roman de Silence*', *Arthuriana*, 24 (2014), 43–70; Christina Fischer, 'Innensicht und Außensicht. Zur Figurenpsychologie in *Chwedyl Iarlles y Ffynnawn (Owein)*', in Cora Dietl, Christoph Schanze, Friedrich Wolfzettel and Lena Zudrell (eds), *Emotion und Handlung im Artusroman* (Berlin/Boston: Walter de Gruyter 2017), pp. 99–115; Erich Poppe, 'Love, Sadness and Other Mental States in the Middle Welsh *Owain* (and Related Texts)', *Journal of the International Arthurian Society*, 8 (2020), 38–60.

25 The concept of 'hyperfocus' remains ill-defined, but is a general term applying to states that reflect 'one's complete absorption in a task, to a point where a person appears to completely ignore or "tune out" everything else'; Brandon K. Ashinof and Ahmad AbuAkel, 'Hyperfocus: the Forgotten Frontier of Attention', *Psychological Research*, 85 (2021), 1–19 (1); see also Ashinof and AbuAkel, 'Hyperfocus', 2, for four criteria that are usually associated with hyperfocus states in secondary literature.

26 Roberts, '*Peredur Son of Efrawg*', 63.

27 For a recent overview of previous studies of *Peredur*'s structure, see Lloyd-Morgan, '*Historia Peredur*', and references in n. 9 (above). To this might be added Jonathan Miles-Watson's analysis of the *Peredur* narrative as a complex of distinct (but thematically interconnected) myths, although he still sees the text as one story; see Jonathan Miles-Watson, *Welsh Mythology: A Neostructuralist Analysis* (Amherst NY: Cambria Press, 2010), pp. 123–64. He sees the Empress figure as a Sovereignty goddess, following Goetinck's analysis (p. 134). The idea was proposed at an earlier point in Roger Sherman Loomis, *The Grail from Celtic Myth to Christian Symbol* (Cardiff: University of Wales Press, 1963); see the criticism in Maartje Draak's review of the volume in *Medium Aevum*, 35 (1966), 260–4, esp. 263–4.

28 The episodes are differentiated in Sioned Davies's translation, but without commentary. It will be shown below that the separation of the episodes is dictated by the narrative, even though there is no division between Episode I and Episode II marked in any of the surviving manuscript witnesses, and only the break between Episode II and Episode III is given in the White Book and Red Book.

29 Brief overviews of the episodes unique to the Welsh text can be found in Lloyd-Morgan, '*Historia Peredur*', p. 148; and Lowri Morgans, '*Peredur son of Efrawg*: The Question of Translation and/or Adaptation', in *A Handbook of Arthurian Romance*, pp. 403–14 (pp. 409–10). A detailed discussion is provided on pp. 27–31 of this book.

30 Lloyd-Morgan, '*Historia Peredur*', p. 148. See also discussion of the possible parallels between *Peredur* and Chrétien's *Yvain* in Annalee C. Rejhon, 'The "Mute Knight" and the "Knight of the Lion". Implications of the Hidden Name Motif in the Welsh *Historia Peredur vab Efrawc* and Chrétien de Troyes's *Yvain ou le Chevalier au Lion*', *Studia Celtica*, 20 (1985–6), 110–22. I am grateful to the anonymous reviewer of the University of Wales Press for this reference. There are numerous discussions of the relationship between the Welsh and French versions of the *Owain/Yvain* story; see, for instance; Tony Hunt, 'Some Observations on the Textual Relationship of *Li Chevaliers au Lion* and *Iarlles y Ffynnawn*', *Zeitschrift für Celtische Philologie*, 33/1 (1974), 93–113; Erich Poppe, '*Owein*, *Ystorya Bown*, and the Problem of "Relative Distance": Some Methodological Considerations and Speculations', in Lloyd-Morgan (ed.), *Arthurian Literature XXI*, pp. 73–94. For an up-to-date discussion and introductory bibliography on the subject, see Regine Reck, '*Owain* or *Chwedyl Iarlles y Ffynnawn*', in Lloyd-Morgan and Poppe (eds), *Arthur in the Celtic Languages*, pp. 117–31.

31 Since the narrative is identical in all manuscripts, with only minor variation in detail, the text quoted throughout the discussion of the structure is from Glenys Goetinck's edition and Sioned Davies's translation of the Long Version for ease of reference. Glenys Goetinck's edition includes the text of Peniarth 7 and Peniarth 14 in the Appendix, at pp. 160–81, and 182–7, but as a transcription, without editorial intervention on matters of punctuation, capitalisation, expansion of abbreviations or word division. I quote it only where it is necessary to discuss differences between the short and long versions at the level of detail. For an alternative edition of these manuscripts, see Vitt, '*Peredur*'.

32 For a discussion of these instructions, see Bollard, 'Theme and Meaning', 78–9. Notable is Bollard's observation that while the punctuation in Goetinck's edition and modern translations appear to indicate that the mother is telling him that to make love to women against their will would make him a better man, following the manuscripts enables us to shift that

punctuation to indicate that even if his courtship is not accepted, he will be a better man for it; Bollard, 'Theme and Meaning', 91 n. 9. Sioned Davies's translation follows the former interpretation, *The Mabinogion*, pp. 66–7.
33 Goetinck (ed.), *Historia Peredur*, pp. 15, 162.
34 Goetinck (ed.), *Historia Peredur*, pp. 15, 16; Davies (trans.), *Mabinogion*, p. 70.
35 Kibler (trans.), *The Story of the Grail*, p. 397.
36 Goetinck (ed.), *Historia Peredur*, p. 16; Davies, trans., *Mabinogion*, p. 70.
37 Goetinck (ed.), *Historia Peredur*, p. 16; Davies, trans., *Mabinogion*, p. 70–1.
38 Goetinck (ed.), *Historia Peredur*, p. 16; the first phrase is almost identical in the Peniarth 7 version, with the difference that the reprimand, *ceryd*, is characterised as *mawr* ('great'), Goetinck (ed.), *Historia Peredur*, p. 162; Davies (trans.), *Mabinogion*, p. 71.
39 Both uncles are related to Peredur through his mother. This constitutes another significant cultural reference, as the sister's son had a special status; see Thomas Charles-Edwards, *Early Irish and Welsh Kinship* (Oxford: Oxford University Press, 1993), p. 179. The importance of the relationship in Chrétien's romance was discussed in William A. Nitze, 'The Sister's Son and the *Conte del Graal*', *Modern Philology*, 9 (1912), 1–32. Ned Sturzer suggests that this character's identification as a foster sister is problematic, because 'it is quite unexpected that Peredur was ever sent out to fosterage'; Sturzer, 'Inconsistencies', 129. However, this is not an inconsistency at all if we consider the possibility that the foster sister might be older than the hero and might have been fostered at his parents' court, before Efrawc's demise (hence she would remember Peredur who would have been too young at that point to remember her, and hence she would remember the dwarfs being those of his father and mother, while he did not).
40 Goetinck (ed.), *Historia Peredur*, p. 16; Davies (trans.), *Mabinogion*, p. 71.
41 Goetinck (ed.), *Historia Peredur*, p. 18; Davies (trans.), *Mabinogion*, p. 72.
42 Goetinck (ed.), *Historia Peredur*, p. 19; Davies (trans.), *Mabinogion*, p. 72. In Chrétien's text there is another adventure at this point, after the first castle, that of the Dispossessed Countess, blonde in the French and brunette in Peredur, which occurs in Episode I(C) of *Peredur*. Cf. analysis in Lovecy, '*Historia Peredur*', pp. 176–77.
43 Goetinck (ed.), *Historia Peredur*, p. 19; Davies (trans.), *Mabinogion*, p. 72–3.
44 Goetinck (ed.), *Historia Peredur*, p. 20; Davies (trans.), *Mabinogion*, p. 73. This scene is discussed in greater detail in Chapters 4 and 5.
45 Goetinck (ed.), *Historia Peredur*, p. 21; Davies (trans.), *Mabinogion*, p. 73.
46 Goetinck (ed.), *Historia Peredur*, p. 22; Davies (trans.), *Mabinogion*, p. 74.
47 For a discussion of this character, see Chapter 6.
48 Chrétien de Troyes, *Le Conte du Graal*, ll. 1657–2865, 3628–3931; ed. and trans. by Méla, pp. 992–1028, 1050–9; Kibler (trans.), *The Story of the Grail*, pp. 403–14 and 426–7.

49 Goetinck (ed.), *Historia Peredur*, p. 22; Davies (trans.), *Mabinogion*, p. 74.
50 Goetinck (ed.), *Historia Peredur*, p. 23; Davies (trans.), *Mabinogion*, p. 75.
51 See discussion in Lloyd-Morgan, 'Narrative Structure in *Peredur*', 206–7; the episode is further mentioned on p. 100 of this book.
52 Chrétien de Troyes, *Le Conte du Graal*, ll. 1768–72, 2852; ed. and trans. by Méla, pp. 996, 1027; Kibler (trans.), *The Story of the Grail*, p. 403, 417.
53 Goetinck (ed.), *Historia Peredur*, p. 25; Davies (trans.), *Mabinogion*, p. 76. Note that here, too, there are differences between the Welsh and French narratives – in the French text the maiden goes to Perceval for help of her own accord, having steeled herself for the ordeal, and tells him explicitly not to assume that she was offering herself to him despite her being half-naked, while in the Welsh version she is forced by her household to do so, as they propose this as the only solution to her problem. For the scene in the French text, see Chrétien de Troyes, *Le Conte du Graal*, ll. 1903–2025; ed. and trans. by Méla, pp. 999–1003; and Kibler (trans.), *The Story of the Grail*, pp. 405–6. It is also worth noting that while in the Welsh text, the maiden leaves reassured after their chaste conversation, in the French version, she spends the night with Perceval in his bed: '*Ensin jurent tote la nuit / Li uns lez l'autre, boche a boche*' (ll. 2022–3) ('Thus they lay side by side with lips touching all night long, until morning came and day dawned') (Kibler (trans.), p. 407). One might argue which of the two is more realistic, but I would suggest that the Welsh is more in line with the (perhaps idealised) social conventions of the audience: spending the night would constitute a type of marital union under Welsh laws, and medieval Welsh texts (and *Peredur* in particular) show a very clear aptitude for reflecting medieval Welsh laws; see discussion in Chapter 5.
54 Goetinck (ed.), *Historia Peredur*, p. 26–7; Davies (trans.), *Mabinogion*, p. 77. In Chrétien's version Perceval goes through only two, not three rounds of fighting; Chrétien de Troyes, *Le Conte du Graal*, ll. 2096–624; ed. and trans. by Méla, pp. 1005–21; Kibler (trans.), *The Story of the Grail*, p. 408–14.
55 Goetinck (ed.), *Historia Peredur*, p. 29; Davies (trans.), *Mabinogion*, p. 78. This episode, the large woman and the witches, are discussed in detail in Chapter 6.
56 Goetinck (ed.), *Historia Peredur*, p. 30; Davies (trans.), *Mabinogion*, p. 79.
57 Goetinck (ed.), *Historia Peredur*, p. 30; Davies (trans.), *Mabinogion*, p. 79.
58 Sioned Davies notes that this scene might have been inspired by the Irish *Exile of the Sons of Uisnech*, as black hair is unusual as a beauty ideal in this period, but she does not note that this matches the description of the young woman who offers herself to Peredur earlier in the episode; Davies (trans.), *Mabinogion*, p. 247. In the fourteenth century, Dafydd ap Gwilym praises a black-haired girl in the poem 'Dyddgu', and while it is remotely possible that Dafydd was inspired by the description in *Peredur*, it may be worth

reconsidering our assumptions regarding medieval Welsh beauty stereotypes; for the text and English translation of 'Dyddgu', see Poem 86, ed. by A. Cynfael Lake, *www.dafyddapgwilym.net* (last accessed 13 July 2021).

59 Goetinck (ed.), *Historia Peredur*, p. 31; Davies (trans.), *Mabinogion*, p. 79.

60 Goetinck (ed.), *Historia Peredur*, p. 35; Davies (trans.), *Mabinogion*, p. 82.

61 The foundational text for the mathematical study of fractals is Benoît Mandelbrot, *The Fractal Geometry of Nature* (New York: Freeman, 1982). An accessible explanation of fractals and fractal structures can be found in Benoît M. Mandelbrot, 'A Geometry Able to Include Mountains and Clouds', in N. Lesmoir-Gordon (ed.), *The Colours of Infinity: The Beauty and Power of Fractals* (London: Springer, 2010), pp. 38–57; generally, the essays in Lesmoir-Gordon, *The Colours of Infinity*, provide an accessible introduction to fractals.

62 For a definition of fractals, see Ian Stewart, 'The Nature of Fractal Geometry', in Lesmoir-Gordon, *The Colours of Infinity*, pp. 2–23 (p. 4). See also the description, in the context of an investigation of fractals in art, in Nicoletta Sala, 'Fractal Geometry in the Arts: An Overview Across the Different Cultures', in Miroslav M. Novak (ed.), *Thinking in Patterns: Fractals and Related Phenomena in Nature* (New Jersey, London: World Scientific, 2004), pp. 177–88 (p. 177).

63 Note that the importance of triadic patterns in this text (though not as its primary structuring principle) has been observed previously. Ian Lovecy has remarked that 'the events which come (usually incrementally) in threes: three blows against the column, three fights in the Circular Valley, three summonses from the Empress, three challenges from three men with three cups, and a need to seek a man who will fight three times', are all indicative of oral tradition; Lovecy, '*Historia Peredur*', p. 176. In the present book the 'Circular Valley' is referred to as the 'Round Valley'; see pp. 27–8 and 66–8 of this book.

64 In this tripartite structure, which is also composed mostly of triadic elements, there is only one potential narrative tangle, in Episode I(C), the scene of Peredur's contemplation of the raven on the snow; but this almost certainly refers to the besieged maiden in the castle; see Lloyd-Morgan, 'Narrative Structure in *Peredur*', 206–7.

65 Mandelbrot, 'A Geometry Able to Include Mountains and Clouds', pp. 44–5; the Sierpiński gasket is also referred to as a Sierpiński triangle, it is named after the Polish mathematician Wacław Sierpiński (1882–1969). For a brief entry on Sierpiński, see the Koninklijke Nederlandse Akademie van Wetenschappen *Digitaal Wetenschapshistorisch Centrum* Past Members page, *www.dwc.knaw.nl/biografie/pmknaw/?pagetype=authorDetail&aId=PE00002984* (last accessed 13 July 2021).

66 Sala, 'Fractal Geometry in the Arts', pp. 181–2, figures 10a and 10b.

67 These are mapped in Lloyd-Morgan, 'Narrative Structure in *Peredur*', 202–15.

68 'Mathematical objects are idealized models of certain features of the real world; they are not real things, and they do not correspond exactly to real things', as Ian Stewart puts it; 'The Nature of Fractal Geometry', p. 4. He also points out that the fact that the Earth is not a perfect sphere does not make the sphere any less useful as a model for it.
69 Stewart, 'The Nature of Fractal Geometry', p. 4.
70 For art using fractals to imitate chaotic structures, see Sala, 'Fractal Geometry in the Arts'.
71 Stewart, 'The Nature of Fractal Geometry', pp. 4, 5. Ceridwen Lloyd-Morgen describes the plot of *Peredur* as 'bewildering array of events'; Lloyd-Morgan, 'Narrative Structure in *Peredur*', 201.
72 See p. 5 of this book.
73 Examples include the three sets of trades practised by the heroes in *Manawydan*, the Third Branch of the Mabinogi, and the three journeys to the fountain undertaken by Cynon, Owein and Arthur in *Owein*. For *Manawydan*, see discussion in Hughes, 'Tripartite Structure'. See also Thomson (ed.), *Owein*, pp. 2, 24 and 21; *The Mabinogion*, pp. 117, 133 and 131, and discussion in Natalia I. Petrovskaia, 'Où va-t-on pour son aventure? Mondes connus et mondes inconnus dans le roman chevaleresque au Moyen Âge', in D. Buschinger, M. Olivier, T. Kuhnle, F. Gabaude, M-G. Grossel and P. Levron (eds), *Ce qui advient … les déclinaisons de l'aventure*, Médiévales 67 (Amiens: Presses du Centre d'études médiévales de Picardie, 2018), pp. 160–9 (pp. 163–6).
74 Goetinck (ed.), *Historia Peredur*, p. 35; Davies (trans.), *Mabinogion*, p. 82.
75 Sometimes referred to as the 'Circular Valley'; see, for instance, Lovecy, '*Historia Peredur*', p. 176, and quotation on p. 50, n. 63 of this book. This episode is discussed in greater detail in Chapter 2.
76 Goetinck (ed.), *Historia Peredur*, p. 39; Davies (trans.), *Mabinogion*, p. 82.
77 Goetinck (ed.), *Historia Peredur*, p. 40; Davies (trans.), *Mabinogion*, p. 84.
78 One wonders, however, whether this might be a shortened version of an adventure involving a monster and a gold-generating stone found in Episode III; see pp. 29, 30 of this book.
79 Robin Chapman Stacey, 'Gender and the Social Imaginary in Medieval Welsh Law', *Journal of the British Academy*, 8 (2020), 267–93 (286).
80 Natalia I. Petrovskaia, 'Oaths, Pagans and Lions: Arguments for a Crusade Sub-Narrative in *Historia Peredur fab Efrawc*', *Poetica*, 77 (2012), 1–26; the argument is revisited and revised in Chapter 2.
81 Goetinck (ed.), *Historia Peredur*, p. 42; Davies (trans.), *Mabinogion*, p. 86.
82 Goetinck (ed.), *Historia Peredur*, p. 42; Davies (trans.), *Mabinogion*, p. 86.
83 One might speculate that Peredur is in his mid to late teens in all episodes, but even cultural contextual evidence is shaky. It could be suggested that the point at which he leaves home and becomes a knight could be the

approximate age of knighthood in twelfth or thirteenth-century contexts, but there is contradictory evidence on the age of knighting or the beginning of adulthood; see, for instance, discussion in Ruth Mazo Karras, *From Boys to Men: Formations of Masculinity in Late Medieval Europe* (Philadelphia PA: University of Pennsylvania Press, 2003), pp. 12–15, 64. An alternative direction for the argument would be to read Peredur's stay with his uncles as fosterage, and approximate his adventures to the completion of fosterage, but there is insufficient evidence to narrow down a specific age for this, even if we were to assume that the Arthurian hero's biography followed real-world time frames, even if the latter could be established with any certainty, for there is contradictory evidence even in the Irish material, which is richer than the Welsh on this point. See Llinos Beverly Smith, 'Fosterage, Adoption, and God-Parenthood: Ritual and Fictive Kinship in Medieval Wales', *Welsh History Review/Cylchgrawn hanes Cymru*, 16 (1992), 1–35 (8) for the reading of Peredur's stay with his uncles as fosterage; and Thomas Charles O'Donnell, 'The Affect of Fosterage in Medieval Ireland' (unpublished PhD thesis, University College London, 2016), p. 33 on the end age of fosterage in Irish sources and pp. 35–6 on the difficulties of using Irish material to complement the Welsh.

84 Goetinck (ed.), *Historia Peredur*, p. 42; Davies (trans.), *Mabinogion*, p. 86. *Gwyddbwyll* is a Welsh board game that features in a number of prose tales; for more, see, for instance, Jan Niehues, 'All The King's Men? On Celtic Board-games and Their Identification', in Franziska Bock, Dagmar Bronner and Dagmar Schlüter (eds), *Allerlei Keltisches. Studien zu Ehren von Erich Poppe. Studies in Honour of Erich Poppe*, (Berlin: curach bhán, 2011), pp. 45–60.

85 Goetinck (ed.), *Historia Peredur*, p. 44; Davies (trans.), *Mabinogion*, p. 87.
86 Goetinck (ed.), *Historia Peredur*, p. 45; Davies (trans.), *Mabinogion*, p. 87.
87 Goetinck (ed.), *Historia Peredur*, p. 45; Davies (trans.), *Mabinogion*, p. 87.
88 Goetinck (ed.), *Historia Peredur*, pp. 45, 47; Davies (trans.), *Mabinogion*, pp. 88, 89.
89 For a detailed analysis of this episode, see Kiki Calis, 'Peredur and the Valley of the Changing Sheep' (unpublished RMA thesis, Utrecht University, 2018).
90 Goetinck (ed.), *Historia Peredur*, p. 49–50; Davies (trans.), *Mabinogion*, p. 90.
91 For a discussion of the mills, see Andrew Breeze, '*Peredur son of Efrawg* and Windmills', *Celtica*, 24 (2003), 58–64; see also Chapter 2, pp. 70–3, of this book.
92 Goetinck (ed.), *Historia Peredur*, pp. 55–6; Davies (trans.), *Mabinogion*, pp. 93–4.
93 For medieval Welsh 'triads' as mnemonic device, see Brynley F. Roberts, 'Oral Tradition and Welsh Literature: A Description and Survey', *Oral Tradition*, 3/1–2 (1988), 61–87 (63) and the discussion in *TYP*[2], 'Introduction', esp.

pp. lxx–lxxi. Note that these studies refer to the medieval Welsh short texts known as 'triads', not to the extensive system of triadic narrative structuring described in the present chapter as the fractal narrative model. For the mnemonic function of triadic structures in Welsh prose texts, see Lloyd-Morgan, 'Triadic Structures in the Four Branches of the *Mabinogi*', p. 8.

94 For further discussion of this variation, see pp. 97–8, 101–2 of this book.
95 Walter J. Ong, *Orality and Literacy: The Technologizing of the Word* (London and New York: Methuen, 1982), pp. 35, 60–1.
96 Davies, 'Written Text as Performance', esp. p. 137 for considerations of length.
97 Lloyd-Morgan, 'Narrative Structure in *Peredur*', 197, with discussion of similar structures in other prose tales, also n. 20. See also Lloyd-Morgan, 'Triadic Structures', p. 4; and the work of Sioned Davies, cited throughout.
98 Lloyd-Morgan, 'Narrative Structure in *Peredur*', 196.
99 Davies, *Crefft y Cyfarwydd*, p. 90. For discussion of episodic performance over the space of several days, see Davies, *Crefft y Cyfarwydd*, pp. 35–9.
100 As supporting evidence for the estimate given here for the duration of performance of Episode I, the following calculations can be offered. Goetinck (ed.), *Historia Peredur* averages approximately 230 to 240 words per page. Episode I is approximately thirty pages long. The total word count of the episode would be approximately 7,000 words. Average speaking speed is approximately 150 words per minute (wpm), with slightly slower speeds advocated for public speaking at 140 wpm (see, for instance, Baruch College Tools for Clear Speech, *https://tfcs.baruch.cuny.edu/speaking-rate/* (last accessed 15 July 2021)), 7,000 words spoken at a rate of 140 wpm would yield fifty minutes. Speaking tempo varies depending on the purpose of the speech act, and in instances of public speaking can drop as low as 100 wpm (or lower); Anne Karpf, *The Human Voice: The Story of a Remarkable Talent* (London: Bloomsbury, 2007), p. 42. However, oral performance of a narrative is different from public speaking of the political variety and could be expected to be at least somewhat faster. Data on average speech rates and performance speech rates, including recommended rates, varies considerably, and historical data for oral performances of medieval Welsh texts is simply not available; see discussion in S. Davies, 'Written Text as Performance', p. 136; and Sioned Davies, *Four Branches of the Mabinogi: Pedeir Keinc y Mabinogi* (Llandysul: Gomer Press, 1993), p. 22–4.
101 While a comparison of this performance length to contemporary lecture and performance segment lengths might be considered anachronistic, it should be noted that university lectures tend to be delivered in forty-five to fifty-five-minute segments, depending on the university system, and the standard duration for television programmes/series episodes tend to have a similar length, with entertainment programmes and films having a longer duration. Less

controversially, perhaps, one might compare the estimate provided here to the duration of oral performances in still-active traditional folkloric traditions. In Tamil culture, for instance, Bow Song performances fall into two types: the longer, ranging from three to five hours, and the shorter, thirty minutes to an hour in length; Stuart H. Blackburn, 'Oral Performance: Narrative and Ritual in a Tamil Tradition', *The Journal of American Folklore*, 94 (1981), 207–27 (216). Our estimate falls within the shorter category.

102 Mary Carruthers, *The Book of Memory: A Study of Memory in Medieval Culture*, 2nd edn (Cambridge: Cambridge University Press, 2008), p. 102.

103 Roberts, 'Oral Tradition and Welsh Literature'; Sioned Davies, 'Storytelling in Medieval Wales', *Oral Tradition*, 7/2 (1992), 231–57 (esp. 235).

104 Davies, 'Storytelling in Medieval Wales', 235. Her overview of features of oral storytelling in this article does not include mnemonic triadic structures; see, however, her *Four Branches of the Mabionogi*, pp. 24–7. For an analysis of a medieval Welsh tale as 'an expanded triad', see Rachel Bromwich's discussion of *Llud a Llefelys* in *TYP*², pp. xciii–xcv.

105 For the importance of memory in oral composition and recitation, in relation specifically to the medieval Welsh tradition, see Davies, *Crefft y Cyfarwydd*, pp. 29–34.

106 Carruthers, *The Book of Memory*, pp. 22–3, citing Albertus Magnus, *Commentary on Aristotle's De memoria*, tract 2, c.1, in Albertus Magnus, *Opera omnia* IX: *Commentary on Aristotle's De memoria et reminiscentia*, ed. by August Borgnet (Paris: Ludovicum Vives, 1890); trans. by J. Ziolkowski in Carruthers and Ziolkowski (eds), *The Medieval Craft of Memory: An Anthology of Texts and Pictures* (Philadelphia PA: University of Pennsylvania Press, 2002).

107 As Rachel Bromwich observes, memorising an extensive range of material appears to have been part of bardic training; *TYP*², pp. lxii–lxiii. See also the discussion of classical and Latinate mnemonic traditions, citing Carruthers among others, in S. Davies, *Crefft y Cyfarwydd*, p. 33.

108 *TYP*², p. lxxix. See, however, observations in Patrick Sims-Williams, 'The Early Welsh Arthurian Poems', in Rachel Bromwich, A. O. H. Jarman and Brynley F. Roberts (eds), *The Arthur of the Welsh. The Arthurian Legend in Medieval Welsh Literature* (Cardiff: University of Wales Press, 1991), pp. 33–71 at pp. 33–4; and the extensive treatment in Paul Russell, '"Go and Look at Latin Books": Latin and the Vernacular in Medieval Wales', in Richard Ashdowne and Carolinne White (eds), *Latin in Medieval Britain*, Proceedings of the British Academy, 206 (Oxford: Oxford University Press and The British Academy, 2017), pp. 213–46.

109 For a foundational discussion of memorisation processes in oral composition contexts, see Ong, *Orality and Literacy*, esp. pp. 33–6, 57–68.

110 Davies, 'Storytelling in Medieval Wales', p. 233.

111 I am very grateful to Peter Schrijver for this idea of connection between my theory of *Peredur*'s fractal structure on the one hand and the meaning of the term *cyfarwyddyd* as combination of the components *cyf-* and *arwydd* on the other.
112 Davies, 'Storytelling in Medieval Wales', p. 233.
113 Roberts, 'Oral Tradition and Welsh Literature', p. 67.
114 Davies, *Crefft y Cyfarwydd*, pp. 29–34. See especially her overview of twentieth-century scholarship on memorisation processes, pp. 31–2.
115 Hughes, 'Tripartite Structure'.
116 Cf. also Charles-Edwards's argument about the stages of development in 'The Textual Tradition', and p. 123 of this book, for further discussion.
117 To be continued in a separate volume that I am currently working on.
118 For a discussion of prose tale structures reflected in the surviving manuscripts, see Davies, 'Written Text as Performance', pp. 139–40. Since Peniarth 14 breaks off part of the way through Episode I, there is little mileage to be gained from the information that the only coloured initial it has for *Peredur* is the initial *E* marking the beginning of the text; Peniarth 14, p. 180 l. 19.
119 What is treated as an episode break here occurs in Peniarth 7 in the middle of what, based on the capitalisation and punctuation patterns, appears to be treated as a single sentence: 'Ac odyna yd|aethant gaer llion a|r nos gyntaf y doeth peredur gaer llion mal yd|oedynt yn troi yn|ygaer y kyfvarvv ac wynt hagharat law eurawc'; text quoted from Diana Luft et al., *Rhyddiaith Gymraeg*, www.rhyddiaithganoloesol.caerdydd.ac.uk (last accessed 11 July 2021). Compare the White Book reading: 'ac ychoelut a orugant parth a|chaer llion. a|r nos gyntaf y doeth peredur y gaer llion y lys arthur'; Peniarth 4, f. 37r, col. 1, ll. 8–10; Luft et al. (eds), *Rhyddiaith* Gymraeg, www.rhyddiaithganoloesol.caerdydd.ac.uk/en/ms-page.php?ms=Pen4&page=37r (last accessed 11 July 2021). See also the digital facsimile of Peniarth 4 on the NLW website, www.library.wales/discover/digital-gallery/manuscripts/the-middle-ages/white-book-of-rhydderch#?c=&m=&s=&cv=86&xywh=0%2C-422%2C4080%2C4923 (last accessed 11 July 2021).
120 The text in Goetinck (ed.), *Historia Peredur*, p. 175, marks no gap, but skips from section numbers '632' to '637'; Luft et al. (eds), *Rhyddiaith Gymraeg*, marks one folio f. 12 as 'blank', www.rhyddiaithganoloesol.caerdydd.ac.uk/en/ms-page.php?ms=Pen7&page=12r (last accessed 11 July 2021).
121 Peniarth 4, f. 38v, col. 2, ll. 3–4; cf. Luft et al. (eds), *Rhyddiaith Gymraeg*, www.rhyddiaithganoloesol.caerdydd.ac.uk/en/ms-page.php?ms=Pen4&page=38v (last accessed 11 July 2021).
122 See the digital facsimile on the NLW website at f. 38v (slide 90).
123 Peniarth 4, f. 42v, col. 1, ll. 27–9.

124 Episode break between Episode II and Episode III marked with a large coloured initial at f. 167v, col. 1 l. 26; for the break between Episode I and Episode II, see f. 166v col. 1 ll. 12–13.

125 Davies, 'Written Text as Performance', p. 140.

126 The scene is compared to Chrétien's text in detail in Claude Luttrell, 'Le Conte del graal et d'autres sources françaises de l'*Historia Peredur*', *Neophilologus*, 87 (2003), 11–28 (19–20).

127 See p. 22, and further discussion on pp. 105–10 and Chapter 5 of this book.

128 Goetinck (ed.), *Historia Peredur*, p. 57; Davies (trans.), *Mabinogion*, p. 94.

129 Goetinck (ed.), *Historia Peredur*, p. 57; Davies (trans.), *Mabinogion*, p. 95; compare Chrétien de Troyes, *Le Conte du Graal*, ll. 4615–35; ed. and trans. by Méla, p. 1079; Kibler (trans.), *Story of the Grail*, p. 438.

130 Goetinck (ed.), *Historia Peredur*, p. 58; Davies (trans.), *Mabinogion*, p. 95. A location is given in the French as *pui qui est soz Mont Esclaire* 'peak below Montesclere'; Chrétien de Troyes, *Le Conte du Graal*, l. 4636; ed. and trans. by Méla, p. 1079; Kibler (trans.), *Story of the Grail*, p. 439. There is an additional reference in the French to *l'Espee aus Estranges Ranges* ('the Sword of Strange Straps'), but this is not picked up on in the Welsh (Chrétien de Troyes, *Le Conte du Graal*, l. 4642).

131 Goetinck (ed.), *Historia Peredur*, p. 58; Davies (trans.), *Mabinogion*, p. 95.

132 Goetinck (ed.), *Historia Peredur*, p. 58; Davies (trans.), *Mabinogion*, p. 95.

133 Chrétien de Troyes, *Le Conte du Graal*, ll. 4677–84; ed. and trans. by Méla, p. 1081; Kibler (trans.), *Story of the Grail*, p. 439.

134 Goetinck (ed.), *Historia Peredur*, p. 58; Davies (trans.), *Mabinogion*, p. 95. In the French, this is the king of Escavalon; Chrétien de Troyes, *Le Conte du Graal*, l. 4721; ed. and trans. by Méla, p. 1082; Kibler (trans.), *Story of the Grail*, p. 440.

135 Frank Brandsma, *The Interlace Structure of the Third Part of the Prose Lancelot* (Cambridge: D. S. Brewer, 2010), p. 16; for more on interlace, see esp. pp. 16–22 and pp. 27–8. The literature on the medieval French narrative technique is extensive. See, for instance, Douglas Kelly, *The Art of Medieval French Romance* (Madison WI: University of Wisconsin Press, 1992), pp. 282–3. For use of this technique in Chrétien and his continuators, see Bruckner, *Chrétien Continued*, esp. pp. 19–20, 40–1, 50–65, 180. For an argument for interlace patterns (thematic, rather than temporal interlace) in medieval Welsh texts, see J. K. Bollard, 'The Structure of the Four Branches of the Mabinogi', *Transactions of the Honourable Society of Cymmrodorion 1974–75*, (1974–5), 250–76.

136 See also Luttrell, 'Le Conte del graal et d'autres sources françaises', 21–2. The differences highlighted here are not mentioned by Luttrell.

137 Goetinck (ed.), *Historia Peredur*, p. 60; Davies (trans.), *Mabinogion*, p. 96. The Welsh is intensified by the use of two derogatory terms: *achenoges*, feminine

form of *achenog* ('beggar'), but also used derogatively, *GPC* s.v. *achenog*; and *putain*, derived directly or via Middle English from French *putain* s.f. ('prostitute'); *GPC* s.v. *putain*; *DMF* s.v. *putain*.
138 See pp. 141–5 of this book.
139 The data on greetings in *Peredur* as well as in the other two Welsh Arthurian narratives with French equivalents, *Owain* and *Gereint*, collected by Froukje Kooistra as part of the Master Apprentice programme at Utrecht University in 2021–2 under my supervision has confirmed the complete absence of similar insults or indeed of any insulting address in these texts. I am grateful to Froukje Kooistra for this information.
140 For a similar argument in relation to the Irish tradition, see Ruairí Ó hUiginn, 'The Background and Development of *Táin Bó Cúailnge*', in James P. Mallory (ed.), *Aspects of the Táin* (Belfast: December Publications, 1992), pp. 29–67 (pp. 61–2); and especially Patricia Kelly, 'The *Táin* as Literature', in Mallory (ed.), *Aspects of the Táin*, pp. 69–102 (pp. 70–1). I am grateful to Peter Schrijver for pointing out the parallel.
141 Goetinck (ed.), *Historia Peredur*, p. 61; Davies (trans.), *Mabinogion*, p. 96.
142 See also discussion in Luttrell, 'Le Conte del graal et d'autres sources françaises', 25.
143 Goetinck (ed.), *Historia Peredur*, p. 61; Davies (trans.), *Mabinogion*, p. 97.
144 Goetinck (ed.), *Historia Peredur*, p. 61; Davies (trans.), *Mabinogion*, p. 97. Given this address and the insult to the lady who kept company with Gwalchmai earlier in the text, the Continuation seems to be more inclined to the use of coarse language than Episodes I to III.
145 Goetinck (ed.), *Historia Peredur*, p. 62; Davies (trans.), *Mabinogion*, p. 97.
146 It is tempting to suggest that *caer uoel* implies religious habitation, since *moel* can mean not only towerless of buildings but 'bald' or 'tonsured' of people; *GPC* s.v. *moel*. Could it be a fort of tonsured ones?
147 Luttrell, 'Le Conte del graal et d'autres sources françaises', 12–13.
148 Luttrell, 'Le Conte del graal et d'autres sources françaises', 13.
149 Luttrell, 'Le Conte del graal et d'autres sources françaises', 14–15.
150 Goetinck (ed.), *Historia Peredur*, p. 67; Davies (trans.), *Mabinogion*, p. 100.
151 Sir John Rhŷs, *Studies in the Arthurian Legend* (Oxford: Clarendon Press, 1891), p. 3; see also his summary of and commentary on the Fortress of Wonders sequence, pp. 105–9; for the text of *Culhwch ac Olwen*, see Rachel Bromwich and D. Simon Evans (eds), *Culhwch and Olwen: An Edition and Study of the Oldest Arthurian Tale* (Cardiff: University of Wales Press, 1992); for more on Malory, see Chapter 4 of this book.
152 Goetinck (ed.), *Historia Peredur*, p. 68; Davies (trans.), *Mabinogion*, pp. 100–1.
153 Goetinck (ed.), *Historia Peredur*, p. 69; Davies (trans.), *Mabinogion*, p. 101.
154 Goetinck (ed.), *Historia Peredur*, p. 69; Davies (trans.), *Mabinogion*, p. 101.

155 Goetinck (ed.), *Historia Peredur*, p. 70; Davies (trans.), *Mabinogion*, p. 102; for more on the procession, see Chapter 4 of this book.
156 Goetinck (ed.), *Historia Peredur*, p. 70; Davies (trans.), *Mabinogion*, p. 102.
157 See comment in Davies (trans.), *Mabinogion*, p. 249.
158 For an edition, see Stephen J. Williams (ed.), *Ystoria de Carolo Magno o Lyfr Coch Hergest* (Cardiff: University of Wales Press, 1930); for a translation, see Robert Williams (trans.), 'The History of Charlemagne. A Translation of "Ystorya de Carolo Magno", With a Historical and Critical Introduction', *Y Cymmrodor*, 20 (1907); a more recent edition and translation of the *Cân Rolant* only, is Annalee Rejhon (ed. and trans.), *Cân Rolant: The Medieval Welsh Version of the Song of Roland*, University of California Publications in Modern Philology CXIII (Berkeley CA: University of California Press, 1984). For a discussion of the Cycle, see Erich Poppe, 'Charlemagne in Wales and Ireland: Some Preliminaries on Transfer and Transmission', in Jürg Glauser and Susanne Kramarz-Bein (eds), *Rittersagas: Übersetzung, Überlieferung, Transmission*, Beiträge zur nordischen Philologie 45 (Tübingen: A. Francke, 2014) pp. 169–90; Petrovskaia, *Medieval Welsh Perceptions of the Orient* (Turnhout: Brepols, 2015), pp. 77–128.
159 See discussion in Petrovskaia, *Medieval Welsh Perceptions of the Orient*, pp. 78–9, 84, 87–91.
160 Luttrell, 'Le Conte del graal et d'autres sources françaises', 14–15.
161 Luttrell, 'Le Conte del graal et d'autres sources françaises', 23–4.
162 Luttrell, 'Le Conte del graal et d'autres sources françaises', 17.
163 Cf. also a similar argument made on slightly different grounds by Glenys Goetinck in *Peredur*, p. 79.
164 See pp. 107–9 of this book; and for a more general overview of such circulation of themes see John Carey, *Ireland and the Grail* (Aberystwyth: Celtic Studies Publications, 2007).
165 Lloyd-Morgan, '*Historia Peredur*', p. 149.
166 There has been a general trend in medieval studies to reconsider earlier harsh judgements of individual authors' or redactor's competence. The recent re-evaluation of Sir Thomas Malory as creative adaptator is a case in point; see Ralph Norris, 'Malory and His Sources', in Megan G. Leitch and Cory James Rushton (eds), *A Companion to Malory* (Cambridge: D. S. Brewer, 2019), pp. 32–52 (p. 50).
167 One thinks in particular of the various revivals and reboots of popular 1980s movie and television franchises.
168 Mandelbrot, *The Fractal Geometry of Nature*, p. 9.

2

THE GEOGRAPHY AND LANDSCAPES OF *PEREDUR*

This chapter is devoted to the discussion of the possible geographical setting of the various episodes of the tale, focusing in particular on Episodes I to III of the Short Version. Unlike their medieval French counterparts by Chrétien de Troyes, the medieval Welsh tales of *Owain*, *Gereint* and *Peredur* tend to be more firmly anchored in the geography and landscape of the real world.[1] That is not to say that *Peredur* is immediately, clearly and precisely mappable onto the real world, but it will be argued here that there is more realism in the text in respect to its spatial setting than it is usually given credit for.[2] It is also worth remembering that what might appear to be a rather vague geography in the medieval French romances, may not be in fact so vague if we remember that it follows the rules not of topographical route maps (or their digital equivalents that we are now used to) but of itineraries, where one could, in fact, 'turn right' from Caerleon and find oneself in Brittany.[3]

In contrast to the distinctly mappable real-world geography of *Gereint*, for instance, there are not many identifiable place names or easily recognisable geographical locations in *Peredur*. The only two easily identifiable placenames are *Caer Loyw* ('Gloucester') and *Caerlion* ('Caerleon'), the seat of Arthur's court. As has already been observed, Caerleon provides the setting for the start and end points of various episodes of *Peredur*.[4] Since the only other identifiable place name, Gloucester, is mentioned in Episode I, the discussion in this chapter will follow the order of the episodes. Some attention will also be paid to the landscapes of *Peredur*, including man-made features such as castles, manors, nunneries and mills. As Muriel A. Whitaker observes, 'realistic aspects are drawn from contemporary models' in medieval literary descriptions of castles, and this observation can be extended to topographical descriptions generally.[5] *Peredur* is a strikingly realistic account, despite some elements of the supernatural, such as gold-generating stones, monsters or disappearing maidens on mounds (all found in Episode III). The human characters appear and indeed function as normal human beings: avoiding conflict when the opponent appears suspiciously confident (and therefore probably has a hidden advantage), as all of Arthur's knights do in Episode I(A); asking awkward questions when drunk, as Peredur does when he asks how the Black Oppressor lost his eye; and becoming stroppy when in intense discomfort, as Cai does after being unseated and having his arm and collarbone broken by Peredur.[6]

In Episode I(C) Peredur proceeds to learn the use of arms at the court of the witches of Gloucester. There is no particular reason, given their name, not to suppose that this might have been imagined by the audience to be in Gloucester. We will return to the question of whether they are 'witches' in Chapter 6. Together with Caerleon, the seat of Arthur's court, this presents two anchor points for the narrative of Episode I, both located in the south. Another location that can be identified, if it is set in real-world geography, is in the episode of the besieged dark-haired young countess in Episode I(C) (the first of the triad of distressed women), whose court receives sustenance from a nearby nunnery.[7] The castle itself is described as 'kaer vawr eidoawc a thyreu kadarn amyl arnei' ('a great ivy-covered fortress with many strong towers').[8]

Given the presence of references to real-world locations (Caerleon and Gloucester) in the tale, it seems reasonable to suggest that there might be a possibility that the nunnery in question was meant as a reference to a real-world location, or at least supposed to invoke known locations for the audience, to serve as a model. This possibility is reinforced by the fact that only three nunneries are known for certain to have existed for any significant period of time in medieval Wales: the Cistercian houses of Llanllŷr and Llanllugan, and the Benedictine priory of Usk.[9] Llanllŷr came under the remit of Strata Florida, and Llanllugan of Strata Marcella.[10] All three were fairly small establishments, counting at times as little as three and at most about fifteen nuns throughout their history.[11] Usk appears to have been founded for a community of five, but by around 1284 could have had more, possibly as many as thirteen.[12]

The small scale of these monastic communities allows us to read the description of the frugal meal in *Peredur* in a slightly different light:

Nyt oed bell yn ol hynny, ef a welei dwy vanaches yn dyuot y mywn, a chostrel yn llawn o win gan y neill, a chwe thorth o vara cann gan y llal.

'Arglwydes,' heb wy, 'Duw a wyr na bu y'r gwfent hwnt heno namyn y gymeint arall o uwyt a llyn.'[13]

Not long after that he saw two nuns entering, one carrying a flagon full of wine and the other six loaves of white bread.

'Lady', they said, 'God knows, tonight the convent over there has only this amount again of food and drink'.[14]

This frugal repast in the castle serves the lady, her four companions and Peredur. One might also add to that number the nineteen lads who had kept him company until the lady and her companions arrived.[15] This would bring the total to twenty-five people, sharing the six loaves of bread. A sparse repast, indeed, although some ink might be spilt debating the size of the loaves.[16] If the convent had only the same again, this suggests that the community would have had roughly the same number of people. Given the attested size of Welsh convents this is unexpected, because if the audience was used to the idea of a nunnery being a small community of five to ten people, the division of the food described here might not seem so fair (or frugal). It might be objected that the medieval audience might not have necessarily expected the same kind of logic from a text as a modern audience, but since in this case the text does not specify the number of nuns for the meal in question, it is presumably relying on the audience's ability to draw on some kind of contextual knowledge. Such contextual knowledge on the part of the audience might not have been necessarily based on Welsh foundations exclusively. It is worth also considering women's convents that existed in the March for the sake of comparison.

Minchinhampton Priory in Gloucestershire appears to have been occupied by nuns, but the size of the establishment is uncertain.[17] In Herefordshire we find the Augustinian Priory of Limebrook, founded towards the end of the twelfth century, as well as the somewhat later Aconbury (initially Hospitaller).[18] Aconbury was only founded in the second decade of the thirteenth century, and the completion of the buildings took place even later, making it slightly too late for a direct reference, let alone for assumed audience background knowledge for *Peredur*.[19] In any case, both appear to have been comparable in size to Welsh nunneries. By contrast, a reasonably large monastic institution, such as the double monastery of Amesbury in Wiltshire, could house more than seventy nuns.[20]

Despite the small numbers of nuns attested for both Welsh and Marcher foundations, this does not mean that these foundations were consistently small. Populations could fluctuate, as attested by the example of Buckland (Devon), which appears to have started off with eight nuns in the 1180s and had as many as fifty in 1300 (with the population dropping again by the time of the Dissolution).[21] If the possibility of population fluctuation, even on a smaller scale, was to be taken into account in drawing conclusions on the basis of attested numbers for the Welsh and Marcher feminine monastic houses, it might be possible to suggest that at least at some point in their history such houses might have had more nuns.[22] Indeed, for Usk, given that in 1284 Archbishop Peckham recommended the appointment of two treasuresses, it seems reasonable to suppose that the community would have numbered more than the thirteen individuals given as the maximum count by modern scholars.[23] Such a possibility could also provide the reference in *Peredur* with the necessary context. While a community of six or even ten nuns sharing twelve loaves of bread equally with the twenty-five people in the castle might seem somewhat uncharitable, supposing that the community at the monastery was also in the realm of twenty to twenty-five souls would yield a more reasonable balance.[24]

Poverty in general and specifically the scarcity of food, appears to have been a feature of these monasteries, and for that of Usk in particular the problems resulting from armed conflict are attested to in the writings of Adam of Usk.[25] It is also tempting to take the nuns' presence at the castle in the context of the 1284 criticism by Archbishop Peckham, who noted upon visitation of the priory that the nuns spent too much time outside the nunnery and among laity.[26] These references are not contemporary to the composition of Episode I (unless it was composed immediately before the writing of the late-thirteenth century Peniarth 7), but do provide some much-needed context. While I would not go so far as to suggest that the nunnery in *Peredur* can be identified, and can be identified as one of the Welsh or Marcher nunneries, it is worth noting that the locations of Usk, Amebury and perhaps even Limebrook would be consistent with the apparent southern geographical focus of Episode I. Usk Priory is within walking distance of two castles, Usk and Abergavenny, three minutes' and three hours' walk respectively, according to Google Maps.[27] This should not be taken as a suggestion that the events of the episode are taking place at one of the two castles (Usk, in particular, would not necessarily have had multiple towers at the time), but rather to give an approximate idea of the type of topographical and cultural context within which the episode is set.[28] As Robert Patterson points out, 'the ideal in baronial headquarters was for them to include castle, monastery, and borough', and thus for the twelfth or thirteenth-century audiences of *Peredur* to find a monastic institution within walking distance of a castle is likely to have been expected.[29] Three hours' walk may perhaps be too far for a location described as 'yr govent yngot' (early version) or 'yr govent hwnt' (later version), but the distance of an hour or two's brisk walk seems a reasonable suggestion.[30] It may be impossible to reconstruct what images the text may have invoked in its medieval audiences, but the landscape of the March and the area north-east of Gloucester, and lying east of the Severn as we follow it north, in the mid-twelfth to mid-thirteenth centuries may well present a suitable chronotope.[31]

After this adventure and his encounter with the maiden of the tent, Peredur finds himself in a devastated area of land with only one house. The episode runs as follows:

> Ac ar vynyd y wrthaw ef a welei gastell, a pharth a'r kastell y doeth a gwan y porth a'y wayw a oruc. Ar hynny llyma was gwineu telediw yn agori y porth, a meint milwr a'e prafter yndaw, ac oetran mab arnaw. Pan daw Peredur y'r neuad, yd oed gwreic vawr delediw yn eisted y mywn kadeir a llawuorynyon yn amhyl yn y chylch, a llawen uu y wreicda wrthaw. A phan uu amser mynet y uwyta, wynt a aethant. A gwedy bwyta,
> 'Da oedd itti, vnben', heb y wreic, 'mynet y gyscu y le arall.'
> 'Pony allaf I gyscu yma?'
> 'Naw gwidon, eneit,' heb hi, 'yssyd yma ac eu tat ac eu mam gyt ac wynt. Gwidonot Kaer Loyw ynt, ac nyt nes inni erbyn y dyd an dianc noc an llad. Ac neur deryw udunt gwerescyn a diffeithaw y kyfoeth, onyt yr vn ty hwnn.'[32]

On a mountain not far from him he could see a castle. And he made for the castle and hammered on the door with his spear. Then behold, a handsome auburn-haired lad opening the door, in stature and strength a warrior, but in age a boy. When Peredur came into the hall there was a large, handsome woman sitting in a chair and numerous handmaidens about her. And the good lady made him welcome. And when it was time to go to eat, they went. And after eating, 'You would do well, lord,' said the lady, 'to go elsewhere to sleep'.

'Can't I sleep here?'

'There are nine witches here, friend,' she said, 'together with their father and mother. They are the witches of Caerloyw. And by daybreak we shall be no nearer to making our escape than to being killed. And they have taken over and laid waste the land, except for this one house.'[33]

Assuming the *gwidonot* of Gloucester are based in Gloucester, or at least Gloucestershire, it is tempting to try to identify the castle described in this passage. Given that Peredur had set out on his journey from Arthur's court in Caerleon, and that the witches threatening the castle or manor are based in Gloucester, there does not seem to be any particularly solid reason to imagine that the action in this episode takes place anywhere other than south Wales, and probably around the Severn valley. Even so, it is highly unlikely for the stronghold in this passage to be identifiable as one of the surviving Norman castles. Neither Chepstow nor Berkeley castles, for instance, are positioned high enough to be described as *ar vynyd* ('on a mountain'). In general, the area around the Severn is quite low-lying with few elevations that could be described as mountains (although given the higher population density in that area the image of a land 'laid waste' would be all the more impactful in the text).[34] Further, the fact that the building or building complex is referred to as both *kastell* ('castle') and *ty* ('house') could point to a fortified manor house rather than a classical turreted and crenelated stone castle.[35]

As N. J. G. Pounds observes, there was a pattern among the nobility of the March to request a royal licence to build a castle even if what they were building was only a manor house that would not have required building permits.[36] These licences, which were licences to crenellate, were a matter of status, and the buildings that were constructed with such licences were not necessarily fortified towers.[37] Given that there would have been a large number of these and they would not necessarily have survived to this day, this particular house is probably not identifiable even if a real place was meant here. It is possible that a real place or at least a real situation is referred to in the passage. The phenomenon described with the words 'Ac neur deryw udunt gwerescyn a diffeithaw y kyfoeth, onyt yr vn ty hwnn' ('And they have taken over and laid waste the land, except for this one house') is echoed in C. G. Harfield's discussion of Doomsday Book references: 'land or houses had been laid waste because of the construction of a castle.'[38] In the urban environment, one of Harfield's examples is Gloucester Castle itself, but Peredur is probably not visiting the city of Gloucester in this episode, or at least not yet, for he will travel to Gloucester with the *gwidonot* later.[39] Given that there is a distinct association between castle-building and destruction in both rural and urban contexts, it is not inconceivable that the lady of the house is referring to the fact that the *gwidonot* had recently conquered the region and are in the process of building a castle (laying waste to the land in the course of that activity). The use of the Doomsday Book for context is perhaps not without risk, especially given the uncertain date of composition for *Peredur* and its individual episodes. However, there is no compelling reason to think that the economic impact of building a castle would have changed so drastically as to make the comparison invalid. It is worth noting here that the reference to 'laying waste', at least in the Welsh text, appears to mean specifically demolition of human habitation and buildings, and not, as one might assume from the English word, the transformation of the surrounding natural environment into a barren and inhospitable one.[40]

While I do not intend to claim that the reference here is to an identifiable historical episode, one wonders if it might not have been perceived by the audience as a typical example of Norman encroachment into Wales: Norman powers based in a Marcher lordship expanding into Welsh territory and laying waste to the countryside in order to build a new castle, leaving only one or two isolated manors intact. At the very least, we can conclude that the medieval audience of this text would have had much more of the necessary knowledge of cultural, political and economic context for this passage than we have today. This is consistent with what is known of the text's use of medieval Welsh law.[41] Thus, it is conceivable that the audience might have been able to identify a context or real-life parallels for this situation, even if it did not refer to an actual real-life location or historical event.[42]

Since, as the argument in Chapter 1 suggests, Episodes I to III of the Short Version do not need to adhere to a sense of continuity or uniformity, despite their common start and end points in Caerleon, it is possible to argue that even without particular differentiation signalling different locations, they may have different geographical settings (and different chronotopes). In the overview of the episodic structure of the Short Version in Chapter 1, I have already suggested that Peredur's travels in

Episode II may have taken him far from home.[43] There are no geographical indications, however, of the location of his adventures, although there is some topographical description.

In previous publications, I have presented an analysis of this episode suggesting that it may have been intended to represent a mini-crusade, and thus involve travel to the East.[44] This was founded on the following considerations. In the first place, the episode presents a battle with and conversion to Christianity of non-Christians. At the beginning of Episode II, Peredur, rejected by Angharad, swears to her that he will abstain from speaking to any Christian until she changes her mind: "'Minheu a rodaf vyg cret,' heb y Peredur, 'na dywedaf inheu eir vyth wrth Gristyawn, hyny adefych titheu arnat vyg caru yn uwyhaf gwr'" ("'And I give my word,' said Peredur, 'that I will never utter a word to any Christian until you confess that you love me best of men'").[45] The episode shows internal consistency, as Peredur upholds this oath through speaking only to non-Christians, although in the case of the inhabitants of the Round Valley he seems to have forgotten about his oath and recollected it, with relief at not having broken it, only once they tell him they are not Christian.[46] While it is possible to read his expression of relief as a redactor's awkward attempt to fix an inconsistency, it should be noted that if this were the case, the redactor could have easily added a similar reference at the start of the interaction. As the text stands, and following the general policy adopted in this book of giving the medieval redactors the benefit of the doubt, there are two possibilities.[47] One is that wherever Peredur was, he would have expected non-Christians and is simply relieved by the confirmation (this is the reading locating the action in the East). The second is to suggest that it was not the redactor but the hero (possibly at this stage a teenager, or at least a very young man) who was forgetful in his exuberant enthusiasm for adventure. In Episode II(B) after the serpent with the ring encounter, the redactor remembers to tell the audience that Peredur kept going without speaking to a Christian.[48] He also remains mute in Episode II(C). The second consideration on which the interpretation of this episode as a crusade echo was based, was that of the representation of the Round Valley, which could be seen as an echo of circular world maps or round maps of Jerusalem. I am now inclined to see this part of the argument as specious, but the third consideration, the exotic use of the lion as gatekeeper, does provide a further indication of general 'easternness' and is worth revisiting and elaborating further before returning once more to discussing the valley's inhabitants.[49]

At the entrance to the Round Valley, Peredur encounters and battles a ferocious lion, who serves as gatekeeper for the non-Christians. This appears to be an exotic element, associated with oriental travel in medieval romance specifically.[50] The image of the lion also has other associations, however, including as a symbol of courage and more specifically of kingship (influenced partly by the bestiary tradition), and also in association with the theme of the grateful beast, classical in origin but enormously popular in medieval Europe.[51] The motif of the grateful lion appears, for instance, in *Le Chevalier au Lion* of Chrétien de Troyes and in its Welsh equivalent, *Owain*.[52] There, the hero rescues a lion from a serpent, and the grateful lion follows him and helps him on his subsequent adventures. However, it has been argued recently by Isabelle Valade, Luciana Cordo Russo and Lee Raye that there is a pattern to medieval Welsh representations of lions, namely as ferocious and violent beasts, that even tempered the image of the grateful lion in *Owain*.[53] They have thus demonstrated that the bestiary type of lions do not provide a good parallel for the representations of the animal in medieval Welsh literary texts, even where they have French equivalents and possibly models.[54]

A ferocious lion similar to the one in *Peredur* in its antagonistic position vis-à-vis the hero appears in Chrétien's *Perceval* in the later section of that narrative, devoted to Gauvain, who encounters it in a magical hall, where he is attacked first by mechanical arrows then by the lion.[55] The use of this animal as a gatekeeper (instead of, for example, the more usual human or canine gatekeeper) underlines the strangeness of the valley and its occupants.

The valley itself is described as being 'on the other side of a great mountain', and inhabited by giants ('*cewri*').[56] Representation of Saracens as giants is sufficiently common in medieval literature, also occurring in medieval Welsh (in the translated Charlemagne texts), to make the identification fairly uncontroversial.[57] Non-Christian giants, however, also occur in texts relating to areas closer to home, in particular in the *Historia regum Britanniae* of Geoffrey of Monmouth, and these homegrown giants are worth investigating.[58] *Peredur* giants have been read as an echo of Geoffrey's indigenous giants by Susan Aronstein, who reads them as scions of a 'surviving indigenous culture', opposing Peredur as Welshman assimilated into Norman colonial culture.[59]

My original counterargument was that Peredur acts in Arthur's interests, converts the giants and sends them to become Arthur's vassals, which is difficult to read as Norman colonialism (at least in a Welsh text), because of the association of Arthur with British power opposed to the incomers (whether Saxon or Norman) in Welsh literary tradition.[60] The non-Christian giants of Geoffrey's *Historia regum Britanniae* were removed by Brutus well before Arthurian times.[61] However, even the *Historia regum* giants appear to be the product of assimilation, as they incorporate a reference to Gog and Magog.[62] While I would not venture to suggest that Episode II presents us with Gog and Magog, it is worth highlighting that Peredur finds the valley of giants behind a *mynyd mawr* ('great mountain'), and it is behind two such mountains that Alexander had imprisoned Gog and Magog according to medieval legend.[63] Thus, it may be possible to suggest multiple strands of influence in the representation of the Round Valley, though it might be impossible to determine the precise combination or extent of the individual references (or degree of their recognisability to the medieval audience).[64] Regardless of the source of influence on the depiction of the Round Valley giants, the various pieces of evidence tend to point to distant and exotic travel. The evidence includes the exotic lion; non-Christians; Peredur's assumption in communicating with them that they would not be Christian; conversion; and the apparent time Peredur spent away. The latter can be seen in the inability on the part of Arthur's court to recognise him.

The latter point in general highlights a pronounced difference between Episode I and Episode II. Whereas in Episode I everyone knew Peredur (and most were his relatives), in Episode II he appears to have travelled to lands where no one knows him. While this does not in itself constitute evidence of Eastern travels, it does seem to point to the fact that he has now ventured beyond his own corner of Britain. It will be seen that the geography of Episode III also plays out along similar lines.

Episode III appears to combine what seem to be features of man-made landscapes that could be local to Wales, with references to Eastern locations: India, and possibly Constantinople. It also stands out from the two other episodes in its heavier reliance on supernatural events, locations and creatures. In tone, it is very different from the others. Some of the cultural contextual elements belonging to the realm of man-made landscapes have been used previously in attempts to date the hypothetical unit of *Peredur* as a whole.[65]

The beginning of Episode III is reminiscent of the beginning of what is perhaps the most famous of medieval Welsh literary texts, and the entry point for most students of medieval Welsh language, *Pwyll Pendeuic*

Dyuet, also known as the 'First Branch of the Mabinogi'.[66] Both Pwyll and Peredur use hounds to hunt a stag. Both are separated from their companions. Pwyll's pack and stag lead him to an encounter with another pack and hunter, Arawn, king of Annwn (the Welsh name for what is usually interpreted as the Otherworld). Peredur, on the other hand, follows his dog, which kills the stag 'in a deserted place'.[67] The similarity to the beginning of *Pwyll* may suggest that the hero might be about to enter the Otherworld.[68] Another indication that he has somehow crossed a border is that his response to a lady at the Oppressor's court who offers him marriage is 'Ny deuthum i o'm gwlat, arglwydes, yr gwreicca' ('I did not come from my country, lady, to take a wife').[69] It is possible that Peredur is still in Arthur's lands and by '*gwlat*' he means his own personal original place of origin, but it is also possible that his *gwlat* is Arthur's land, and somehow while hunting near Caerleon he had already left it. In terms of real-world geography, the latter is not entirely improbable, as he could easily have crossed from Wales into *Lloegyr* ('England'), or more accurately the March, since this was a border region, and Caerleon itself had changed hands a number of times in the twelfth century alone.[70] Rather than arguing that the episode setting is purely otherworldly and devoid of real-world geographical anchoring, or alternatively attempting to divest each element of its potential otherworldly connotations, the suggestion here is to see in Episode III a combination of influences and references. The elements of the otherworldly are here intertwined with elements of the real world, both in terms of geography and man-made landscapes, and in terms of characters, such as the Empress, who will be discussed in Chapter 3. The rest of the episode, with its string of magical elements, up to the encounter with the miller and the Empress (on which more to follow), seems to support this view. The realistic and consistent element in the episode is Peredur's lack of armour and weapons, since he would not have had any on his hunt.

The one-eyed black-haired Oppressor is bad-humoured and violent, but quite human in his characteristics, since he is no Cyclops but is described explicitly as a man who had lost an eye in an encounter with a monster.[71] The monster, a serpent living in a cairn, on the *Cruc Galarus* ('Mountain of Mourning'), is in possession of a magic gold-generating stone.[72] The notion of the cairn inside the mountain is suggestive of a prehistoric burial chamber, such as the rock-cut tombs of Carn Llidi and similar sites in Pembrokeshire.[73] Mounds and prehistoric burial sites appear to have specific otherworldly associations in medieval Welsh (and Irish) texts, and the cairn of the serpent may thus be a further indication that the geography of Episode III is otherworldly, or at least has the hero travel the liminal space touching on the Otherworld in multiple locations.[74]

In general, this episode is much more reminiscent of other native medieval Welsh tales. From the dwelling of the one-eyed Oppressor, Peredur travels to the court of the three Sons of the King of Suffering. These are killed daily by a cave-dwelling or lake-dwelling monster (referred to in the previous discussions as the *Adanc*), and daily brought back to life by their three sisters by immersion in a tub of warm water.[75] The similarity of this to the Cauldron of Rebirth of *Branwen uerch Lyr* (the 'Second Branch of the Mabinogi') has been remarked on in previous discussions.[76] One is put in mind of *Branwen* again at the mention of the *llechwayw gwenwynic* ('poisonous stone spear'), with which the cave monster kills its opponents.[77] Once the monster is killed, Peredur finds himself in an otherworldly valley, complete with colour-changing sheep, a half-burning tree and a remarkably royal-looking squire on a mound (another *cruc*), with three roads leading from the mound.[78] The potential otherworldly connotations of mounds have already been mentioned. A similar mount-sitting personage, who has been previously identified as an otherworldly figure but who appears to be a combination of otherworldly and exotic (being an amalgamation of a Cyclops and a sciapod), is encountered in *Owain*.[79]

Another figure who appears on a suspiciously otherworld-invoking mound (again, a *cruc*), is the maiden who gives the hero a magic stone that makes him invisible to the spear-hurling monster of the cave.[80] This figure, who remains unnamed at this point in the narrative, appears to possess supernatural powers, for not only is her stone magic, but she herself disappears having given Peredur his stone and the instructions to go and find her 'parth a'r India' ('towards India').[81] In the final passage of the episode this is discovered to be the same individual as the Empress of 'Constantinople'. The character has previously been interpreted as an incarnation of the goddess of Sovereignty.[82] It is probable that this is another example of an amalgamation of influences. The character is further discussed in Chapter 3, as the figure offers opportunities to explore possible historical allusions in the text. References grounded in contemporary culture abound in that particular section of the episode, and one of these relates specifically to man-made landscapes.

On arriving in the valley occupied by the tents of the Empress, Peredur encounters a landscape of watermills and windmills. Based on this, Andrew Breeze has put forward the argument that the presence of a reference to windmills superficially points to a composition date of no earlier than *c*.1200.[83] Given my argument in Chapter 1 of this book regarding the independence of Episodes I to III from each other, were Breeze's date to be accepted, it would relate only to Episode III.

The mills are introduced as follows: 'Ac ef a deuth y dyffryn afon, teccaf a welsei eiroet, a llawer o pebylleu amliw a welei yno. A ryfedach ganthaw no hynny gwelet y sawl a welei o velineu ar dwfyr a melineu gwynt'[84] ('He came to a river valley, the fairest he had ever seen, and he could see many pavilions there of different colours. But he was more surprised to see the number of watermills and windmills').[85] Particularly interesting for our purposes is the combination of windmills and watermills in the references in this text. The later version of the text specifies 'melineu ar dwfyr a melineu gwynt' ('watermills and windmills'), while the earlier version of Peniarth 7 gives 'melynev amyl a llawer o velinev gwynt' ('numerous mills and many windmills') [my translation].[86] Regardless of the date at which the tale was composed (or the windmill reference inserted), Peniarth 7, written in the second half of the thirteenth century, dates to the time when windmill-building was at its height.[87] While it appears that windmills were introduced in England around 1185, the peak of windmill-building occurred in the middle of the thirteenth century.[88] Indeed, there are few references to windmills in English sources before 1200.[89] In that context, it may be important that in the world of the narrative, it appears that these windmills and watermills represent temporary, or at any rate new, constructions, built in response to new demand, as the miller explains to Peredur:

> Gofyn a oruc y'r melinyd py achaws yd oed y dygyfor hwnnw. Y dywawt y melinyd wrth Peredur, 'Mae y neill peth; ae tydi yn wr o bell, ae titheu yn ynuyt. Yna y mae amherodres Cristinobyl vawr, ac ny myn honno namyn y gwr dewraf, canyt reit idi hi da. Ac ny ellit dwyn bwyt y'r sawl vilyoed yssyd yma, ac o achaws hynny y mae y sawl velineu.'[90]

> He [Peredur] asked the miller why there was such a crowd of people. The miller said to Peredur, 'It is either one or the other: either you are a man from afar or else you are mad. The empress of great Constantinople is there, and she wants only the bravest man since she has no need of wealth. And it was impossible to

carry food to the several thousands that are here, and that is why there are all these mills'.[91]

Peniarth 7 refers to watermills simply as 'mills', specifically describing only 'windmills', meaning that the latter may have been perceived as a novelty. By the time that the text represented by the White Book and the Red Book had become established, windmills were a common enough sight, and it might be reasonable to suggest that 'watermills' would also need to be specified as they were no longer the default type of mill.[92] In terms of the date of composition, there is no particular need to suppose much of a delay in the introduction of windmill technology to Wales. It was the Cistercians who were particularly active in the spread of technological advancements through their abbey network (especially in application to their own land holdings), and mills in particular are attested on Cistercian land throughout Europe.[93] Given the tight structure of the order and the degree of the development that their network had reached in Wales in this period, a delay in the application of windmill technologies specifically on their Welsh lands would require special explanation.[94] It therefore seems reasonable to suppose that windmills, like other technological advances used by the Cistercians, made their way to Wales and the March first onto the Cistercian order's own holdings and then spread to their neighbours.

While it is difficult to pinpoint a location for this episode of *Peredur*, the landscape of mills is extremely suggestive. If Peredur had not travelled far from Caerleon and remains in Britain, it is not impossible that the landscape invoked by the combination of mills is to be found somewhere along the Severn. If he did travel 'in the direction of India', following the prompt of the mysterious maiden earlier in the episode, then the Severn landscape could well have provided inspiration for the author (and a reference point for the audience) in imagining a mill-filled river valley further away. There is some evidence for the Severn landscape. John Langdon's study of watermills and windmills in the West Midlands has shown a pattern to the mill-building in Southern Worcestershire, where, in Landgon's words 'especially on manors next to the Severn … windmills may have been a better alternative than setting up watermills on a major river'.[95] Yet it was the southern stretch of the Severn that is considered to have presented one of the greatest concentrations of watermills in Britain.[96] A landscape dominated by mills would be striking enough to merit special mention, regardless of whether technological innovation (windmills) was involved. Stretches of land with a particularly high density of mills, of which the southern stretch of the Severn was one, could have as much as one mill for every 500 metres.[97] Such a sight would be impressive, even today.

It must be noted in this context that Andrew Breeze suggests a southeastern location for the romance on the basis of windmill landscapes in Glamorgan and Pembrokeshire at a slightly later period.[98] Evidence that he further lists to illustrate the presence of windmills in Wales shows that by the fourteenth and fifteenth centuries these were probably fairly widespread throughout the country.[99] Regardless of which area we take as the setting of the text, the impression made on its medieval audiences would have been informed by their knowledge of these landscapes.

The discussion in this chapter has shown that the three episodes of the Short Version take place in widely differing geographical settings. The only common element is the hero's base at Arthur's court in Caerleon. Episode I takes place locally, among characters familiar with, if not to, the hero, and is anchored at its other extreme by the reference to Gloucester. There are no supernatural elements (we will return to the 'witches' in a later chapter) in this episode, and the human landscape is recognisable and realistic. While the geography of Episode II is vaguer and it is more difficult to pin-point its location, there is sufficient evidence to tentatively suggest that the hero travels abroad, and that the context of his oath suggests he travels far abroad into non-Christian lands. Meanwhile, Episode III offers a combination of otherworldly elements and landscapes that are recognisable and have real-world equivalents in Wales. Its setting seems more similar to the other Welsh native tales than are the settings of Episodes I and II. Yet it is also very modern, for it refers to windmills, which would have been a recent technological introduction at the time of writing of the text's earliest manuscript, Peniarth 7. The mills thus provide our first glimpse of a real-world historical context. Further possible allusions to historical events and characters, which are also found in this episode, will be discussed in Chapter 3.

Notes

1 For a discussion of the vague topography of Chrétien's romances, see Corinne J. Saunders, *The Forest of Medieval Romance: Avernus, Broceliande, Arden* (Cambridge: D. S. Brewer, 1993), pp. 60–80. For discussions of geography in the Welsh texts, see Helen A. Roberts, 'Court and *cyuoeth*: Chrétien de Troyes' *Erec et Enide* and the Middle Welsh *Gereint*', *Arthurian Literature*,

21 (2004), 53–72; Oliver Padel, *Arthur in Medieval Welsh Literature* (Cardiff: University of Wales Press, 2013), pp. 61–2; Natalia I. Petrovskaia, 'Real and Imaginary Towns in Medieval Wales', in by Marie-Françoise Alamichel (ed.), *Les villes au Moyen Âge en Europe occidentale – (ou comment demain peut apprendre d'hier)* (Paris: LISAA Editeur, 2018), pp. 355–70; Erich Poppe, 'Ystorya Geraint fab Erbin', in Lloyd-Morgan and Poppe (eds), *Arthur in the Celtic Languages*, pp. 132–44 (pp. 133–4).

2   Sioned Davies, for instance, writes of the Welsh 'romances' that these give 'no clear geographical boundaries to [Arthur's] kingdom, and the action takes place in a somewhat unreal, daydream-like world'; Davies. (trans.) *The Mabinogion*, p. xxiv. It will be shown here that for at least two of *Peredur*'s episodes, the world is less like a daydream and more topographically like medieval Wales than might be assumed at first glance. Goetinck points out that *Peredur*, *Owain* and *Gereint* are less geographically detailed than other native Welsh prose narratives; Goetinck, *Peredur*, p. 1 (note that Goetinck considers *Peredur* and others to be native compositions, p. 2). For geography and topography of the native medieval Welsh texts, see, for instance, Patrick Sims-Williams, 'The Irish Geography of *Culhwch ac Olwen*', in D. Ó Corráin et al. (eds), *Sages, Saints and Storytellers: Celtic Studies in Honour of James Carney* (Maynooth: An Sagart, 1989), pp. 412–26; J. Hunter, 'Dead Pigs, Place Names, and Sir John Rhŷs: Reconsidering the Onomastic Elements of *Kulhwch ac Olwen*', *Proceedings of the Harvard Celtic Colloquium*, 11 (1991), 27–36; A. Joseph McMullen, 'Three Major Forts to Be Built for Her: Rewriting History through the Landscape in *Breuddwyd Maxen Wledig*' *Proceedings of the Harvard Celtic Colloquium*, 31 (2011), 225–41.

3   The allusion is to Erich Auerbach's discussion of the vague geography of Chrétien's *Yvain*; E. Auerbach, *Mimesis: dargestellte Wirklichkeit in der abendländischen Literatur*, 5th edn (Bern: Dalp, 1971), p. 125. For the observation that medieval romances followed the itinerary tradition in descriptions of voyages, see Helen Cooper, *The English Romance in Time: Transforming Motifs from Geoffrey of Monmouth to the Death of Shakespeare* (Oxford: Oxford University Press, 2004), p. 68. For further discussion and references, see Petrovskaia, 'Où va-t-on pour son aventure?'.

4   See p. 19 of this book; citing Brynley Roberts's analysis of the tale's structure.

5   Muriel A. Whitaker, 'Otherworld Castles in Middle English Arthurian Romance', in Robert Liddiard (ed.), *Late Medieval Castles* (Woodbridge: Boydell & Brewer, 2017), pp. 393–408 (p. 393).

6   For the latter, see Goetinck (ed.), *Historia Peredur*, p. 32; Davies (trans.), *Mabinogion*, p. 80. Cai's 'geireu dic keinuigenvs' ('angry, jealous words') to Gwalchmai, when the other claims to be able to bring Peredur to Arthur with kind words after everyone else had failed, are usually taken as indications of Cai's unpleasant character. However, in his defence, it must be said that while

it might be suggested that he brought his injuries on himself by being rude to Peredur, Gwalchmai's quip that 'Ny dylyei neb kyffro marchawc vrdawl y ar y medwl y bei arnaw yn aghyfartal ... A'r aghyfartalwch hwnnw, ac atuyd, a gyfaruu a'r gwr a amwelas ag ef yn dywethaf' ('No one should distract an ordained knight from his thoughts in a discourteous way ... such discourtesy, perhaps, was shown by the man who saw him last') clearly refers to Cai, and does so in a manner suspiciously reminiscent of the modern 'not to point fingers, but ...', usually delivered with emphatic finger-pointing, which may well have been as much a provocation in the twelfth century as it is today. One suspects that the ideal knight and negotiator Gwalchmai might have come across to the medieval audience (and to Cai) as annoyingly smug. This view echoes the interpretation of Goetinck, *Peredur*, pp. 4, 6, 9.

7 For a slightly different reading of the reference to the nunnery and scarcity of food in this episode, see Glenys Goetinck, '*Peredur* ... Upon Reflection', *Études Celtiques*, 25 (1988), 221–32 (227).

8 Goetinck (ed.), *Historia Peredur*, p. 22; Davies (trans.), *Mabinogion*, p. 74.

9 For a discussion, see Jane Cartwright, *Feminine Sanctity and Spirituality in Medieval Wales* (Cardiff: University of Wales Press, 2008), pp. 177–81; Jane Cartwright, 'The Desire to Corrupt: Convent and Community in Medieval Wales', in Diane Watt (ed.), *Medieval Women and their Communities* (Toronto: University of Toronto Press, 1997), pp. 20–48 (pp. 20–2); David H. Williams, *The Welsh Cistercians* (Leominster: Gracewing, 1997) pp. 7–8.

10 Cartwright, *Feminine Sanctity*, p. 178.

11 Cartwright, *Feminine Sanctity*, p. 181.

12 Cartwright, *Feminine Sanctity*, pp. 181–2.

13 Goetinck (ed.), *Historia Peredur*, p. 23. The early version of the tale, attested in Peniarth 7, has a similar wording: 'Ac ar hynny ef awelai dwy vanaches yndyuot ymewn achostrel ynllawn owin ygan yneill achwethorth ouara cann gan y llall adywedut wrth y vorwyn arglwydes duw awyr hep wynt nabu yr govent yngot heno ovwyt a diawt namyn kymyn arall hyn'; Goetinck (ed.), *Historia Peredur*, p. 166.

14 Davies (trans.), *Mabinogion*, p. 75.

15 Goetinck (ed.), *Historia Peredur*, p. 23.

16 There is some evidence that the size of bread made by bakers, as well as the export of bread (particularly into Wales) was regulated, at least in urban environments, towards the later Middle Ages; John S. Lee, 'Grain Shortages in Late Medieval Towns', in Ben Dodds and Christian D. Liddy (eds), *Commercial Activity, Markets and Entrepreneurs in the Middle Ages* (Woodbridge: Boydell Press, 2011), pp. 63–80 (pp. 71–2). However, whether such regulation applied in the period in which Episode I was produced, and whether it applied to bread made for personal consumption (provided that the nuns produced their own bread), are points that would require further investigation.

17 See *https://arts.st-andrews.ac.uk/monasticmatrix/monasticon/minchinhampton-female-needs-verification* (last accessed 27 January 2023).
18 *Monasticon*, University of St Andrews, 2021, *https://arts.st-andrews.ac.uk/monasticmatrix/monasticon/limebrook* (last accessed 13 June 2021).
19 See *https://arts.st-andrews.ac.uk/monasticmatrix/monasticon/aconbury* (last accessed 13 June 2021). The priory, nevertheless, had a history associating it with the theme of starvation, as it was founded by Margaret de Lacy (daughter of William de Braose) in memory of her mother and elder brother who had starved to death in captivity; see Susan Mary Withycombe, '"O mihti meiden! O witti wummon!": the early English Katherine as a model of sanctity', *Parergon*, 9 (1991), 103–15 (106).
20 The Amesbury count is from the mid-thirteenth century, see *https://arts.st-andrews.ac.uk/monasticmatrix/monasticon/amesbury-double-monastery*.
21 See *https://arts.st-andrews.ac.uk/monasticmatrix/monasticon/buckland* (last accessed 27 January 2023).
22 Thus, it may be possible that there were more religious women in Wales at any one point than the extremely conservative number of approximately thirty-five suggested by Cartwright, *Feminine Spirituality*, p. 182.
23 Cartwright, *Feminine Spirituality*, p. 184; Cartwright cites Knowles and Hadcock's estimate of thirteen nuns as the population during Peckham's visit as the 'more optimistic estimate', Cartwright, *Feminine Spirituality*, p. 182; citing David Knowles and Richard Neville Hadcock, *Medieval Religious Houses: England and Wales* (London: Longman, 1971), p. 267.
24 The conventional counts might not necessarily include the entire population of a monastery, as it may exclude monastic servants.
25 Quoted and discussed in Cartwright, *Feminine Spirituality*, p. 184.
26 Cartwright, *Feminine Spirituality*, p. 184.
27 Google Maps, *www.google.com/maps* (last accessed 12 July 2021).
28 For a brief description of the castles, see John R. Kenyon, *The Medieval Castles of Wales* (Cardiff: University of Wales Press, 2010), pp. 96, 149–51.
29 Robert B. Patterson, *The Earl, The Kings and the Chronicler: Robert Earl of Gloucester and the Reigns of Henry I and Stephen* (Oxford: Oxford University Press, 2019), p. 95.
30 The words *yngot* ('nearby/there') and *hwnt* ('yonder') both indicate proximity; see *GPC* s.v. *yngod* and s.v. *hwnt*.
31 I use the term as defined by Mikhail Bakhtin as 'the intrinsic connectedness of temporal and spatial relationships'; Mikhail M. Bakhtin, 'Forms of Time and of the Chronotope in the Novel: Notes toward a Historical Poetics', in Michael Holquist (ed.), *The Dialogic Imagination: Four Essays by M. M. Bakhtin*, trans. by Caryl Emerson and Michael Holquist, University of Texas Press Slavic Series 1 (Austin TX: University of Texas Press, 1981), pp. 84–258 (p. 84). We return to the Severn basin on pp. 64 and 71–2 of this

book. For a different set of arguments linking the composition of *Peredur* (seen as a single whole) to the Severn basin, see Goetinck, '*Peredur* ... Upon Reflection', 230, 231.

32 Goetinck (ed.), *Historia Peredur*, p. 29.
33 S. Davies (trans.), *Mabinogion*, p. 78.
34 For a discussion of population density, see Max Lieberman, *The Medieval March of Wales: The Creation and Perception of a Frontier, 1066–1283* (Cambridge: Cambridge University Press, 2010), pp. 29–30.
35 A castle with towers is described in another episode of *Peredur*, discussed on p. 60 of this book. For a brief discussion of the terminology, see Anthony Emery, *Discovering Medieval Houses* (Oxford: Shire Publications, 2011), p. 6.
36 N. J. G. Pounds, *The Medieval Castle in England and Wales: A Social and Political History* (Cambridge: Cambridge University Press, 1990), p. 104.
37 Emery, *Discovering Medieval Houses*, p. 11.
38 C. G. Harfield, 'A Hand-List of Castles Recorded in the Domesday Book', *The English Historical Review*, 106 (1991), 371–92 (373).
39 Harfield, 'A Hand-List', 373, 377.
40 See pp. 138–40 of this book.
41 See Chapter 5 and further references therein.
42 For a similar reading of a different text, suggesting that Gawain's journey through North Wales in *Sir Gawain and the Green Knight* would have presented elements to its readers that would have been familiar within their cultural context, see Joshua Byron Smith, '"Til þat he neʒed ful neghe into þe Norþe Walez": Gawain's Postcolonial Turn', *The Chaucer Review*, 51 (2016), 295–309. For more on possible historical contextual reference in another episode of *Peredur*, see discussion in Chapter 3.
43 See pp. 28–9 of this book.
44 See Petrovskaia, 'Oaths, Pagans and Lions'; and Petrovskaia, *Medieval Welsh Perceptions of the Orient*, pp. 169–71, 176–80.
45 Goetinck (ed.), *Historia Peredur*, pp. 35–6; Davies (trans.), *The Mabinogion*, p. 82.
46 Goetinck (ed.), *Historia Peredur*, p. 39; Davies (trans.), *The Mabinogion*, p. 84.
47 For discussion of the redactor's possible interference in other aspects of this episode, see Lovecy, '*Historia Peredur*', pp. 177–8.
48 Goetinck (ed.), *Historia Peredur*, p. 40; Davies (trans.), *The Mabinogion*, p. 85.
49 Petrovskaia, 'Oaths, Pagans and Lions', 7–8.
50 Petrovskaia, 'Oaths, Pagans and Lions', 7; with reference to John K. Wright, *Geographical Lore of the Time of the Crusades: A Study in the History of Medieval Science and Tradition in Western Europe*, American Geographical Research Series XV (New York: American Geographical Society, 1925), p. 296; Geraldine Heng, *Empire of Magic: Medieval Romance and the Politics of Cultural Fantasy* (New York: Columbia University Press, 2003), pp. 49, 158.

51 For the former aspect, for instance, the discussion in Margaret Haist, 'The Lion, Bloodline, and Kingship', in Debra Hassig (ed.), *The Mark of the Beast: The Medieval Bestiary in Art, Life, and Literature* (New York: Routledge, 2013; originally published by Garland Publishing, 1999), pp. 3–21. The grateful lion story in a form very similar to that of Chrétien's text is found, for example, in Letter 100 of Peter Damian; see K. Reindel (ed.), *Die Briefe des Petrus Damiani*, Monumenta Germaniae Historica: Briefe der deutschen Kaiserzeit IV, 4 vols. (Munich: Monumenta Germaniae Historica, 1983–93), vol. III, pp. 113–14; Owen J. Blum (trans.), *Peter Damian: Letters*, 6 vols (Washington WA: Catholic University of America Press, 1989–2005), vol. V, pp. 118–19. For more on this, specifically in the context of discussions of the lion in Chrétien's narrative, see Tony Hunt, 'The Lion and Yvain', in P. B. Grout et al. (eds), *The Legend of Arthur in the Middle Ages: Studies Presented to A. H. Diverres by Colleagues, Pupils and Friends* (Cambridge: D. S. Brewer, 1983), pp. 86–98; Julian Harris, 'The Rôle of the Lion in Chrétien de Troyes' Yvain', *PMLA*, 64/5 (1949), 1143–63; A. G. Brodeur, 'The Grateful Lion: A Study in the Development of Medieval Narrative', *Publications of the Modern Language Association of America*, 39 (1924), 485–524; William A. Nitze, 'Yvain and the Myth of the Fountain', *Speculum*, 30 (1955), 170–9; Petrovskaia, 'Oaths, Pagans and Lions', 7–8 and notes on 24; and most recently in Piero Andrea Martina, 'Les aventures avec le lion: *Huon d'Auvergne*, *Yvain* (et les autres …)', *Reinardus: Yearbook of the International Reynard Society*, 26 (2014), 107–24 (15–18, with further bibliography in n. 26 on 115).

52 For the episode introducing the lion, see Chrétien de Troyes, *Le Chevalier au Lion*, ll. 3348–483, in C. Méla (ed.), *Chrétien de Troyes: Romans* (Paris: Livre de Poche, 1994) pp. 705–936, at pp. 821–6; *The Knight with the Lion (Yvain)*, in *Arthurian Romances*, trans. by Kibler, pp. 295–380, at pp. 337–8; see also *Owein: or, Chwedyl Iarlles y Ffynnawn*, pp. 25–8; Davies (trans.), *Mabinogion*, pp. 133–6.

53 Isabelle Valade, Luciana Cordo Russo and Lee Raye, 'Uses of the Supernatural in the Middle Welsh *Chwedyl Iarlles y Ffynnawn*', *Mirabilia: electronic journal of antiquity and middle ages*, 23 (2016), 168–88 (180–2), www.raco.cat/index.php/Mirabilia/article/view/321023 (last accessed 7 February 2023).

54 The argument relates specifically to the story of *Owain*, equivalent of Chrétien's *Le Chevalier au lion*; see Isabelle Valade et al., 'Uses of the Supernatural', 181–2. See also the discussion of a helpful lion that occurs in the Irish context, in *Tochmarc Emire*, where it appears to belong to the folktale 'helpful animal' variety, with possible, but very tenuous links to the 'grateful lion' story; in Marie-Louise Theuerkauf, 'Dragon Slayers and Lion Friends: Intertextual Considerations in *Tochmarc Emire*', *Aigne*, 5 (2014), 80–94 (82–7).

55 See Chrétien de Troyes, *Le Conte de graal*, ll. 7767–88; Méla (ed.), *Le Conte du Graal*, p. 1171; Kibler (trans.), *The Story of the Grail*, p. 477.

56 Goetinck (ed.), *Historia Peredur*, p. 37; Davies (trans.), *The Mabinogion*, p. 83. For studies of giants in Welsh cultural contexts, see Chris Grooms, *The Giants of Wales: Cewri Cymru* (Lewiston NY: Edwin Mellen Press, 1993) and, more recently, Harry Armstrong, 'Giant Minds: A Study of the Emotions, Rational Thought and Self-Awareness of Giants in Middle High German and Middle Welsh Literature' (RMA thesis, Utrecht University, 2020).

57 See, for instance, Cyril Meredith-Jones, 'The Conventional Saracen of the Songs of Geste', *Speculum*, 17 (1942), 201–25 (205); Suzanne Conklin Akbari, *Idols in the East: European Representations of Islam and the Orient, 1100–1450* (Ithaca NY and London: Cornell University Press, 2009), pp. 164, 167, 172–3; Sylvia Huot, *Outsiders: The Humanity and Inhumanity of Giants in Medieval French Prose Romance* (Notre Dame IN: University of Notre Dame Press, 2016), esp. pp. 80–96, 197–200. See also Petrovskaia, *Medieval Welsh Perceptions of the Orient*, p. 176 and n. 25 for further references.

58 The most recent edition of the *Historia regum* is Geoffrey of Monmouth, *The History of the Kings of Britain*, ed. by Reeve and trans. by Wright.

59 Aronstein, 'Becoming Welsh', 161–2.

60 Petrovskaia, *Medieval Welsh Perceptions of the Orient*, p. 171.

61 Geoffrey of Monmouth, *History*, pp. 26–7.

62 See Paul Russell, 'Geoffrey of Monmouth's Classical and Biblical Inheritance', in Joshua Byron Smith and Georgia Henley (eds), *A Companion to Geoffrey of Monmouth* (Leiden: Brill, 2020), pp. 67–104 (pp. 95–8); see also discussion in Victor I. Scherb, 'Assimilating Giants: The Appropriation of Gog and Magog in Medieval and Early Modern England', *Journal of Medieval and Early Modern Studies*, 32 (2002), 59–84 (65–8).

63 Goetinck (ed.), *Historia Peredur*, p. 36. Davies (trans.), *The Mabinogion*, p. 82

64 Russell makes this point in relation to classical giant influences in Geoffrey; Russell, 'Geoffrey of Monmouth's Classical and Biblical Inheritance', p. 98. Harry Armstrong has recently suggested that the manner in which Peredur's giants of the Round Valley are represented is reminiscent of the representation of non-Christians in the Welsh Charlemagne Cycle; Armstrong, 'Giant Minds', pp. 48–9. For an earlier discussion, see Petrovskaia, *Medieval Welsh Perceptions of the Orient*, p. 170.

65 See p. 71 of this book.

66 R. L. Thomson (ed.), *Pwyll Pendeuic Dyuet* (Dublin: DIAS, 2003), p. 1; Davies (trans.), *Mabinogion*, pp. 3–21.

67 Davies (trans.), *Mabinogion*, p. 86.

68 For a comparison between Pwyll's adventure and Peredur's, in relation to all Episodes of *Peredur*, see Goetinck, *Peredur*, pp. 214–18, 266–7. According to Goetinck, Peredur 'enters a world of enchantment', p. 245, but she does not draw the connection to Pwyll here.

69 Goetinck (ed.), *Historia Peredur*, p. 46; Davies (trans.), *Mabinogion*, p. 88.
70 See R. R. Davies, *The Age of Conquest: Wales, 1063–1415* (Oxford: Oxford University Press, 1987), pp. 160, 275.
71 For a summary, see p. 29 of this book, and Goetinck, *Peredur*, p. 47. The matter-of-fact nature of the interaction, with the drunk Peredur and the irritable Oppressor, is remarked on by Goetinck, *Peredur*, p. 247.
72 Goetinck, *Historia Peredur*, p. 45; cf. Davies, *The Mabinogion*, p. 87.
73 See Glynn E. Daniel, *The Prehistoric Chamber Tombs of England and Wales* (Cambridge: Cambridge University Press, 1950), pp. 46–8.
74 *Pwyll's* mound ('*gorsedd*') of Arberth once more provides the Welsh context; for discussions of this and of the Irish otherworldly geography, see John Carey, 'Time, Space, and the Otherworld', *Proceedings of the Harvard Celtic Colloquium*, 7 (1987), 1–27, esp. 5–6 and 13. For discussion of prehistoric monuments in medieval Welsh literature, see Brigid Ehrmantraut, 'Of Mice and Mounds: Prehistoric Monuments in the Literature of Medieval Wales', *Cambrian Medieval Celtic Studies*, 81 (2021), 93–111.
75 Goetinck (ed.), *Historia Peredur*, p. 46; Davies (trans.), *Mabinogion*, p. 88.
76 Davies (trans.), *Mabinogion*, p. 248 n. 88; Goetinck, *Peredur*, pp. 248–9. For a discussion of the cauldron in connection to the grail, see Carey, *Ireland and the Grail*, pp. 46–7, 79–90. For an edition of *Branwen*, see Derick S. Thomson (ed.), *Branwen uerch Lyr* (Dublin: DIAS, 1961).
77 Goetinck (ed.), *Historia Peredur*, p. 47; Davies (trans.), *Mabinogion*, p. 89. In *Branwen*, King Bran is killed by a poisoned spear; Thomson (ed.), *Branwen*, pp. 14–15; Davies (trans.), *Mabinogion*, pp. 22–34 (p. 32). See also discussions in Goetinck, *Peredur*, pp. 299–300; and Loomis, *The Grail*, pp. 56–7, 140–5. For more on Bran, see the discussion in Chapter 4.
78 Goetinck (ed.), *Historia Peredur*, p. 48; Davies (trans.), *Mabinogion*, p. 89. For a recent discussion of the episode, see Calis, 'Peredur and the Valley of Changing Sheep'.
79 For a discussion of the giant herdsman of *Owain*, see Natalia I. Petrovskaia, 'Die Identität des Riesen in Owein – Die Herrin der Quelle', in Ronny F. Schulz and Silke Winst (eds), *Riesen: Entwürfe und Deutungen des Ausser/Menschlichen in mittelalterlicher Literatur* (Vienna: Fassbaender, 2020), pp. 419–38; and Natalia I. Petrovskaia, 'Cross-legged Gods and One-legged Foresters', in Franca Ela Consolino, Lucilla Spetia and Francesco Marzella (eds), *Aspetti del meraviglioso nelle letterature medievali. Aspects du merveilleux dans les littératures médiévales — Medioevo latino, romanzo, germanico e celtico* (Turnhout: Brepols, 2016), pp. 357–69.
80 Goetinck (ed.), *Historia Peredur*, p. 47; Davies (trans.), *Mabinogion*, p. 89.
81 Goetinck (ed.), *Historia Peredur*, p. 47; Davies (trans.), *Mabinogion*, p. 89.
82 See, in particular, Goetinck, *Peredur*, pp. 147–9, 257; for counterarguments, see Petrovskaia, *Medieval Welsh Perceptions of the Orient*, pp. 162–3.

83 Breeze, '*Peredur son of Efrawg* and Windmills', 58. John Carey refers to this as evidence for the tale post-dating Chrétien's romance; Carey, *Ireland and the Grail*, p. 245, n. 3. It is possible, however, for the reference to windmills to be an interpolation. Furthermore, since what is here identified as Episode III has no correspondence to Chrétien's romance in any case, argument regarding the relationship between the texts depending on this section of *Peredur* would remain inconclusive.
84 Goetinck (ed.), *Historia Peredur*, p. 52.
85 Davies (trans.), *The Mabinogion*, p. 92.
86 Goetinck (ed.), *Historia Peredur*, pp. 52 and 179.
87 John Langdon and James Masschaele, 'Commercial Activity and Population Growth in Medieval England', *Past & Present*, 190 (2006), 35–82 (51).
88 Breeze, '*Peredur son of Efrawg* and Windmills', 59. For a discussion of the history of milling in England, and the involvement of religious orders, see Adam Lucas, *Ecclesiastical Lordship, Seigneurial Power and the Commercialization of Milling in Medieval England* (Farnham: Ashgate, 2014); For discussion of mills in Wales, see R. R. Davies, *The Age of Conquest*, pp. 154–5.
89 See, for instance, John Salmon, 'The Windmill in English Medieval Art', *Journal of the British Archaeological Association*, 6/3 (1941), 88–102 (88–9).
90 Goetinck (ed.), *Historia Peredur*, p. 53.
91 Davies (trans.), *The Mabinogion*, p. 92.
92 A contemporary parallel might be offered by our use of 'car' for a petrol car/combustion engine car, and 'electric car' for a car with an electric engine. The former is the default option because it has been around considerably longer.
93 Jean Gimpel, *La révolution industrielle du Moyen Âge* (Paris: Editions du Seuil, 1975), pp. 41, 66–9; Constance Hoffman Berman, 'Agriculture and Economies', in Mette Birkedal Bruun (ed.), *The Cambridge Companion to the Cistercian Order* (Cambridge: Cambridge University Press, 2012), pp. 112–24 (p. 118–19).
94 For a brief overview of the structure, administration and close internal ties within the Cistercian order, see Emilia Jamroziak, 'Centres and Peripheries', in Bruun (ed.), *The Cambridge Companion to the Cistercian Order*, pp. 65–79 (pp. 69–73).
95 John Langdon, 'Water-Mills and Windmills in the West Midlands, 1086–1500', *Economical History Review*, 44/2 (1991), 424–44 (433–4).
96 Gimpel, *La révolution industrielle*, pp. 16–17.
97 Gimpel, *La révolution industrielle*, p. 17; the calculation is based on the Wylye in Wiltshire and refers to watermills only. It may not be unreasonable to suppose that the landscape described in this episode of *Peredur*, with its combination of windmills and watermills, could have been equally or more densely built.
98 Breeze, '*Peredur son of Efrawg* and Windmills', 62.
99 Breeze, '*Peredur son of Efrawg* and Windmills', 62.

3

HISTORICAL CONTEXT AND THE EMPRESS

Peredur's three episodes have distinct chronotopes. Some indications of the importance of the historical and cultural context to our understanding of these texts can already be seen in the discussion of the tales' man-made landscapes – manors, nunneries and mills – explored in Chapter 2. More historical context is hinted at in the various female figures encountered particularly in Episodes I and III. There is a striking proliferation of women in power. The besieged countess who is Peredur's love in Episode I is explicitly stated to be her father's heir. The large woman whose household is threatened by the 'witches' of Gloucester, is clearly the master of her house. In Episode III, on his way to the cairn monster, Peredur meets the *Iarlles y Kampeu* ('Countess of the Feats), whose retinue the hero overthrows and who marries Edlym Gleddyf Goch.[1] All of these women appear to be – temporarily or otherwise – masters of their lands. At the end of Episode III, the highest-ranking of them all, the Empress, is introduced, who also appears to be wielding power in her own right, although surrounded by advisors.

The Empress's position at the culmination of the story makes of her a figure of some significance in this episode. Her marriage to the hero, and her earlier appearance as the mysterious maiden on the mound, have led to interpretations in light of the Sovereignty Theory.[2] One possible alternative is to see in this figure an allusion to individuals of circumstances recognisable to a medieval Welsh audience of the early to mid-thirteenth century.[3] The identification of the Empress as a figure at least inspired by Empress Matilda, who was the daughter of Henry I of England and widow of Henry V of the Holy Roman Empire, and whose claim on the English throne found support in the March (led by her half-brother

Robert of Gloucester) and also in Wales, offers an alternative to the Sovereignty Theory.[4]

It is not necessary to see the Empress as a fictionalised representation of Matilda herself, but given the heavily fictionalised representations of historical figures found elsewhere in Welsh literature, it does not seem to be impossible. The heavily fictionalised representation of Magnus Maximus in *Breudwyt Macsen Wledic* as the crowned Emperor of Rome, is one example that comes to mind.[5] There is another parallel between *Breudwyt Mascen* and Episode III, in that Elen is named *amherodres* ('empress'), before she marries the emperor.[6] This is particularly interesting in the context of Matilda's use of the title, since although she was married to the emperor, she herself had never been crowned by the Pope, only by a bishop, though she and her husband regarded him as papal legate.[7]

While references to women inheriting and ruling lands in Episode I must be dismissed for the purposes of analysing Episode III if we are to be consistent in reading these as independent texts, they do seem to point to the same cultural context, and a view that a woman could inherit and rule land. There are multiple examples contemporary to Matilda of women wielding power at the level of kingdoms and of earldoms.[8] Despite this, the view appears to be prevalent among scholars that, to quote Catherine Hanley's recent biography of Matilda, 'She lived at a time when daughters were thought to be lesser value than sons, and many noble (even royal) families did not bother to record their births with any care'.[9] This does not apply to Wales, as daughters are listed in medieval Welsh genealogical tracts, and inheritance sometimes traced through the female line, especially to boost prestige.[10] However, as Robin Chapman Stacey observes, originally Welsh women were not allowed to inherit land under Welsh law (with the exception of a single text), or to rule land as widows, and where women did inherit for lack of male heirs, the custom is considered to have been imported from England via the March.[11] There is, however, ample evidence from the twelfth century of noblewomen inheriting land in Europe outside Wales (the royal examples are a separate matter, discussed later in this chapter).[12] Within Episode III itself, a precedent is also set in the figure of the Countess of the Feats for female rule. The proliferation of female heirs and rulers in both Episode I and Episode III, therefore, might be regarded as a Norman cultural import. We should also not forget Peredur's mother ruling her land as a widow in the beginning of Episode I. The representation in these texts of a world where the traditionally male-gendered role of the ruler was occupied by various females serves to counterbalance the male-orientated and male-dominated representation that we find in the Welsh Laws of the Court.[13] An important implication of this contrast is that we may need to re-evaluate our views of real-world gender roles in medieval Welsh governance, or at least adjust our ideas of how gender roles were imagined by contemporaries. Although the *Peredur* episodes are fiction and depict an imaginary world, the Welsh laws also represent, as Robin Chapman Stacey formulates it, 'an imagined construction of reality rather than a faithful reproduction of it', carrying the views and wishes of the lawyers as much as, if not more, than they reflect real-world customs.[14] The conflict here is therefore not between a description of the real world in the laws and one of an imagined world in *Peredur* episodes, but rather between two idealised representations of two different ideals, both based in some way on reality. If the law books represented to some degree the wishful thinking of the lawyers, as Stacey argues, then we are left with the question of what the Arthurian text might represent.

There are a number of possibilities. One is to follow Andrew Breeze's reasoning in his discussion of what appear to be female-gendered themes in the Four Branches and postulate a female author (or, perhaps, less controversially a female patron) for Episodes I and III.[15] Given the contrast with the male-centred agenda of the laws, however, reading a feminist intentionality into the *Peredur* episodes would lead us, in this case, to postulating a kind of medieval proto-feminism expressed in the text, with all the dangers of anachronistic thinking. A second option is to perceive these fictional narratives as a mirror representation of the world, inverting the balance of power structures to achieve a sense of wonderous otherworldliness. This may be a viable solution to Episode III, with its invisibility stones, gold-generating magic, cave-dwelling monsters, colour-changing sheep and burning trees, but it does not seem to apply equally well to Episode I, with its conspicuous absence of otherworldly markers. Indeed, because Peredur never seems to leave the immediate vicinity of Arthur's court and the courts of various relatives, with real-world place names anchoring the narratives to Caerleon and Gloucester and thus south Wales and the March, the world depicted in that text can be seen as idealised at best, but not as otherworldly. A third option is to see the proliferation of female rulers in these episodes as an exaggerated reflection of the reality that would have been familiar to the intended medieval audience. If Episodes I and III were associated with the south and perhaps even lands bordering on the March, one might expect the audience to be familiar with the Marcher customs of female inheritance, and of widows administering their husbands' lands, which would have been seeping into Wales at the time, probably in that region. The sheer number of women in that position in the text could be accounted for by the simple fact that the situation would have made the female ruler vulnerable, precisely because she would not have been able to lead her own people into battle.[16] Such scenarios yield themselves particularly well to the intervention of the knightly protagonist: if the castle lacks a lord, it lacks, in essence, a military protector. If it has a lord, then the individual would have to be either too old to do battle, incapacitated in some way or simply incompetent, in order to allow the hero to perform his function. This is a less effective scenario and is, indeed, found only in the *Peredur* Continuation. The king who imprisons Peredur on suspicion of being his daughter's lover or prospective lover, is challenged by an earl who, in possession of two earldoms, 'cyn gadarnet yw a brenhin' ('is as strong as a king').[17] Peredur takes part in the battle anonymously on several consecutive days, finally killing the earl.[18] Reference to the king himself is conspicuously absent from the narrative at this point: we are not told of his actions (if there are any) on the battlefield. In terms of storytelling, the scenario simply presents more difficulties. Nevertheless, it must be emphasised that these practicalities are relevant only if the choice is between situations that would not have appeared alien to the audience. Women inheriting and ruling earldoms need not have been as frequently encountered a phenomenon as it is in Episodes I and III, but there would have to have been precedents.

While this argument, seeking a model in the real world to provide context for the audience, does not necessarily have to extend to the Empress, it is illustrative that there were, at royal level, examples of female rulers in the twelfth century. Doris Edel in her analysis of Medb's conversation with Ailill at the beginning of the Irish epic *Táin Bó Cúailnge* ('The Cattle-Raid of Cooley'), reading the character in light of Matilda's struggle for the throne, gives two contemporary examples as parallels. These are Melisende of Jerusalem and Urraca of Léon-Castilla, who succeeded Alfonso VI in 1109.[19] Both Melisende and Urraca had succeeded in holding on to royal power largely in spite of their husbands.[20] Urraca, like Matilda, appears to have used the imperial title, originally introduced in the chancery of her father Alfonso VI, calling herself *imperatrix* of all Spain (before reverting to the title of 'queen').[21] Another example of a female heir is the queen Petronilla of Aragon, whose father, Ramiro II, had abdicated in her favour in 1137 when she was only a year old, betrothing her to Count Ramon Berenguer of Barcelona.[22]

In her discussion of the possible reflection of Matilda in Medb of the pillow-talk episode in *Táin Bó Cúailnge*, Edel observes that 'one of the problems of female succession was that if the woman became queen in her own right, her husband would claim the title of king'.[23] Nevertheless, the actual situation was much more complex (and less openly disadvantageous to women).[24] Henry I appears to have nominated Matilda as his heir, rather than Matilda and her husband Geoffrey of Anjou as a couple.[25] Geoffrey's father Fulk had difficulties establishing himself as joint ruler of the kingdom of Jerusalem alongside his wife Melisende – the heir to the previous king – despite the fact that in his case the agreement had been precisely joint rule, and that Fulk would be not merely consort to the queen but himself king.[26] Had the default situation been that the consort would become king and co-ruler, as Edel seems to imply, there would have been no need for Baldwin to give his prospective son-in-law assurances as to his status. Conversely, the lack of acknowledgement of Geoffrey's status as prospective co-ruler by Henry would also not have been problematic. We can thus conclude that the elevation to co-ruler for a male consort of a female heir was optional in cases where he did not himself have at least a tangential claim to the throne. In each of these cases, there appears to have been some struggle for power between the queen and other individuals, be it her consort or other claimants to the throne. In the latter case, there is no discernible difference between these instances and examples of male pairs of competing candidates for the throne. It is only the struggle with the spouse that differentiates these medieval female rules from their male counterparts.

The issue of joint rule and inheritance by marriage in twelfth-century political reality provides a useful context for Episode III. While the hero's ascension to rule through marriage has previously lent itself to interpretation in light of the 'sovereignty theory', with the female figure in the narrative read as the 'sovereignty goddess', it seems that it rather reflected contemporary concerns. Peredur, after he marries the Empress, rules jointly with her for fourteen years at the conclusion of Episode III.[27] If, at the time, Wales was only beginning to introduce female inheritance as a Marcher-inspired innovation, one might wonder whether the Empress (both Matilda and her literary echo in this text) and the various ruling countesses in Episodes I and III were intended to provide a form of literary propaganda for the idea.[28]

Such contemporary concerns might link the production of Episode III (and perhaps also Episode I) to areas bordering on the March, as those most likely to be subject to Anglo-Norman cultural influence. It is interesting in this connection to return to the issue of geography, within this historical-political context, and to consider the place name associated with the Empress in this text. We have seen in Chapter 2 that the landscape of mills might be associated with the Severn, perhaps in the south, but the question remains of where the Empress comes from. Two of the manuscripts containing the tale, the White Book and the Red Book, have the reading 'amherodres Cristinobyl vawr' ('Empress of great Constantinople').[29] The third manuscript, however, that contains the episode with the Empress, namely, the manuscript with the shorter version of the text, Peniarth 7, has the reading '*Corsdinobyl*'.[30] The word is generally assumed to mean Constantinople, so the Empress is called 'Empress of Constantinople' in all translations and discussions of the text. I have previously suggested that the readings are the result of a process of scribal corruption that ran as follows:[31]

- *Constantinobyl* → *Const[ant]inobyl*: eye-skip or failure to expand an abbreviation.
- *Constinobyl* → *Corstinobyl*: confusion between *n* and *r*, common in certain insular scripts.
- *Corstinobyl* → *Cristinobyl*: an attempt to read significance into the name or failure to correctly associate it with Constantinople.

This reconstruction of the possible stages of alteration assumes that *Constantinople* is the original reading that was corrupted. I would like to add here that this reconstruction is supported by the fact that the reading of the intermediate stage, *Constinobyl*, is in fact attested in the Grail triad of Peniarth 50, quoted in the Introduction of this book, evidence that I was unaware of when I first proposed this sequence.[32] It is also attested in a late fifteenth-century poem by Ieuan ap Huw Cae Llwyd.[33] However, it is possible that the *Peredur* readings might not derive from Constantinople, while the others do. It is also worth pointing out that both of the other examples are much later than the *Peredur* texts, dating from the mid to late fifteenth century. Using these as supporting evidence for the intermediate stage of the reconstructed process is therefore problematic. The possibility thus remains that *Constantinople* may not be the term of origin for *Cristinobyl* at all. From the perspective of our interest in the cultural context of the text, regardless of the etymology, the redactors and audiences of the text might not have been able to make the connection between *Cristinobyl* and Constantinople in any case.[34]

Alterations to place names relating to distant locations are not uncommon in medieval Welsh texts. Before proceeding any further with the investigation, therefore, it seems necessary to examine, at least briefly, the use of the *Constantinople* place name in Welsh texts, and specifically to examine the occurrence of the variants corresponding to the ones that we have in *Historia Peredur*. Table 2 presents all the variants of what may have originally been *Constantinople* from medieval Welsh manuscripts containing prose texts. In addition to the manuscripts of *Peredur*, the terms occur in the following manuscripts: Aberystwyth, NLW, Peniarth 8 (s. xiii/xiv); Peniarth 10 (s. xiv[med.]); Peniarth 15 (s. xiv/xv); and Oxford, Jesus College MS 119 (1346).[35] Table 2 normalises initial mutations.[36] The name of the text in which the reference occurs is found in the right-hand column.[37]

In the first place, the recognisable term *Constantinobyl* occurs in a number of Welsh texts: the geographical treatise *Delw y Byd*; the *Life* of St Catherine; and the Welsh translation of the Letter of Prester John. For these texts, the identification of the place name as Constantinople is also straightforward because of the nature of the texts. *Delw y Byd* also preserves the alternative reading *Constantinapoli*, which is devoid of interest for this discussion as it simply retains the case-ending of the original Latin.[38] The term *Corsdinobyl*, which we find in the Peniarth 7 version of *Peredur*, is the term used in the same manuscript to refer to Constantinople in the Charlemagne texts (where it is identifiable as Constantinople, since these are translations). We also find it, with a slight spelling variation, in the Red Book versions of the same texts, as well as in *Delw y Byd*. In all these cases, the references are unambiguously to Constantinople. The reading *Cristinobyl*, however, remains unique to *Peredur*.

Given that the version in Peniarth 7 has the *Corsdinobyl* form recognisable elsewhere as a reference to Constantinople, it is possible that is what is meant here. The Long Version in the White Book and Red Book could conceivably represent a corrupted reading of the same. What remains unclear, however, is whether a medieval audience would have been able to recognise the reference in this form, or whether this represents a level of corruption that would have made recognition impossible. If the term was no longer recognised as referring to Constantinople, one might suppose a possible alternative identification.

Table 2: Occurrence of 'Constantinople' terms in medieval Welsh manuscripts

Readings	MS location	Text
Cristinobyl	Pen. 4 f. 41r col. 162 l. 12	*Historia Peredur*
	RB f. 169r col. 686 l. 7	
Corstinabyl	RB f. 112v col. 467 l. 21	*Cân Rolant*
	RB f. 149r col. 606 ll. 19–20	*Pererindod Siarlymaen*
	RB f. 150r col. 609 l. 23	*Pererindod Siarlymaen*
	RB f. 150r col. 610 l. 40	*Pererindod Siarlymaen*
	RB f. 150v col. 611 l. 4	*Pererindod Siarlymaen*
	RB f. 154r col. 626 l. 7	*Pererindod Siarlymaen*
	Pen. 10 f. 5r l. 20	*Pererindod Siarlymaen*
	Pen. 10 f. 7r l. 38	*Pererindod Siarlymaen*
	Pen. 10 f. 7v l. 10	*Pererindod Siarlymaen*
	Pen. 10 f. 13v l. 34	*Pererindod Siarlymaen*
	Pen. 10 f. 41v l. 26	*Cân Rolant*
Corstinobyl	RB f. 245v col. 986 l. 24	*Delw y Byd*
	RB f. 251v col. 1011 l. 14	*Brut y Saeson*
	Pen. 5 f. 91v col. 129 l. 22	*Pererindod Siarlymaen*
	Pen. 5 f. 93r col. 135 l. 11	*Pererindod Siarlymaen*
	Pen. 5 f. 93v col. 137 l. 17	*Pererindod Siarlymaen*
	Pen. 5 f. 102r col. 171 l. 16	*Cân Rolant*
	Pen. 5 f. 93v col. 137 ll. 28–9	*Pererindod Siarlymaen*
	Pen. 5 f. 99v col. 161 ll. 14–15	*Pererindod Siarlymaen*
Corsdinobyl	Pen. 7 f. 15r col. 45 l. 24	*Historia Peredur*
	Pen. 7 f. 16v col. 51 l. 28	*Pererindod Siarlymaen*
	Pen. 7 f. 17r col. 54 l. 16	*Pererindod Siarlymaen*
	Pen. 7 f. 17v col. 56 l. 16	*Pererindod Siarlymaen*
	Pen. 7 f. 37r col. 133 l. 4[39]	*Cân Rolant*
	Pen. 8 p. 2 l. 24	*Pererindod Siarlymaen*
	Pen. 8i p. 19 ll. 21–2	*Pererindod Siarlymaen*
	Pen. 8ii p. 3 l. 29	*Pererindod Siarlymaen*
Constinapoli	RB col. 123v col. 510 l. 24	*Delw y Byd*
Constantinobyl	Pen. 5 p. 2v l. 37	*Delw y Byd*
	Pen. 5 p. 21v l. 21	*Buchedd Catrin*
	Pen. 15 p. 115, l. 29	*Gwlad Ieuan Vendigeid*
	Pen. 15 p. 138, l. 17	*Buchedd Catrin*
	Jesus MS 119 f. 137v, l. 3	*Gwlad Ieuan Vendigeid*

The empress of Constantinople who was closest to the time of our earliest manuscript – the thirteenth-century Peniarth 7 – was the mid-eleventh century Empress Theodora.[40] However, there appears to be no particular reason for Welsh audiences to be interested in this character.[41] I have previously suggested that *Cristinobyl vawr* could be rendered as 'the great [something] of Christ'.[42] While *-obyl* appears to derive from *-polis*, based on the reconstruction of the scribal corruption, this would not necessarily have been recognised in medieval Welsh contexts, and it would not necessarily have been seen to mean 'city'; however, since it would have been recognisable as a place name, Jerusalem seemed a viable possibility.[43] Even if the place name was interpreted as a reference to Jerusalem, which I see as unlikely given that there is no indication that Jerusalem was ever referred to by such a term in medieval Welsh, Matilda's association with Jerusalem through her father-in-law, Fulk, provided a tentative connection.[44] An alternative possibility is that the original term may have been *Chrysopolis*, the site of Constantine I's victory over his rival Licinius, which was originally a different city on the opposite bank from Constantinople but came to be a district incorporated into the latter (subsequently known as Scutari, then Üsküdar).[45] We might also be dealing with conflation of the two place names.

It seems possible, however, given the ambiguity of this corrupted form of the geographical reference, to suggest that the Empress of *Cristinobyl* may represent an amalgamation of Matilda with Melisende of Jerusalem. Indeed, the Latin Kingdom of Jerusalem had a history of female rulers, which made it very different from medieval Western kingdoms.[46] Knowledge of this phenomenon may have spread in Britain in the course of Matilda's own struggle for power, since her claims of inheritance were based on her father's recognition of her as heir for lack of legitimate male heirs, which is exactly the parallel to the pattern of female queenship in the Latin Kingdom of Jerusalem. Alternatively, such histories might have been brought to Wales by returning crusaders after the Third Crusade at the end of the twelfth century.[47] In either case, information would have been available in Wales well before the writing of Peniarth 7, our earliest *Peredur* manuscript. As such, if the reference was not explicitly to Matilda, we might suppose that the Empress is intended merely as a fictional, vaguely oriental sovereign representing an orientalist fantasy *avant la lettre*.

Interpreting the Empress straightforwardly as a fictionalisation of Matilda is also possible. In this reading, the multitude of tents could represent Matilda's forces during her stay in the Marcher territories of her brother, Robert of Gloucester.[48] Indeed, it is also possible to see the explicit reference to a wise man who counselled the Empress and brought Peredur to her, as a literary reflection of Earl Robert, the main Marcher magnate whose contacts in Wales had brought Welsh allies to the Empress's side at the Battle of Lincoln.[49] His function as counsellor to both Henry I and later Matilda, as strategist for the war with Stephen, and patron of literature (including, famously, Geoffrey's Arthurian opus *Historia regum Britanniae*), combine to create an image that may easily have given rise to a literary wise counsellor incarnation.[50] The idea that the Empress's wise man may be a reflection of Earl Robert may seem fanciful on its own, but it fits with the rest of the picture if we take the view that the Empress is a reflection of Matilda.

Whether the Empress is to be seen as Matilda or as an agglomeration of female rulers of the twelfth century, or even as a distant echo of the queens of the Kingdom of Jerusalem, matters to some extent to our understanding of the relationship of Peredur legends and Chrétien's romance. I have previously suggested that the version that reached Chrétien either did not yet contain the episode discussed here, that he removed the episode, or that the episode did not make it into his version as that version was never completed.[51] Since it is only Episode I that appears to correspond with the French text, it simply appears as if Episodes II and III never made it to the Continent. As Goetinck notes, 'medieval compilers were more inclined to interpolation than rejection of episodes'.[52] Whether they belonged to a different tradition, or were composed after Episode I made its way to the Continent, we cannot know for certain. Given the possible crusade references in Episode II, and the references to windmills (and possibly Matilda) in Episode III, it may be that we are dealing with two episodes that were composed towards the end of the twelfth or even the beginning of the thirteenth century, and would thus be contemporaneous with, or later than, *Perceval*. There is no internal indication in Episode I that would point to such a late date of composition, but the proliferation of independent women in power may indicate mid to late twelfth-century origins. It is entirely possible that it could have been composed in the twelfth century and represented the first *Peredur* story.[53]

Episode I also appears to contain traces of other, possibly earlier stories. These are almost impossible to reconstruct based on available information. However, since they are indications of possible other

Arthurian narratives, it seems worthwhile to investigate these possibilities. The following chapter, therefore, engages with the older stratum of narratives. We move from twelfth-century historical context and possible late twelfth to early thirteenth-century composition of Episodes II and III, back in time to the lost tales hinted at in Episode I.

Notes

1 Goetinck (ed.), *Historia Peredur*, p. 50; Davies (trans.), *The Mabinogion*, p. 90.
2 For example, see Ian C. Lovecy, 'The Celtic Sovereignty Theme and the Structure of *Peredur*', *Studia Celtica*, 12–13 (1977–8), 133–46; Goetinck, 'The Female Characters'.
3 The date of composition of this episode may be earlier, but given the late thirteenth-century date of the manuscript and the reference to windmills, the early thirteenth century seems to be the safest conservative estimate.
4 The identification was first proposed in Petrovskaia, 'Dating *Peredur*' (238–9 for Welsh support of Matilda's claim); for a similar argument in relation to Irish sources, proposing that Medb's pillow-talk contest with Ailill in the *Táin Bó Cúailnge* is to be read as a parallel to the contest between Matilda and Stephen, see Doris Edel, 'Medb of Crúachain and the Empress Matilda: literature and politics in 12th-century Leinster', *Zeitschrift für celtische Philologie*, 64 (2017), 19–58. For biographies of Matilda, see Marjorie Chibnall, *The Empress Matilda: Queen Consort, Queen Mother and Lady of the English* (Oxford: Blackwell, 1991); and more recently Catherine Hanley, *Matilda: Empress, Queen, Warrior* (New Haven CT and London: Yale University Press, 2019).
5 Brynley F. Roberts (ed.), *Breudwyt Maxen Wledic* (Dublin: Dias, 2005); for discussions, see Patrick Sims-Williams, 'Some Functions of Origin Stories in Early Medieval Wales', in T. Nyberg et al. (eds), *History and Heroic Tale: A Symposium* (Odense: Odense University Press, 1985), pp. 97–131; Martin Rockel, 'Fiktion und Wirklichkeit im *Breuddwyd Macsen*', in Hildegard L. C. Tristram (ed.), *Medialität und mittelalterliche insulare Literatur* (Tübingen: Gunter Narr, 1992), pp. 170–81 (p. 174).
6 See discussion in Petrovskaia, 'Dating *Peredur*', 230.
7 Chibnall, *The Empress Matilda*, pp. 32–3; Hanley, *Matilda*, pp. 26–7.
8 For a discussion of female inheritance in medieval Europe, see, for instance, David Herlihy, 'Land, Family, and Women in Continental Europe, 701–1200', in Susan Mosher Stuard (ed.), *Women in Medieval Society* (Philadelphia PA: University of Pennsylvania Press, 1976), pp. 13–45 (pp. 22–3, 26–32); Michael T. Clanchy, *England and Its Rulers, 1066–1307*, 4th edn (Malden, Oxford and Chichester: Wiley Blackwell, 2014), pp. 185–6 (with reference to

Matilda). For an examination of the degree to which medieval women shared in power (in the sense covered by the medieval legal concept of *potestas*), see Georges Duby, 'Women and Power', in Thomas N. Bisson (ed.), *Cultures of Power: Lordship, Status, and Process in Twelfth-Century Europe* (Philadelphia PA: University of Pennsylvania Press, 1995), pp. 69–85 (esp p. 70 for the issue of inheritance). For female rulers contemporary to Matilda, Melisende of Jerusalem and Urraca of Castilla, see discussion and associated references, p. 86 of this book. For a study of female rulers from a global perspective, see Elena Woodacre (ed.), *A Companion to Global Queenship* (Leeds: ARC Humanities Press, 2018), and especially the 'Introduction' of this book for an overview of the field.

9 Hanley, *Matilda*, p. 2. Matilda's first husband, the emperor, inherited his Italian lands from a woman: Matilda of Canossa, Hanley, *Matilda*, pp. 24–5. See also discussion of female power in Amalie Fößel, 'The Political Tradition of Female Rulership in Late Medieval Europe', in Judith M. Bennett and Ruth Mazo Karras (eds), *The Oxford Handbook of Women and Gender in Medieval Europe* (Oxford: Oxford University Press, 2013), pp. 68–83.

10 See Ben Guy, *Medieval Welsh Genealogy: An Introduction and Textual Study* (Woodbridge: Boydell Press, 2020), for instance, pp. 60, 74, 82–3, 90–1, 165, 205.

11 See Robin Chapman Stacey, *Law and the Imagination in Medieval Wales* (Philadelphia PA: University of Pennsylvania Press, 2018), p. 72 and Stacey, 'Gender and the Social Imaginary', 280 and esp. n. 64 for the reference to the legal tract. The allowance for widows to inherit in the absence of eligible male heirs, present in the Blegywryd redaction of the Welsh laws, which is southern, is likely to be due to Anglo-Norman influence; Stephen J. Williams and J. Enoch Powell (eds), *Cyfreithiau Hywel Dda yn ôl Llyfr Blegywryd (Dull Dyfed)*, 2nd edn (Cardiff: University of Wales Press, 1961), p. 75.24–5; by way of contrast, in the north, in Gwynedd, no such allowance was made; Sir John Edward Lloyd, *A History of Wales: From the Earliest Times to the Edwardian Conquest* (London: Longmans, 1948), vol. 1, p. 300, n. 83. I am grateful to Paul Russell for this information and references.

12 Hanley, *Matilda*, pp. 143–4.

13 For a recent discussion of gender balance in the Welsh laws, see Stacey, 'Gender and the Social Imaginary'.

14 Stacey, 'Gender and the Social Imaginary', 270, 274.

15 Andrew Breeze, 'Did a Woman Write the Four Branches of the Mabinogi', *Studi Medievali*, 38 (1997), 679–705.

16 See, for instance, Hanley, *Matilda*, pp. 122–3, 133–4, 239–41.

17 Goetinck (ed.), *Historia Peredur*, p. 64; Davies (trans.), *Mabinogion*, p. 98. The strength here refers presumably to the size of the earl's armies.

18 Goetinck (ed.), *Historia Peredur*, p. 65; Davies (trans.), *Mabinogion*, p. 99.

19 See Edel, 'Medb of Crúachain', 33, 49–52. Urraca and Melisende are discussed as contemporary parallels to Matilda also in Hanley, *Matilda*, pp. 58–9, 145–6.
20 For more on these queens, in the context of a broader discussion of medieval female rulership, including later medieval examples, see Fößel, 'The Political Tradition of Female Rulership', pp. 75–7. For discussion of Melisende in the context of female succession in the Kingdom of Jerusalem in the twelfth and thirteenth centuries, see Hayley Bassett, 'Regnant Queenship and Royal Marriage Between the Latin Kingdom of Jerusalem and the Nobility of Western Europe', in Elena Woodacre (ed.), *A Companion to Global Queenship* (Leeds: ARC Humanities Press, 2018), pp. 39–52.
21 Bernard F. Reilly, *The Kingdom of Léon-Castilla Under King Alfonso VII 1126–1157* (Philadelphia PA: University of Pennsylvania Press, 1998), p. 136–7.
22 Hanley, *Matilda*, pp. 146–7. For more on Petronilla, see William Clay Stalls, 'Queenship and Royal Patrimony in Twelfth-Century Iberia: the Example of Petronilla of Aragon', in Theresa M. Vann (ed.), *Queens, Regents and Potentates* (Cambridge: Academia Press, 1993), pp. 49–61 (p. 50 for the abdication and marriage).
23 Edel, 'Medb of Crúachain', 33.
24 The history of the status of the male consort in the medieval period has not been studied extensively; for analysis of the later examples, see Charles Beem and Miles Taylor (eds), *The Man Behind the Queen Male Consorts in History* (New York: Palgrave Macmillan, 2014).
25 Edel, 'Medb of Crúachain', 29 n. 51, and 51–2; see Chibnall, *The Empress Matilda*, pp. 56, 60; Hanley, *Matilda*, pp. 59, 64–5.
26 For the promise made to Fulk, see Hans E. Mayer, 'Studies in the History of Queen Melisende of Jerusalem', *Dumbarton Oaks Papers*, 26 (1972), 93–182 (99).
27 Goetinck (ed.), *Historia Peredur*, p. 56; Davies (trans.), *The Mabinogion*, p. 94.
28 Given the engagement of Earl Robert in literary patronage with, as Robert Patterson argues, precisely those goals in the Anglo-Norman cultural environment, it would not be entirely implausible to suggest that similar efforts were being made in the Welsh; Patterson, *The Earl*, pp. 178–80.
29 Goetinck (ed.), *Historia Peredur*, p. 53; Davies (trans.), *Mabinogion*, p. 92.
30 Goetinck (ed.), *Historia Peredur*, p. 80.
31 In Petrovskaia, 'Dating *Peredur*', 232.
32 See pp. 4–5 of this book.
33 See Helen Fulton, 'The Encomium Urbis in Medieval Welsh Poetry', *Proceedings of the Harvard Celtic Colloquium*, 26/27 (2006–7), 54–72, at 66–8 for the poem, translation and discussion.
34 Petrovskaia, 'Dating *Peredur*', 232.
35 For dates, see Huws, *Medieval Welsh Manuscripts*, pp. 58–60.

36 For initial mutations affecting nouns in Welsh, see D. Simon Evans, *A Grammar of Middle Welsh* (Dublin: DIAS, 1964), pp. 14–17.
37 This table is an expanded version of the table originally published in Petrovskaia, 'Dating *Peredur*', which only included readings from manuscripts that also contain *Peredur* and made some omissions.
38 For retention of Latin case endings in *Delw y Byd*, see Natalia I. Petrovskaia (ed.), *Delw y Byd: A Medieval Welsh Encyclopedia* (London: MHRA, 2020), p. 20. For an earlier edition of the complete text, see Henry Lewis and P. Diverres (eds), *Delw y Byd (Imago Mundi)* (Cardiff: University of Wales Press, 1928).
39 Spelt with superscript *r*.
40 Goetinck, *Peredur*, p. 36; A. P. Kazhdan et al., *Oxford Dictionary of Byzantium* (Oxford, 1991) vol. 3, p. 2038.
41 Petrovskaia, 'Dating *Peredur*', 238.
42 Petrovskaia, 'Dating *Peredur*', 237.
43 Petrovskaia, 'Dating *Peredur*', 237.
44 Petrovskaia, 'Dating *Peredur*', 237–8; Chibnall, *Empress*, pp. 15–16, 55–6, 70.
45 Thomas Russell, *Byzantium and the Bosporus: A Historical Study, From the Seventh Century BC until the Foundation of Constantinople* (Oxford: Oxford University Press, 2017), pp. 62, 81; Michael Grant, *Constantine the Great: The Man and His Times* (New York: Barnes & Noble, 1993), p. 119.
46 Bassett, 'Regnant Queenship'.
47 For discussion of Welsh participation in the Third Crusade, see Kathryn Hurlock, *Wales and the Crusades, c. 1095–1291* (Cardiff: University of Wales Press, 2011), pp. 58–91; and Petrovskaia, *Medieval Welsh Perceptions of the Orient*, pp. 49–76.
48 Matilda had originally stayed as Robert of Gloucester's guest Bristol after arriving in Britain but moved to Gloucester (where the castle was held by Miles of Gloucester for the crown) in 1140; Hanley, *Matilda*, pp. 123–4.
49 Hanley, *Matilda*, pp. 139–40. Robert of Gloucester appears to have achieved peace with his Welsh neighbours in around 1135×1137; see Patterson, *The Earl*, p. 134.
50 For more on Robert of Gloucester, see Patterson, *The Earl*, esp. pp. 48–9 and 178–80 for literary patronage.
51 Petrovskaia, 'Dating *Peredur*', 241.
52 Goetinck, *Peredur*, p. 79.
53 See also Goetinck, '*Peredur* … Upon Reflection', 231 for a suggestion of a twelfth-century date of composition (for *Peredur* seen as a single unit).

4

LITERARY CONTEXT:
PEREDUR AND SOME LOST TALES

In addition to the various individual episodes that can be treated almost as independent stories loosely bound together within each frame narrative of the three *Peredur* episodes, the text contains a number of references that seem to point to further narratives, which function, in Brynley F. Roberts's words, 'as hooks for the reciter and his audience to introduce or demand other stories'.[1] Although it may not be possible to reconstruct these narratives with any great certainty, in some cases there is sufficient external evidence to suggest some possible forms that the narrative referred to might have taken.[2]

One such reference occurs towards the opening of the tale, in the scene of Peredur's initial meeting with the three knights of Arthur's court, and concerns the purpose of their journey. In Chrétien's version, the knights appear to be in pursuit of five knights and three maidens. '*Veïs tu hui en cele lande .V. chevaliers et .III. puceles?*' ('Have you seen five knights and three maidens cross this clearing today?'), asks the first of these knights of Perceval, who is too busy admiring the knights' accoutrements to respond to the query.[3] The Welsh version, characteristically, has no indication of damsels in distress, but rather provides a tantalising hint at another story: '*Sef oedynt, Gwalchmei uab Gwyar a Gweir uab Gwestyl ac Owein uab Uryen, ac Owein yn kadw yr ol, yn ymlit y marchawc a ranassei yr aualeu yn llys Arthur*'[4] ('Who were they but Gwalchmai son of Gwyar and Gwair son of Gwystyl and Owain son of Urien, and Owain bringing up the rear, pursuing the knight who had shared out the apples in Arthur's court').[5] The reference itself is almost identical in the Peniarth 14 version of the text, with the exception of the order of the knights – Gwalchmai is bringing up the rear and later engages in conversation with Peredur (whereas in the Long Version this role is Owain's).[6] We are never told who the knight of the apples was, what the issue with the apples might have been, or whether they had ever caught up with the knight. As Sioned Davies observes in the notes to her translation of the passage, 'There are no references elsewhere to the sharing of apples in Arthur's court'.[7] Nevertheless, this reference appears very similar to the incidental reference to additional branches of the *Mabinogi* present in *Manawydan* and to the triads present in the Four Branches and *Culhwch*.[8] It seems inadvisable, in this light, to reject out of hand the possibility that this passage might refer to another episode or tale.

The episode might at first glance seem irrecoverable, for as Davies observes, there are no such references in the Welsh tradition. However, there is a narrative tradition concerning poisoned apples, linked specifically to Arthur's court. An objection that might be raised to this parallel is that there is no specific reference in *Peredur*'s Episode I to the apples having been poisoned. However, this does not seem an unreasonable suggestion, since poisoned apples are a fairly common literary motif and would, in this case, explain why the one who handed out these apples at court would be pursued by three knights. There would have to be something wrong with the apples for that to happen. The motif is therefore worth investigating.

The most famous example of the episode involving knights, apples and the Arthurian court, occurs in what is perhaps the most influential of fifteenth-century Arthurian narratives, Malory's *Morte Darthur*, in Book XVIII, Chapter 3, known as the 'poisoned apple episode'.[9] In Malory's version, poisoned apples are present at the banquet hosted by Guinevere and she is subsequently blamed for the poisoning.[10] In this episode, the Queen organises a banquet for twenty-four knights, including Gawain, who had a great predilection for fruit and for apples and pears in particular, and one Sir Pinel le Savage, who held a grudge against Gawain for killing his brother. Pinel poisons apples at the feast, but another knight, Sir Patryse, eats them and is poisoned. Guinevere, as the host, is suspected. The text of the episode as it is in Malory is as follows:

> So the quene lete make a pryvy dyner in London unto the Knyghtes of the Rownde Table, and all was for to shew outwarde that she had as grete joy in all other knyghtes of the Rounde Table as she had in Sir Launcelot. So there was all only at that

dyner Sir Gawyne and his brethren, ... Sir Kay le Senysciall, Sira Madore de la Porte, Sir Patrise (a knyghte of Irelonde), Sir Alyduke, Sir Ascamoure, and Sir Pynell le Saveayge, whych was cosyne to Sir Lameroke de Galis, the good knyght that Sir Gawayne and hys brethirn slew by treson. And so thes foure and twenty knyghtes sholde dyne with the quene in a prevy place by themselff, and there was made a grete feste of all maner of deyntees.

But Sir Gawayne had a custom that he used dayly at mete and at supper: that he loved well all maner of fruyte, and in especiall appyls and pearys. And therefore whosomever dyned other fested Sir Gawayne wolde comonly purvey for good fruyte for hym; and so ded the quene: for to please Sir Gawayne she lette purvey for hym all maner of fruyte. For Sir Gawayne was a passyng hote knygt of nature, and thys Sir Pyonell hated Sir Gawayne bycause of hys kynnesman Sir Lamorakes dethe; and therefore, for pure envy and hate, Sir Pyonell enpoysonde sertayn appyls for to enpoysen Sir Gawayne.

So thys was well yet unto the ende of mete, and so hit befylle by myssefortune a good knyght, Sir Patryse, which was cosyn unto Sir Mador de la Porte, toke an appyll, for he was enchaffed with hete of wyne. And hit myssehapped hym to take a poysonde apple. And whan he had etyn hit he swall sore tylle he braste, and there Sir Patryse felle downe suddeynly dede amonge hem. Than every knyght lepe frome the bourde ashamed and araged for wratthe nyghe oute of hir wittis, for they wyst nat what to sey; consyderynge Queen Gwenyvere made the feste and dyner they had all suspeccion unto hir.[11]

This quotation omits the list of names of the knights present at the feast for the sake of saving space. It must be noted in the context of reading this episode as a possible reflection of earlier, and specifically Welsh tradition, that the number of *foure and twenty knyghtes* present at the fatal feast in Malory's text corresponds to the number in the text *Pedwar Marchog ar Hugain Llys Arthur* ('Twenty-four knights of Arthur's Court'), which survives among the triads.[12] The Welsh text survives in Llanstephan 28, written by Gutun Owain in 1455, although this is probably a copy based on an exemplar belonging to an older tradition.[13] It must be acknowledged that correspondences between the Welsh list and the list in Malory (omitted in the quotation) are more likely to be due to the shared French exemplar of Malory and the Welsh list (in the Vulgate Cycle) than to any possible ancient Welsh source underlying a hypothetical common tradition, although the *Pedwar Marchog ar Hugain* text does seem to have an early substratum.[14] The correspondence that matters, however, and that is echoed in *Peredur* and thus probably does represent an early, Welsh, source (which would have influenced Malory at many removes), is the number of the knights. While it might be, at a push, dismissed as a coincidence, the fact remains that it is twenty-four knights of Arthur's court who are present at the fateful banquet in Malory's *Morte*, listed in *Pedward Marchog ar Hugain* and, crucially, appear in Episode I of *Peredur*. In the scene in Episode I(C) where Peredur contemplates the blood and the raven in the snow, and thinks on his beloved, he is accosted by a lad, then by twenty-four knights, and finally by Cai, before Gwalchmai finally succeeds in bringing him to Arthur: 'Ac ol yn ol ef a doeth petwar marchaw[c] ar hugeint, ac nyt attebei ef y'r vn mwy no['e] gylid, namyn yr vn gware a phob vn, y wan ar vn gossot tros [pedrein] y varch y'r llawr' ('Twenty-four knights came in succession, and he would not answer one more than another, but treated each one the same – he threw each one with a single thrust over his horse's crupper to the ground').[15] While I would not wish to push this correspondence too far, it does seem to support the possibility that there might have been some common shared literary tradition reflected in Malory's 'poisoned apple episode' and *Peredur*'s Episode I, justifying the argument that we might look at apple episodes in and around Malory's text for possible approximations of the lost apple story alluded to in *Peredur*.

There are two earlier Arthurian texts, the French prose *Mort Artu* (part of the Vulgate Cycle) and the English stanzaic *Le Morte Arthur* (a verse composition composed before 1460, presenting an abridged adaptation of the same) which contain the same episode and have been shown to have served as Malory's model.[16] In the stanzaic *Morte Arthur* the perpetrator is a squire and no motivation for the crime is provided. The key section of the episode runs as follows:

> A squier in the court hath thought
> That ilke day, yif that he might,
> With a poison that he hath wrought
> To slay Gawain, yif that he might;
> In frut he hath it forthe brought

> And set before the queene bright;
> An apple overest lay on loft,
> There the poison was in dight.[17]

The French version of the episode runs as follows:

> Et en une chambre delez la sale avoit un chevalier qui avoit non Avarlan et haoit monseigneur Gauvain de mort et avoir fruit envenimé, dont il cuidoit monseigneur Gauvain fere morir. Si li fu avis que s'il en enveoit a la reïne, ele l'en donoroit plus tost que a nul autre; et se il en menjoit, il en morroit tantost. La reïne prist le fruit, qui de la traïson ne se gardoit, si en dona a un chevalier qui estoit compains de la Table Reonde et avoit non Gaheris de Karaheu …[18]

> In an adjacent room was a knight named Avarlan, who mortally detested Sir Gawain, and he had some poisoned fruit with which he planned to cause Gawain's death. He thought that if he sent some of it to the queen, she would give it to Gawain before anyone else; and if he ate it, he would die immediately.
> The queen, without suspecting the treachery, took the fruit, but she gave it to a knight of the Round Table named Gaheris of Carahew.[19]

The knight in question does not survive. In this narrative, as in the other ones discussed here, Gawain is the target, and in each case Gawain survives unharmed. If this type of narrative lay behind the reference in *Peredur*, one might suggest that Gwalchmai's prominent role in the Peniarth 14 scene of the pursuit may be a reflection of the fact that this is an adventure of his. Although the earliest version of the text in Peniarth 7 had lost this section of the text, in light of the fact that it is Gwalchmai, not Owain (as in the White Book and Red Book texts), who afterwards helps Peredur remove the armour of the knight who had insulted the queen, it is probable that in that text it was Gwalchmai who had engaged in conversation with Peredur at this point and mentioned the apples.[20] If the distribution of apples at Arthur's court is to be taken as a reference to a pre-existing story, the change to the character who makes the reference (Gwalchmai in the early version to Owain in the later) might be an indication that either the tradition was fluid, or that, by the time that the

Long Version came to be, the story of the apples had already been lost and the reference no longer associated with Gwalchmai.

Returning to the later poisoned apple narratives, a difficulty in identifying this episode as the reference in *Peredur* lies in the fact that the French version of the story refers only in general terms to fruit, while apples are specified only in the English texts. However, it is possible that were apples to be the specific fruit in the hypothetical common source, *fruit* could be the variant. There are a number of similar poison narratives in French *chansons de geste*, and in each of which the poisoned fruit are apples, although the details of the episodes are quite different.[21] Neither in these, nor in the various versions of the 'poisoned apple episode' of the *Morte Darthur*, is there any sharing out or dividing of the apples involved. However, another episode involving poisoned apples, identified by Yolande de Pontfarcy as a possible parallel to the 'poisoned apple episode', does involve sharing out apples and might therefore provide the missing link to the tradition hinted at in *Peredur*. The episode in question is a passage in Geoffrey of Monmouth's *Vita Merlini*, where a woman pursuing Merlin lays poisoned apples out in the grass, but he shares them out to his friends instead.[22] The following quotation corresponds to the section of text describing the episode itself.[23] It is followed in the text by the explanation that the apples had been left there by a jealous woman:

> Deinde super teneras solito conspeximus herbas
> in rivo fontis redolentia poma jacere.
> Mox ea collegit qui primus adiverat iste
> porrexitque michi subito pro munere ridens.
> Ergo distribui data quia non suffecit acervus.
> Riserunt alii quibus impertita fuerunt
> meque vocant largum cupidis quoque faucibus illa
> agrediendo vorant et pauca fuisse queruntur.
> Nec mora, corripuit rabies miserabilis istum
> et cunctos alios qui mox ratione carentes
> more canum sese lacerant mordendo vicissim.
> Stridunt et spumant et humi sine mente volutant.
> Denique digressi sunt illinc, more lupino
> complentes vacuas miseris ululantibus auras.
> Hec michi non illis velut estimo poma dabantur,
> postmodo seu didici …

Then we saw fragrant apples lying on the soft grass of the familiar bank of the spring. The man who had first come upon them quickly gathered them and gave them to me, laughing over our unexpected present. I handed the gift of apples round my friends but left myself without any, because the pile was not large enough. Those who had received apples laughed and called me generous. Then they eagerly fell to and ate them up, complaining that there were so few.

In a moment a pitiable madness seized this man here and all the others. Soon they were out of their minds, bit and scratched each other like dogs, screamed, foamed at the mouth and rolled demented on the ground. Then they dispersed and went off, filling the air with their pitiful howlings, like wolves.

I think that these apples had been a gift intended for me, not for them; and I later learnt that this was so.

The term used for the distribution of the apples is *distribuere* ('distribute'), which has the same range of meanings as the Welsh *rannu* ('to divide, separate, part' and 'distribute, share out, contribute').[24] As de Pontfarcy points out, the Latin *pomum*, which can mean 'apples', can also more generally mean 'fruit'.[25] The Latin text can be seen not only as the link between the French and English versions of the 'poisoned apple episode' (because of the fruit-*pomum*-apple link) but also as a mediator between these and the Welsh text, because it presents a different setting for poisoned apples entirely, but also crucially contains a reference to sharing out the apples, which are not shared out in the 'poisoned apple episode', but are rather left on the table to be taken. The Welsh text also stands out from the other texts discussed here in its reference to pursuit. As de Pontfarcy observes, what the *Vita Merlini* and the *Mort Artu* episodes have in common is the impunity of the culprit, who is not even pursued.[26]

It might be argued that the reference in *Peredur* does not have enough information to firmly establish its relationship to the 'poisoned apple episode'. However, if we set out the key components of the episode following the comparative analysis of de Pontfarcy and Donaldson, it becomes apparent that most of the necessary information is provided in that one brief reference in *Peredur*. This should not be surprising, given that in medieval Wales an established tradition for shorthand references to narratives is well-attested in the triads.[27] Table 3 lays out these variants.

Table 3: Comparison of poisoned apple episodes

	Malory	Fr. *Mort Artu*	Stanzaic *Morte Arthur*	*Vita Merlini*	*Peredur*
Fruit shared out	No	No	No*	Yes	Yes
Fruit poisoned	Yes	Yes	Yes	Yes	Unknown
Apples *versus* Fruit	Apples	Fruit	Apples	Fruit/Apples	Apples
Culprit pursued	No	No	No	No	Yes
Arthurian setting	Yes	Yes	Yes	No	Yes
Culprit a knight	Yes	Yes	No (squire)	No (woman)	Yes
Gawain character directly involved	Yes (intended victim)	Yes (intended victim)	Yes (intended victim)	No	Yes (pursuer)

In the stanzaic *Morte Arthur* Guinevere effectively shares out the fruit, since the plate is put in front of her and she hands the fruit to the Scottish knight instead of Gawain. However, in Table 3 sharing is marked in the negative, since there is no specific reference to all fruit being shared out among multiple individuals. Arguably, however, Guinevere simply had not got that far, as the first recipient collapsed.

De Pontfarcy argues, based on the similarities outlined, that the French *Mort Artu* derived its episode of the poisoned apples from Geoffrey's narrative. I would venture to suggest tentatively that, based on the comparison presented, it might be possible that the apple story hinted at in the opening of *Peredur* also belongs to the same tradition, and is in fact closer to the *Mort Artu* than it is to Geoffrey's text. Unless other apple narratives come to light this suggestion must, perforce, remain tentative. Nevertheless, it offers some hope that it may be possible to reconstruct other allusions to apparently lost material, or to offer, at least, some sense of what type of narrative the medieval audiences of the text might have been reminded of when hearing these references.

Another mystery of a similar ilk is offered by the procession of the head, witnessed by Peredur at his second uncle's castle in Episode I. No book about *Peredur* can avoid discussing the fact that this is the one version of what seems to be the Perceval/Grail story that appears not to have a mystic object featured in its procession scene on the lines of Chrétien's *graal* or Wolfram von Eschenbach's *lapsit exilis*.[28] Peredur sees a bleeding lance and a head on a salver, which is mourned loudly by those present, but his host offers no explanation and Peredur asks no questions. The issue of the questions is examined in detail in Chapter 5, where the argument is made that, in contrast with Grail romances proper, in this instance the hero acted correctly by not asking questions. In this second part of the present chapter, the matter of the head will be addressed and its possible literary allusions unpacked. It is worth remembering that in Episode I (and thus in the Short Version of *Peredur*) there is no explanation provided for this procession, nor is the head identified. If, as is my thesis here, Episode I is a self-sufficient narrative, this lack of explanation presents an interpretative problem for the modern reader. The following discussion will explore the literary associations that this scene may have invoked in its medieval audience.

The scene in Episode I that presents the equivalent of Chrétien's Grail procession runs as follows:

> Ac neill law y ewythyr yd eistedawd Peredur, ac ymdidan a orugant. Ar hynny, ef a welei deu was yn dyuot y'r neuad ac o'r neuad yn mynet y ystauell, a gwayw ganthunt anuedrawl y veint, a their ffrwt ar y hyt yn redec o'r mwn hyt y llawr. A phan welas pawb y gweisson yn dyuot yn y wed honno, llefein a drycyruerth a gymerth pawb yndunt, hyt nat oed hawd y neb y diodef. Ny thorres y gwr ar y ymdidan a Pheredur beth oed hynny, nys gofynnwys ynteu idaw.
>
> Gwedy tewi yspeit vechan, ar hynny, llyma dwy vorwyn yn dyuot y mywn a dyscyl vawr y rygthunt, a phen gwr ar y dyscyl, a gwaet yn amhyl yg kylch y pen. Ac yna diaspedein a llefein a oruc pawb, hyny oed anhawd y neb bot yn vn ty ac wynt.[29]

> Peredur sat down next to his uncle, and they talked.
> Suddenly he could see two lads entering the hall, and from the hall they proceeded to a chamber, carrying a spear of huge proportions, with three streams of blood running from its socket to the floor. When everyone saw the lads coming in this way, they all began weeping and wailing so that it was not easy for anyone to endure it. Yet the man did not interrupt his conversation with Peredur. The man did not explain to Peredur what that was, nor

did Peredur ask him about it. After a short silence, suddenly two maidens entered with a large salver between them, and a man's head on the salver, and much blood around the head. And then they all shrieked and wailed so that it was not easy for anyone to stay in the same building.[30]

The version preserved in Peniarth 7 is virtually identical, but contains some telling differences in detail:

> Ac ymdidan aorugant o hyn_n_y allan Ac ar hyn_n_y ef awelei dev was yn dyuot y mewn. athrwy ynevad yn mynet i ystauell agwaew mawr ganthu_n_t ac atheirfrwt owaet aryt ypaladyr Affan weles ytylwyth hyn_n_y dryc ar verthv aorugant hyt nadoed hawd ev gwarandaw Ac nythorres ygwr gwynnllw_y_t ar ymdidan affared*ur* yr hynny Nydwawt ygwr ype_r_ed*ur* pabeth oed hynny nysgovynnawd pe_r_ed*ur*. Ac yn agos y hyn_n_y wynt awelynt yndyuot ymewn dwy vorwyn adysgyl vawr ganthvnt aphe_nn_ gwr arnei yn waed lyt. Ac yna onewyd enynnv dryc aruayth aoruc ytylwyth.[31]

> And they conversed thenceforth. And upon that he saw two lads coming inside, and going through the hall to the room, and a big spear with them, and three streams of blood staining the spear. And when the kinsfolk saw that they wailed so, that it was not easy to listen to them. And the grey-haired man did not pause the conversation with Peredur on that account. The man did not say to Peredur what that was nor did Peredur ask. And shortly after that they saw coming in two girls with a big dish with a man's bloody head on it. And then again the family lamented. (My translation)

The differences between the passages are minor but illustrative. In the earlier version of Peniarth 7 the spear is merely described with the standard word *mawr* ('big' or 'large'), whereas by the time it arrived in the White Book and the Red Book, it had become 'anuedrawl y veint' ('of huge proportions'). The Long Version is also vaguer in its designation of those who are performing the loud wailing, designating them merely as '*pawb*' ('everyone'). The word used in Peniarth 7 is *tylwyth*, which can mean 'household', but also 'kinsfolk' or 'extended family'.[32] The key point here is the kinship, and the issue will become important in the discussion of the issue of Peredur's unasked questions in Chapter 5. It will be argued that Peredur was right not to ask questions because he is bound by Welsh customs (codified in law), which specify that such questions asked at the wake of a kinsman constitute formal insult. That the head probably belongs to a kinsman of Peredur's is an interpretation dependent not on the explanation provided in Chrétien-reliant Continuation in the Long Version, which is irrelevant for the interpretation of Episode I as it stands in Peniarth 7 in any case, but regarding the context: Peredur is in the house of a man who has just identified himself as his maternal uncle, with the whole household mourning.

The probable identity of the head as belonging to Peredur's unidentified kinsman notwithstanding, the mention of the bloody spear and the severed head in this passage also evokes literary associations. The most immediate of these is with the figure of Bran, or Bendigeidfran, the giant king of the Island of Britain who is killed by a poisoned spear and afterwards beheaded in the tale of *Branwen*, the 'Second Branch of the Mabinogi'.[33] Bran is frequently mentioned in discussions of the Grail legends and in discussions of *Peredur*. It has been suggested that Bran is the prototype of the lame Fisher King, and the Cauldron of Rebirth is the prototype of the Grail.[34] Examining some of the later Continental French Grail romances, John Carey observes that not only are there severed heads present in a number of texts that cannot derive from *Peredur* (or vice versa), but that all appear to link the head directly or indirectly with characters whose names derive from Bran.[35] In the *First Continuation*, heads of boars are present at a feast in the castle of a character named *Bran de Lis*, while in *Perlesvaus* there is a head that is identified as the son of Brun Brandalis.[36] Carey suggests that both names derive from Bran uab Llyr, and that in each case the presence of the head at a feast is a trace of the influence of the scene in *Branwen*, where Bran's severed head is good company for the survivors of the war with Ireland.[37] Such links with the name of Bran provide context for the links that exist elsewhere between Bran's head specifically and the Arthurian legend. As Rachel Bromwich observes, 'the marvelous qualities of Brân's severed head appear to have been his most prominent characteristic in the underlying mythology connected with him'.[38] This characteristic appears to have extended into the later tradition, as Bran's head features in Triad 37, which in the expanded Red Book version connects him to the Arthurian world. The quotation below extracts the sections of the triad relevant to Bran:[39]

Tri Matkud Ynys Prydein:
Penn Bendigeituran uab Llyr, a guduwyt yn y Gwynuryn yn Llundein, a'e wyneb ar Ffreinc. A hyt tra uu yn yr ansavd y dodet yno ny doei Ormes Saesson byth y'r Ynys honn;

...

Ac Arthur a datkudyavd Penn Bendigeituran o'r Gvynnvryn. Kan nyt oed dec gantav kadv yr Ynys honn o gedernit neb, namyn o'r eidav ehun.

Three Fortunate Concealments of the Island of Britain:
The head of Brân the Blessed, son of Llŷr, which was concealed in the White Hill in London, with its face towards France. And as long as it was in the position in which it was put there, no Saxon Oppression would ever come to this Island;

...

And Arthur disclosed the Head of Brân the Blessed from the White Hill, because it did not seem right to him that this Island should be defended by the strength of anyone, but by his own.

It may be that this represents a lost tradition connecting the Four Branches material with the Arthurian material.[40] The connection, however, is quite tentative, and given that the triad preserved in the other manuscripts contains no reference to the disclosure by Arthur, only to the burial of the head, one might ask how well known this tradition would have been. Rachel Bromwich points out that the wording of the Red Book version corresponds closely to the version of this triad found in *Branwen*.[41] Although the other manuscripts do not contain the reference to Arthur, the fact that they do mention disclosures (even if this is not expanded on) suggests that a tradition was already there. We cannot know whether it was always connected with Arthur.

Brân's association with a lance does not feature as prominently, and not at all in the triad, but it may be worthwhile pointing out the poem of Cynddelw Brydydd Mawr, which refers to 'Rut ongir Bran vab llir lledieith' ('The red spear of Brân son of Llŷr').[42] The description of the spear in Peniarth 7, 'ac atheirfrwt owaet aryt ypaladyr' (which I have translated as 'and three streams of blood staining the spear'), taking *ryt* as pret. 3 sg. of *rhydaf* ('to oxidise', 'to corrode' or 'to dirty'), although it is usually interpreted as the same form of *rhedaf* ('to run') (including of colours).[43] Regardless of the precise translation, the spear is reddened by blood. The fact that the word *rhud* ('red') is used to describe the spear in the poem, and *rhuddaf* is its verbal form 'to redden', suggests the possibility that all these words could have been easily interchanged in the description of the spear, and it may be impossible to reconstruct the original description (if such a thing exists in oral tradition). The Long Version opts for the unambiguous 'yn redec o'r mwn hyt y llawr', translated by Davies as 'running ... to the floor'.

It is not the intention here to suggest that the head brought into Peredur's uncle's court to general expressions of mourning is the head of Bran unearthed by Arthur in his hubris. It is, however, possible that the medieval audiences of Episode I may have been reminded of Bran's head when listening to the tale. Such allusions and associations might also account for the later emergence of the literary tradition associating Bran with the lame Fisher King at whose court Perceval sees the Grail.

The other head present in Welsh literary corpus that was the subject of mourning is the head of Urien Rheged (a historical sixth-century ruler of Rheged), which is the subject of a series of englynion, possibly ninth or tenth century in date, in *Canu Urien*.[44] In the sequence of englynion stanzas known as *Penn Urien*, an unidentified speaker is carrying Urien's head away from the battlefield. The stanzas have been the subject of much discussion, particularly in relation to ambiguity in the line that refers to the killing of Urien or the striking off of his head (afterwards), using the term *llad*, which in Welsh can mean both 'strike' and 'kill'.[45] The death of Urien is attested in multiple sources, including Latin historical texts, and while a full discussion of this tradition would constitute a digression, it is worth noting the possibility that for the medieval audience this might have provided an alternative object of literary associations when a decapitated head appeared at the scene in a narrative context.[46]

The objection might be raised here that the story of Urien's death is not attested in the vernacular prose dating from the time of Episode I's composition, and that it may be a stretch to suggest that the even later medieval audience of Peredur's story may have known of the decapitation of Urien. However, it can be pointed out in response that, like Urien, Peredur is a hero associated originally with the Old North, and furthermore that Peredur's companion Owain vab Urien, who in the Long Version is so kind as to explain to him how knightly accoutrements work and later to help him divest his first kill of his armour, is in original the son of that same Urien Rheged.[47] Owain is mentioned alongside Urien in the so-called 'historical poems' of Taliesin – poems attributed to the sixth-century bard Taliesin and which deal with sixth-century events but were probably composed considerably later.[48] If Peredur and Owain were remembered and assimilated into the Arthurian legend, there is no particularly compelling reason to believe that Urien would have been forgotten entirely. Indeed, he routinely appears in medieval Welsh genealogies, for instance, particularly in the Llewelyn ab Iorwerth genealogy, which Ben Guy dates to *c*.1216×1223.[49]

There is no evidence in the sources that the Old North character of Peredur was ever believed to be related to Owain or Urien, so it is unlikely that the head in his uncle's house is Urien's. (In Chapter 5 we will return to the argument that it would have probably belonged to a kinsman of Peredur's.) However, Urien and Bran would have provided the author(s) and audience(s) with a suitable context in which to read the appearance of the head.

To conclude, while the severed head in *Historia Peredur* is in no way related to the head of Urien, nor to that of Bran, it is important to remember that the audience of the tale may have been aware of one and would almost certainly have been aware of the other. Not only is Bran's head linked to Arthurian legend in the Triads, but the Four Branches of the Mabinogi share at least the later manuscript tradition (White Book and Red Book) with *Historia Peredur*. Urien's head is linked to the Arthurian tradition tangentially via his son, Owain, and *Canu Urien* is also preserved in the Red Book. It may not be advisable to read too much into the presence of all these texts in these later one-book libraries, but the fact that they are there, and that the two manuscripts had at least one common ancestor, implies that the tales had been circulating in the same circles at least in the fourteenth century, and possibly earlier. One does not need to have read Joseph Conrad's *Heart of Darkness* or Margaret Mitchell's *Gone With the Wind* to have a vague sense of what one of those novels is about, and it would perhaps not be too great a stretch to suppose that at least a part of the cultured medieval Welsh audience of *Peredur* would have heard that there were legends of Urien's head and of Bran's.[50] Indeed, the scene in *Peredur* suggests that there may even have been others.

The procession scene not only raises questions about the place of *Peredur* in a broader Welsh literary tradition, with its potential echoes of other characters and legends, but it also provides an insight into the text's relationship with its French counterpart. As will be demonstrated in Chapter 5, this scene lends itself particularly well to reading within the Welsh cultural and legal context.

Notes

1. Roberts, '*Peredur Son of Efrawg*', 70, with reference specifically to this passage in the corresponding n. 18, p. 72.
2. For a parallel problem, involving Malory's lost and oral sources, see Norris, 'Malory and His Sources', p. 43.
3. *Le conte du Graal*, ll. 178–9, ed. by Méla, in Chrétien de Troyes, *Romans*, p. 948; Kibler (trans.), *The Story of the Grail*, p. 383.
4. Goetinck (ed.), *Historia Peredur*, p. 8.
5. Davies (trans.), *The Mabinogion*, pp. 65–6.
6. Goetinck (ed.), *Histria Peredur*, p. 182.
7. Davies (trans.), *The Mabinogion*, p. 245. Cf. Glenys Goetinck's comment: 'the story behind this particular knight has been lost'; Goetinck, *Peredur*, p. 167.
8. For the concept of triads, see p. 5 of this book. For editions of *Manawydan*, see P. K. Ford (ed.), *Manawydan uab Lyr* (Belmont: Ford & Bailie, 2000); and Ian Hughes (ed.), *Manawydan Uab Llyr: Trydedd Gainc y Mabinogi* (Cardiff: University of Wales Press, 2007); for *Culhwch*, see Bromwich and Evans (eds), *Cuhlwch and Olwen*.
9. Sir Thomas Malory, *La Morte d'Arthur*, ed. by P. J. C. Field, vol. 1 (Cambridge: D. S. Brewer, 2013), pp. 793–4; For Malory's influence on later literature, see, for instance, Marylyn Parins (ed.), *Sir Thomas Malory: The Critical Heritage* (London and New York: Routledge, 1987).
10. E. Talbot Donaldson, 'Malory and the Stanzaic *Le Morte Arthur*', *Studies in Philology*, 47 (1950), 460–7, 465; Ryan Muckerheide, 'The English Law of Treason in Malory's *Le Morte Darthur*', *Arthuriana*, 20 (2010), 48–77.
11. Quoted from Sir Thomas Malory, *La Morte d'Arthur*, ed. by Field, vol. 1, pp. 793–4, corresponding to the text of the Winchester manuscript ff. fol. 411v and Caxton's edition XVIII.2–3. For commentary on the differences between the Winchester and Caxton versions, see Field (ed.), *La Morte d'Arthur*, vol. 2, p. 694. The variation is mostly at lexical level and is not pertinent to the present discussion.
12. See *TYP*[2], pp. 250–5 for the text, and pp. cxxxv–cxxxix for discussion.
13. *TYP*[2], pp. cxxxv–cxxxvi.
14. *TYP*[2], p. cxxxviii. The names themselves do not correspond, except for a couple, including Gawain/Gwalchmai.
15. Goetinck (ed.), *Historia Peredur*, p. 31; Davies (trans.), *The Mabinogion*, p. 79.
16. See discussion in Donaldson, 'Malory'; Norris, 'Malory and His Sources', pp. 38–9; Field (ed.), *La Morte d'Arthur*, vol. 2, pp. 685–6. In addition, there is an *exemplum* narrative that also contains a poisoned apple story, found in *Book of the Knight of La Tour Landry*, Chapter 106, which Kenneth Hodges has argued could have furnished Malory with the name of the victim (Sir Patryse, derived from the exemplum's Patrides); Hodges, 'Haunting Pieties: Malory's Use of Chivalric Christian "Exempla" after the Grail', *Arthuriana*, 17 (2007),

28–48 (35). I am grateful to Lidón Prades Yerves for alerting me to this article and Malory's use of the *exemplum*. This *exemplum* has a slightly different plot, involving jealousy and a more intricate crime, setting up its victim to be accused of murder, rather than poisoning her. In the *exemplum*, the poisoned apple is given to a virtuous damsel by a perfidious knight whom she had spurned, and claims a child, the son of her lord, to whom she gives the apple, as its victim. The culprit is challenged to battle by another knight and is defeated. For the text, see Thomas Wright (ed.), *The Book of the Knight of La Tour-Landry*, Early English Texts Society o.s. 33 (London: EETS, 1903); for a summary, discussion in connection to Malory's text, and further references, see Hodges, 'Haunting Pieties', 34–40. The Middle English text published by Caxton in 1484 was based on the fourteenth-century French original, *Livre pour l'enseignement de ses filles du Chevalier de La Tour Landry*. For more on the original text, see John L. Grigsby, 'A New Source of the *Livre du Chevalier de La Tour Landry*', *Romania*, 84 (1963), 171–208; and Anne-Marie de Gendt, *L'Art d'éduquer les nobles damoiselles: Le Livre du Chevalier de la Tour Landry* (Paris: Champion, 2003). Since its only real connection to the texts examined here is in the presence of a poisoned apple and an evil knight, and its possible use by Malory, though it may have correspondences to another text involving jealousy and apples, the *Vita Merlini*, this *exemplum* is unlikely to represent the type of narrative referred to in *Peredur*.

17 Larry D. Benson (ed.), 'Stanzaic Morte Arthur, Part 1', in Larry D. Benson (ed.), *King Arthur's Death: The Middle English Stanzaic Morte Arthur and Alliterative Morte Arthure*, revised by E. E. Foster, Middle English Texts (Kalamazoo: Medieval Institute Publications, Western Michigan University, for TEAMS, in association with the University of Rochester, 1994), ll. 840–7.

18 J. Frappier (ed.), *La mort le roi Artu, Roman du XIIIe siècle*, 3rd edn (Paris: Droz, 1996), p. 76.

19 Translation source, Norris J. Lacy (trans.), *The Death of Arthur*, Lancelot-Grail. The Old French Arthurian Vulgate and Post-Vulgate in Translation 7 (Cambridge: D. S. Brewer, 2010), p. 41. Note, the translation does separate the two paragraphs, the layout of which I have followed here.

20 For the variation, see pp. 21, 31, 33 and 97–8 of this book.

21 Yolande de Pontfarcy, 'Source et structure de l'épisode de l'empoisonnement dans *La mort Artu*', *Romania*, 99 (1978), 246–55 (246–8).

22 de Pontfarcy, 'Source et structure', 248; A. O. H. Jarman, 'The Merlin Legend and the Welsh Tradition of Prophecy', in Rachel Bromwich, A. O. H. Jarman, and Brynley F. Roberts (eds), *The Arthur of the Welsh: the Arthurian Legend in Medieval Welsh Literature* (Cardiff: University of Wales Press, 1991), pp. 117–45 (pp. 133–4).

23 Geoffrey of Monmouth, *Vita Merlini*, ll. 1408–24, ed. and trans. by Basil Clarke, *Life of Merlin* (Cardiff: University of Wales Press, 1973), pp. 128–9.

LITERARY CONTEXT: *PEREDUR* AND SOME LOST TALES

24 Charleton T. Lewis and Charles Short, *A Latin Dictionary* (Oxford: Oxford University Press, 1879), s.v. *dis-tribuo*; *GPC* s.v. *rhannaf*[1]: *rhannu*.
25 de Pontfarcy, 'Source et structure', 250.
26 de Pontfarcy, 'Source et structure', 251.
27 See p. 5 of this book.
28 Discussions of the head and its relationship to Chrétien's grail are numerous. See, for instance, Antonio L. Furtado, 'Geoffrey of Monmouth: A Source of the Grail Stories', *Quondam et Futurus*, 1 (1991), 1–14; Leslie Jones, 'Heads or Grails? A Reassessment of the Celtic Origin of the Grail Legend', *Proceedings of the Harvard Celtic Colloquium*, 14 (1994), 24–38. Other discussions are referred to, where relevant, throughout this chapter. For a general study of the grail legends, see Barber, *The Holy Grail*. For a discussion of Wolfram's grail, see, for instance, A. D. Horgan, 'The Grail in Wolfram's *Parzival*', *Medieval Studies*, 36 (1974), 354–81; and more recently, G. Ronald Murphy, *Gemstone of Paradise: The Holy Grail in Wolfram's Parzival* (Oxford: Oxford University Press, 2006).
29 Goetinck (ed.), *Historia Peredur*, p. 20.
30 Davies (trans.), *The Mabinogion*, p. 73.
31 Goetinck (ed.), *Historia Peredur*, p. 164; I have expanded abbreviations but retained the italic superscript and original capitalisation and punctuation.
32 *GPC*, s.v. *tylwyth*.
33 D. S. Thomson (ed.), *Branwen*, pp. 14–15; Davies (trans.), *Mabinogion*, p. 32.
34 See, for instance, Loomis, *The Grail*, pp. 55–7; Goetinck, *Peredur*, pp. 298–300; and discussion in Barber, *The Holy Grail*, pp. 241, 245–6. The identification of Bran as the Fisher King is supported by the line in a medieval Welsh poem attributed to the legendary figure of Taliesin, which refers to witnessing a thigh being pierced when the speaker was with Bran in Ireland; Thomson (ed.), *Branwen*, p. 37, referring to the more in-depth discussion in Proinsias Mac Cana, *Branwen Daughter of Llŷr: A Study of the Irish Affinities and of the Composition of the Second Branch of the Mabinogi* (Cardiff: University of Wales Press, 1958), pp. 164–5.
35 Carey, *Ireland and the Grail*, p. 253.
36 Carey, *Ireland and the Grail*, p. 253. For the *First Continuation*, see William Roach (ed.), *The Continuations of the Old French* Perceval *of Chrétien de Troyes. Volume 1: The First Continuation* (Philadelphia PA: University of Pennsylvania Press, 1949); and Nigel Bryant (trans.), *The Complete Story of the Grail: Chrétien de Troyes'* Perceval *and its Continuations* (Cambridge: D. S. Brewer, 2015), pp. 79–235.
37 Carey, *Ireland and the Grail*, pp. 253–4.
38 *TYP*[2], p. 285.
39 Text and translation quoted from *TYP*[2], pp. 88–9.

40 For other indications of such a connection, via identification of Bran with Brendan and scattered evidence for Brendan's head, see Carey, *Ireland and the Grail*, pp. 261–2.
41 *TYP*², p. 92; Thomson (ed.), *Branwen*, p. 17; Davies (trans.), *Mabinogion*, p. 34.
42 Quoted with translation in *TYP*², p. 285. For the entire poem, see *Gwaith Cynddelw Brydydd Mawr, I*, ed. by Nerys Ann Jones and Ann Parry Owen, Cyfres Beirdd y Tywysogion III (Cardiff: University of Wales Press, 1991), poem 7 'Marwnad Madog ap Maredudd', pp. 82–91.
43 *GPC* s.v. *rhydaf*, s.v. *rhedaf*.
44 For the text of the poem, see Jenny Rowland (ed. and trans.), *Early Welsh Saga Poetry: A Study and Edition of the Englynion* (Cambridge: D. S. Brewer, 1990).
45 Most recently discussed in Russell, 'Three Notes on *Canu Urien*', *North American Journal of Celtic Studies*, 4/1 (2020), 48–78.
46 For a discussion of the tradition surrounding the death of Urien and its significance for Welsh culture, see Patrick Sims-Williams, 'The Death of Urien', *Cambrian Medieval Celtic Studies*, 32 (1996), 25–56.
47 For an overview of the history of the Owain figure in Welsh literary tradition, see *TYP*², pp. 478–83; for Peredur, see *TYP*², pp. 488–91, esp. 488–9. Owain is also present in the Peniarth 7 version of *Peredur*, but in a minor role (he is swapped with Gwalchmai).
48 *TYP*², p. 479; for the dating and historical relevance of the Taliesin poetry, see Patrick Sims-Williams, 'Dating the poems of Aneirin and Taliesin', *Zeitschrift für celtische Philologie*, 63 (2016), 163–234.
49 Guy, *Medieval Welsh Genealogy*, pp. 160, 202, 225; nor is he forgotten later, as he is also mentioned in sixteenth-century genealogies, Guy, *Medieval Welsh Genealogy*, p. 127.
50 For a similar argument in the context of a discussion of Malory's audiences, see Hodges, 'Haunting Pieties', 32.

5

Peredur and Welsh Law

The mysterious procession witnessed by the hero – which in *Perceval* introduced the Grail to the world, but in *Peredur* features a human head – is one of the most discussed episodes in both the Welsh and the French narratives.[1] It is on the presence of this episode in the Welsh text that its association with the 'Grail romance tradition' hinges. This chapter will show that the Welsh text, and this scene in particular, sits comfortably within medieval Welsh tradition, and specifically within its legal context.

Of particular importance within this episode – and in the scholarly discussions – is, to use Ceridwen Lloyd-Morgan's words, the hero's 'failure to ask the appropriate question'.[2] The two subsequent references to this procession made in *Peredur* are both found in the Continuation.[3] The first of these is made by the Ugly Damsel who appears at Arthur's court at the beginning of the Welsh Continuation.[4] The second reference occurs towards the end of the Continuation, in the episode involving the reappearance of the witches of Gloucester (unique to the Welsh tale). Both subsequent references to the procession match Chrétien's narrative, rather than the Welsh procession, in the details that they give. They have therefore been hitherto understood as confused or interpolated references to the French romance. This interpretation, in turn, has led most to read the scene of the procession itself in the light of the French text, including a general assumption that the hero was wrong not to have enquired after the nature of the things that he was witnessing.[5] This is because Chrétien's narrative includes an explicit condemnation of the hero's silence during the procession scene: 'Mais plus se taist qu'il ne convient' ('But he kept more silent than he should have').[6] *Convenir* in medieval French has the sense of moral obligation as well as of necessity.[7] After the castle and its inhabitants magically disappear the following morning, Perceval meets a cousin, who reprimands him for his inappropriate silence, explaining its disastrous results. Since this pattern is seen in other versions of this story, the scene's function is usually assumed to be the same.[8] We shall see, however, that Peredur meets not a cousin but a foster sister, and her complaint to him is different.[9] This has implications for our reading of the procession scene in the Welsh tale.

The hero's silence in both the French and Welsh versions has been perceived as a failure, on the part of a hero brought up by a woman, to engage in the chivalric masculine society represented by the absent father figure.[10] It is the purpose of the present chapter to suggest some alternative possibilities of interpretation, particularly as to whether we have been right to condemn Peredur's silence out of hand.[11] It will be argued here that Peredur does not fail in this episode. His success follows both the logic of the narrative, for it is predicted when he first comes to Arthur's court, and the logic of Welsh social convention, which we know of from surviving legal texts. Indeed, his success in this episode also follows the pattern seen in other, native, Welsh tales, such as *Culhwch ac Olwen*, where the hero's arrival at Arthur's court anticipates the success of his subsequent mission. Further, as will be demonstrated in this chapter, Peredur's active silence receives not the slightest shadow of condemnation in the earliest surviving version of the story, preserved in Peniarth 7.[12]

The proposed approach is based on a contextual reading of the tale in light of what we might glean of Welsh society and expectations of proper behaviour.[13] It will also be suggested that at least those apparent inconsistencies within *Peredur* as a whole that relate to this episode – particularly those between this episode and those passages in the Continuation that refer back to it – may be the result of design rather than an accident of compilation (or the product of a redactor's incompetence).[14] The arguments presented here have implications that would introduce additional nuance to our understanding of the relationship of the Welsh and French texts.

Preliminary to the analysis, a caveat: it is not the purpose of the present argument to propose any significant revision of the currently dominant view that the Welsh text (or rather, the specific narrative combination surviving in the Long Version as Episode I + Continuation) is heavily influenced by, if not a direct adaptation of, the French text, but rather to engage with the two versions of the story from the perspective of 'relative distance'. The concept, based on an idea expressed by R. L. Thompson in relation to the medieval Welsh *Chwedl Iarlles y Ffynnawn* ('Tale of the Lady of the Fountain'), also known as *Owein* (the equivalent of Chrétien's *Chevalier au lion/Yvain*), was defined and used most effectively by Erich Poppe, and is particularly useful in application to the comparison of Welsh and French versions of the same story, where the exact relationship between the texts is almost impossible to determine.[15] In the case of *Peredur/Perceval*, it will be argued that the relative distance is greater where the differences in the cultural context within which these texts were produced were more pronounced, and depends on which version of *Peredur* we are examining. The attitude towards Peredur's silence differs between the Short Version and the Long Version. Further, the text of Peniarth 14, insofar as it preserves relevant passages, differs from both.

The original instruction against inquisitiveness itself is present in all the surviving versions of the story, but with some notable variation. In the Long Version, it runs as follows:

> a chyt a mi y bydy y wers hon yn dyscu moes a mynut. Ymadaw weithon a ieith dy vam, a mi a uydaf athro it ac a'th urdaf yn varchawc urdawl. O hyn allan, llyna a wnelych; kyt gwelych a vo ryued genhyt, nac amofyn ymdanaw ony byd o wybot y venegi it. Nyt arnat ti y byd y keryd namyn arnaf i, kanys mi yssyd athro it.[16]

> And you will stay with me for a while, learning manners and etiquette. Forget now your mother's words – I will be your teacher and make you a knight. From now on this is what you must do: if you see something that you think is strange, do not ask about it unless someone is courteous enough to explain it to you. It will not be your fault, but mine, since I am your teacher.[17]

In the Peniarth 7 text, which is our only witness to the earliest, Short Version, of the tale, the reference is to possible blame for asking a question rather than for silence.[18] In Peniarth 14 these instructions appear in the last episode, which is contained in the fragmentary manuscript (the text breaks off almost immediately after this scene), and interestingly in that version of the instructions, even the possibility of blame for silence is lacking.[19] In this version, the uncle simply tells Peredur not to ask questions: 'a chyt gwelych beth auo ryued gennyt taw amdanaw an ac na ouyn' ('and if you see that which might be marvellous to you be silent about it and do not fear').[20] There is no reference to fault resting with the teacher, nor with the student, and there is therefore no suggestion that anyone might deem such silence inappropriate.

This injunction against asking a question is not remarked on in most discussions of *Peredur* (except to say that he was following this advice in keeping silent in the procession scene).[21] Joseph A. McMullen argues that Peredur's silence during the procession scene represents a failure that is directly caused by a lack of instruction on the part of his relatives, or by the advice of the first uncle, which McMullen qualifies as 'problematic'.[22] It must be pointed out, however, that if we are not to refer to the French text for comparison, then Episode I of the Short Version of *Peredur* has internal logic. He is instructed to be silent and to not ask questions, he follows that advice and receives no criticism for that (in)action. He leaves the castle with permission the following day, with no suggestion of anything having gone wrong.[23] This is in stark contrast to the mysterious (and mystical) disappearance of the castle the following morning in the French version.

Inconsistencies appear only once we get to the Continuation in the longer version of *Peredur*, preserved in the White Book and the Red Book, where the procession is mentioned on two further occasions. It will be remembered that the shortest version, preserved in Peniarth 7, concludes the story well before those scenes. Because the second earliest and, presumably, fuller version in Peniarth 14 breaks off at an earlier point (before the procession episode), it is uncertain whether it would have contained the Continuation and thus these later references.[24]

As the manuscript tradition stands, therefore, the two later references to the procession episode only occur in the Continuation within the longer version of the tale, which, as we have seen, is widely acknowledged to carry more direct influence from Chrétien's French romance.[25] Whereas in the French text, the hero is immediately criticised for not asking any questions in the procession scene, it is worth re-emphasising the point that this issue is not brought up at all in Episode I, and, indeed, not in the whole of the earliest version of the Welsh text.[26] The foster sister whom Peredur meets immediately after this does not upbraid him about not asking the questions, nor does she make any reference at all to the procession scene. Instead, she accuses him of causing his own mother's demise by leaving.[27] Furthermore, according to the first uncle's original instructions, the implication in the Short Version seems to be that blame can only be attached to asking inappropriate questions, not to silence. The situation is the reverse of that of Chrétien's text and of *Peredur*'s Welsh Continuation in the longer versions of the White Book and Red Book.

A possible point of reference for this phenomenon of the hero's silence may be found in Welsh law. In the context of his discussion of the possibly ninth-century medieval Welsh poem *Canu Urien* (which, as we have seen, also happens to feature a severed head) concerning the death of Urien Rheged and the burial of Urien's body, Paul Russell mentions two legal triads that enumerate the types of insult to a corpse.[28] The second of these, the *gwarthrud kelein* ('dishonourings of a corpse') triad, may also have implications for understanding audience expectations in the plot of *Peredur*. The triad refers to three *gwarthrud* ('shames/dishonourings') that may be inflicted on a body through inappropriate questions. The triad runs as follows: 'Teir gwarthrud kelein yw: gofuyn "pwy ladawd hwnn?", a "phiev yr elor?", a gofuyn "piev y beth newyd hwnn?"' ('The three shames of a corpse are asking "who killed this one?", and "whose is this bier?", and asking "whose is this fresh grave?"').[29]

As Paul Russell observes, this triad:

> has to do with dishonouring and disrespecting the corpse, presumably by turning up at the funeral not knowing who it is and what has happened (the assumption is that you would probably be a kinsman or should at least have done due diligence before turning up at the grave).[30]

The implication is that a kinsman would be aware of the circumstances of the death. One might add that it was probably also expected of the kinsman to know who had been killed (and their degree of kinship). This is an important point, given the prominence of *galanas* in medieval Welsh law, compensation for killing paid by the perpetrator and his kinsmen to the victim's kinsmen, with degree of kinship determining degree of compensation, and the obligation to take vengeance if this were not duly paid.[31] This situation fits *Peredur* perfectly, as the hero arrives at his uncle's house and is presented with a procession that features a severed head.

Reading *Peredur* with Russell's interpretation of the triad in mind throws light not only on the procession scene, but also on the contrast between his action there and Peredur's behaviour in a similarly extraordinary situation involving corpses in Episode III. In the episode of the Sons of the King of Suffering (in Episode III(B-1)), Peredur is confronted with a series of corpses brought back to life using a vat of warm water and precious ointment.[32] In this case, the hero seems to have no qualms about asking what is going on. On the one hand, this might be because these are technically no longer dead bodies. On the other hand, if, as Russell suggests, the injunction in the legal triad applies specifically to kinsmen, then Peredur was bound by it only at his uncle's court. The objection may be that the first uncle did not specify that questions would relate specifically to dead kinsmen, but it is necessary to account for the fact that audience expectations would not be formed by the internal logic of the text only (as ours must often be, for lack of any other information) but also by their own cultural context. It is also worth reminding ourselves that Episode I seems to focus on encounters between Peredur and people who know him, most of whom are related to him, whereas this is not the case in Episode III.[33] Thus, contextually, it would stand to reason – in terms of audience expectations formed by narrative context – that he would avoid risking asking a question about someone in Episode I, as the individual would potentially be a relative.

Echoes of the legal triad tradition can be found elsewhere in *Peredur*, particularly in the scene of the hero's first arrival in Arthur's court in Episode I, where a knight has just struck the queen and snatched a goblet of wine from her hand – two of three ways to insult a queen.[34] As Michael Cichon observes, it is very probable that the latter is a deliberate echo of medieval Welsh law, demonstrating that the audience would have been able to pick up on such references.[35] This makes it even more likely that another such reference, not noted by Cichon in his discussion, is embedded in the tale in Peredur's behaviour at the sight of (part of) a body at his uncle's court.[36] Further supporting evidence can be found elsewhere in Episode I. As Ceridwen Lloyd-Morgan observes, Peredur has a duty to avenge his foster sister's husband (Episode I(B)), and according to the laws, a relative's scream is 'one of the three incitements to revenge', which 'must have had extra resonances for a contemporary audience familiar with the laws'.[37]

In Episode I as it is found in the shortest version of *Peredur*, therefore preserved in the oldest manuscript, and possibly representing an early stage in the development of the narrative, the story consistently presents the hero's actions as correct and unobjectionable. The objections, and the inconsistencies, appear only in the longer versions preserved in the White Book and the Red Book, which contain two further references to the procession, in the added Continuation. The first invokes the procession scene, when the maiden who arrives at Arthur's court refuses to greet Peredur. She chastises him for not asking the question, but crucially, there is no contradiction as to the legal connotations mentioned above. Although the accusation that the maiden lays at Peredur's door is specifically that he did not ask questions, the scene as she invokes it does not contain the head (which was his reason for silence), nor does she mention kinship:

> Pan doethost y lys y brenhin cloff a phan weleist yno y maccwy yn dwyn y gwayw llifeit, ac o vlaen y gwayw dafyn o waet, a hwnnw yn redec yn rayadr hyt yn dwrn y maccwy, ac enryfedodeu ereill, heuyt, a weleist yno, ac ny ofynneisti eu hystyr nac eu hachaws.[38]

> When you came to the court of the lame king and when you saw there the young man carrying the sharpened spear, and from the tip of the spear a drop of blood streaming down to the young man's fist, and you saw other wonders there, too – you did not question their meaning or their cause.[39]

The maiden's reference to what appears to be the procession of *Perceval* rather than that found earlier in *Peredur* has been the subject of some discussion.[40] Lloyd-Morgan observes that whereas in Peredur's story it is the first, not the second, uncle who was lame (and it is the first uncle who instructs Peredur not to ask questions and the second uncle at whose court the procession takes place), it is the Lame King who is associated with the procession in Chrétien's story.[41]

Peredur's response to this apparent French narrative import into the story is strikingly formulaic: 'Myn vyg cret, ny chysgaf hun lonyd nes gwybot chwedyl ac ystyr y gwayw y dywawt y vorwyn du ymdanaw' ('By my faith, I will not sleep in peace until I know the story and significance of the spear about which the black-haired maiden spoke').[42] The first part of the phrase repeats verbatim the lines spoken by Gwalchmai immediately before: 'Myn vyg cret, ny chysgaf hun lonyd nes gwybot a allwyf ellwg y vorwyn' ('By my faith, I will not sleep in peace until I know whether I can set the maiden free').[43] The attention of Gwalchmai and the rest of Arthur's household is on the part of the girl's narrative that tells of a maiden in distress, besieged in her castle, whereas Peredur's interest is in the other part of the story. While I would not wish to press the point too far, it does seem worth noting that the two elements here seem to fall into two categories: imported and native. The first in this pair of elements seems to be a characteristic topos of Continental (French) romance, since no maidens in distress are found in those episodes of *Peredur* that are unattested elsewhere (it should be remembered that the object of the hero's affection, the besieged maiden of Episode I, is Blancheflor in the French text).[44] In general, maidens in distress in Welsh texts tend to appear in those episodes that have French equivalents.[45] It may be argued that the only exception is Branwen; however, her story is not one of a maiden in need of rescue, but of a formal insult in need of recompense, with distinct echoes again in the native legal tradition.[46] Meanwhile, Peredur's attention is drawn to the personal insult in the girl's speech, and the words that he uses are *chwedl* and *ystyr*. These words signify 'story' and 'significance', as in Sioned Davies's translation, but are also the terms used in the Welsh manuscripts to describe the tales themselves: the story of *Owein* is a *chwedl* and that of *Peredur*, a *historia* or *ystoria*.[47] The term *ystyr* can also mean 'history' and 'cause', and thus seems to point to the notion of background/back-story in this instance.[48] The reference to *chwedl* and *ystyr* in the Welsh texts seems to be a short-cut summary of the more extensive response that the challenge elicits from Perceval in the French version: 'Que il ne jerra en ostel / Deus nuiz en trestot son aaige, / … / Tant que il do Graal savra / Cui l'en an sert, et qu'il avra / La Lance qui saigne trovee, / Tant que la verité provee / Li soit dite por qu'ele saigne' ('that he would not spend two nights in the same lodgings as long as he lived … until he had learned who was served from the Grail and had found the bleeding lance and been told the true reason why it bled').[49] If the Welsh is rendering the French here, then *chwedl* refers to the context and purpose (though in this case there is no Grail) and the *ystyr* to the story behind the bleeding lance. The abbreviated form of the adaptation here makes sense in light of the differences between the Welsh and French processions, but it is also not unparalleled elsewhere in the Welsh Continuation. One might think of the insult meted out by her kinsman to the lady keeping Gwalchmai company further on in the text, in response more obviously to the sexual activity taking place in the French text than to the conversation that replaces it in the Welsh.[50]

Giving the competence of the compilers and copyists the benefit of the doubt, we might make sense of the Long Version of the story as it stands if we assume that the difference between the scene at the uncle's house in Episode I and the later summaries in the Continuation is clear not only to us, but is also made intentionally clear for the audience. It is also worth asking whether there is a contradiction between the accusation levelled here against Peredur and his uncle's earlier assurance that all blame would be deflected from the student to the teacher. Perhaps asking questions about the head would have been inappropriate, but should he have asked about the spear?

Alternatively, the Long Version of *Peredur* may represent the type of attempt to bring together and reconcile various versions of the text that have been found in other Welsh texts preserved in the same manuscripts. The examples that spring to mind are the two openings of the *Ystoria Bown o Hamtwn* and the two versions of the encyclopaedic text *Delw y Byd*, both of which feature miscellaneous fragments added after the conclusion of the text from what is very clearly yet another set of different versions.[51] The above examples of this patchwork of collation come from our two manuscripts that contain the longer version of *Peredur*. This brings us ultimately to the theory of multiple layers proposed by Charles-Edwards. He suggests that there was a multi-tiered process of alteration in the development of medieval Welsh text, where a text as copied in 'practitioners' books' was more prone to change, but that 'when they were copied by professional scribes, they left traces in higher-class books, which were more likely to survive'.[52] Thus, the manuscript tradition of *Peredur* illustrates the multilayered fluidity of Welsh texts, where high-end manuscripts produced by professional scribes might contain traces of alterations undergone by the more fluid layer of the tradition, in professionals' books.[53] The White Book and Red Book are high-end manuscripts, and these multiple versions of (sections of) the texts are examples of the same phenomenon.

In the final reference to the procession scene, which occurs during another encounter with the 'maiden', who turns out not to be a 'black-haired maiden' at all, but 'a yellow-haired lad', who had pretended to be a girl, the head is once more mentioned (but there is still only one lad carrying the spear, rather than the original two).[54] The head turns out to be a cousin. This suggests once more that Peredur's silence in the procession scene in Episode I was justified after all, and indeed, no further accusations are brought against him for not asking any questions, nor are these even mentioned. Instead, vengeance is requested and thereafter carried out.

Given the correspondences between the latter two descriptions of the scene and the French, as opposed to the Welsh, version of the story, it seems probable that these references are indeed the result of influence exerted on our narrative by the French text. The similarities between the composition of the longer version of *Peredur* and the multi-version patchworks attested in the same manuscripts suggest the possibility that multiple versions of the tale were brought together here. The process of alteration is visible in the correlation observed between the two elements: the head and the criticism. When the head is mentioned, Peredur is not criticised for his silence. Conversely, when the head is not mentioned, Peredur is criticised.

The tantalising possibility raised by reading the text, in both shorter and longer versions, in light of the Welsh legal tradition, is that Peredur's mistake was a specifically cultural one, and existed only in the longer version of the story and only once the Continuation (of quite probably French origins) was added. This does not necessitate any assumptions about the redactors of the tale necessarily using Welsh law specifically, but rather follows Robin Chapman Stacey's suggestion 'that both legal and literary genres might have been part of a common and constantly evolving narrative tradition'.[55] The only conjecture required, and one that is founded on ample evidence from this and other medieval Welsh prose narratives, is that the redactors and audiences shared the cultural background and knowledge of customs that were also codified in the laws that have survived. If not asking questions about bodies in a kinsman's house was part of custom codified by law, as the triad in Russell's interpretation implies, it seems reasonable to expect that a medieval Welsh audience would be aware of this custom and recognise it in Peredur's behaviour. Peredur had received general instructions not to ask questions, and further sees a head in a kinsman's house. The audience may have been equally curious about the story, but also aware of a taboo on questions in this particular setting. Audience expectations and context are, therefore, key.

Peredur's silence and his uncle's instructions may therefore be read as an avoidance of inappropriate questions, dictated by custom, rather than as an expression of the silence of the colonised voice as proposed by McMullen.[56] McMullen, quoting Ngũgĩ wa Thiong'o on the intricate connections between language and culture, argues that Peredur fails because he is not communicating and not sharing in his culture.[57] However, such a reading has three presuppositions. The first, and perhaps the least problematic, is that the knowledge or understanding of the connection between cultural expression through language and external (colonial) domination is a universal staple, and is automatically expressed by medieval writers. The second presupposition offers the complementary or alternative possibility, that the medieval authors/redactors of the tale, who were responsible for these narrative elements, were aware of the role of communication in culture generally. The third presupposition is that the lack of cultural communication, or to use the terminology introduced to the field of postcolonial studies by Gayatri Chakravorty Spivak, the 'silence' of the 'subaltern', would have been understood as a problem relevant to the situation of Wales in the thirteenth or fourteenth century (whenever we think this tale was being actively formed in transmission).[58]

Leaving aside the first two presuppositions, which to my mind cannot be proven or disproven within the available space or with the available material, I propose to focus on the third. The most immediate problem with this, and one that McMullen addresses with dexterity, is that this tale of presumed cultural silence of the colonised subject is itself an expression of the culture of that same colonised subject.[59] According to McMullen, 'the redactor may be intending to remind his audience about how necessary communication is, especially if, by communicating, a family is also bestowing cultural values onto its youngest members'.[60] The preoccupation with culture seems very modern, but, in any case, it is not a concern unique to a colonial situation (and neither is the concern with teaching the young).

The dissonance in the application of the postcolonial framework to *Peredur* in the context of loss of sovereignty and the silencing of the colonial subject becomes apparent if we go back to the beginnings of postcolonial studies and read the text alongside Spivak's essay, foundational for the field's methodologies.[61] She gives several examples of what she terms the 'epistemic violence' done to the study of the colonial subject, and one of these is the colonial narrative of the codification of Hindu law.[62] Her other, most often quoted example, is of the women involved in the rite that has acquired in the colonial discourse the name of *suttee* and by which it is now mostly known in the West.[63] These women, as Spivak shows, have no say in the story, as their voices are irrecoverable in either the colonial British narrative, or in what she designates as the 'Indian nativist argument'.[64] The first example is particularly interesting in its associations with law, because, in our Welsh tale, the Welsh laws are very visible, regardless of whether the interpretation of Peredur's attitude to inappropriate questions proposed here is accepted or not.[65] The contrast, however, between the examples of the silencing of the colonial subject given by Spivak, and the case of Peredur, is considerable. Peredur may be silent (and my argument is that he has good reason) but the text

Peredur is not silent at all, and not only speaks, but does so in its own native language. The narrative that we are presented with is itself, to some extent at least, the voice of the subaltern (but see the caveat to follow), irrespective of what might be said of any scholarly discussion of the text written in English.

This marks another point at which the application of Spivak's or any other postcolonialist theory to the study of the literary production of the medieval period breaks down, because in dealing with medieval texts we are by default dealing with the elite.[66] For Spivak, 'the floating buffer zone of the regional elite-subaltern, is a *deviation* from an *ideal* – the people or subaltern – which is itself defined as a difference from the elite'.[67] For the study of medieval literature, whether in the colonial context or not, the 'regional elite-subaltern' is for the most part the only visible subaltern. Beyond that is, in Aaron Gurevich's terms, the 'silent majority'.[68] The real subaltern, ultimately, as Spivak pointed out, remains silent.

The solution may be to see the Long Version of *Peredur* not as a colonial production, but as a dual production. The complicated manuscript history of the tale with its shifting relative distance to the French text, may here be more of a help than a hindrance. Taking only the longer version of the text in the postcolonial framework, with the imposition of the later episodes as an external influence of the colonial world (which serve to narrow the 'relative distance' between the Welsh and French versions), releases the earlier part of the tale from the constraints of the fallacies inherent in the application of this framework and of its reading in light of the French text. The procession itself in Episode I is not a colonial experience for anyone. Peredur's silence is not inaction. Peredur acts: he avoids causing insult by asking inappropriate questions about a body in a kinsman's house. Within the text, he is not the silent colonial subject, but a recognisable member of the culture acting in a way that the intended audience of the text would understand.[69] Episode I as it is preserved in the shortest, earliest version of the text in the Peniarth 7 manuscript contains no accusation, no criticism of this action. Indeed, it is also worth noting that *Peredur* is particularly rich in inexplicable events and encounters that remain unexplained and unqueried within the text. Most of these occur in Episode III and are thus unique to the Welsh tale.[70] Thus, the procession scene is also no exception in terms of narrative expectations.

The criticism of this Welsh behavioural pattern is only introduced in the episode that is part of the Continuation, very clearly added in the longer version and inspired by the French text (narrowing the relative distance between the two narratives) – this omits any reference to kinship. When kinship is once again introduced at the end of the Continuation, conversely, no reference is made to the previous criticism of the silence. One possible interpretation is to take our view of *Peredur* as a composite product (consisting of four episodes of different origins that would have been performed separately and did not require a tight structure) further, and suggest that the Continuation – at least as its stands in the manuscripts – was also built on the same principles.[71] The evidence of the other multi-version texts preserved in medieval Welsh manuscripts might be brought in to support this view.

The second possibility is retain our understanding of the structure of *Peredur* as Episodes I–III + Continuation, and for understanding the inconsistencies brought to the whole by the addition of the latter in the Long Version to return to a postcolonial reading of the tale, but one that does not require the medieval audience to perceive themselves as colonial subjects to any greater extent than an awareness of the increased prevalence of foreign influences and imported customs might afford. With an outline of this reading, I will conclude this discussion.

The contrast between Peredur's avoidance of questions, perfectly correct under Welsh law on the one hand, and the courtly environment of much of the rest of the tale on the other, seems to show rather than tell the same stark contrast between Welsh and (Anglo-Norman) French so sharply portrayed in Chrétien's romance. If we consider that the Welsh audience would have perceived Peredur's action as correct in the original scene in Episode I, until the revelation of the cousin's tale at the end of the Continuation (in a description of the procession that notoriously echoes the French rather than the Welsh version of the narrative), the hybrid nature of the tale as it is preserved in the White Book and the Red Book may be seen in a different light. It might be worth considering the possibility that the apparent inconsistencies are the product not of a loss in transmission, nor of incompetence on the part of any redactor or compiler, but of a contrast and conflict between Welsh and French cultures made visible in a narrative's very structure.[72] The addition of the Continuation, derived from the French to the fractal triadic composition comprising Episodes I to III, with only a loose connection, may be a nod by the redactor to the audience.[73] The loose connection is in itself not necessarily a result of inadequacy. Given the penchant of medieval Welsh storytellers for triadic structures, it may not be an accident that the procession scene is repeated three times in the text, with variations.[74] In the first iteration, Peredur was right, as a Welshman, not to ask questions about the head. In the second iteration, Peredur was wrong, in a court anchored in Continental culture, not to ask questions about the distress of his hosts. In the third iteration, Peredur's behaviour in the original scene is ultimately irrelevant, and only his future action of vengeance matters. With the action ending in Gloucester, where the revenge takes place, one is tempted to speculate whether the triad of Welsh-French-Marcher that becomes visible in this structure is not rather intentional than fortuitous.[75] In light of the importance of the Marcher lords of Gloucester to the politics of the twelfth and thirteenth centuries, including the many instances of clashes between the English kings and Welsh rulers, the use of the place name in connection to ideas of treachery and vengeance is probably no accident. To give one example, a number of Welsh rulers who had attended the council at Gloucester in 1175 were, in subsequent years, victims of ambush (even when travelling under safe passage from the English king).[76] I do not propose this event as a specific reference point for the narrative, but rather as an illustration of the type of associations that the place name may have invoked for the medieval Welsh audience. We have already explored the geography of the narrative and we will return to the subject of the 'witches' of Gloucester, and the lady of the manor that they attack in Episode I, in the discussion of female characters in Chapter 6.

To conclude this discussion, the interpretation of Peredur's silence as a perfectly acceptable avoidance of inappropriate questions, dictated by Welsh social order and customs, has an implication that has the potential to disturb the established paradigm. Peredur vab Efrawc, in Wales, acts in accordance with law and custom in remaining silent at the sight of a head at a relative's house. Perceval, known as *li galois* ('the Welshman'), acts inappropriately in the French courtly context of Chrétien's narrative by remaining silent in exactly the same way. As has been noted in many discussions of the French romance, the epithet *galois* seems to be associated with ignorance, simplicity, stupidity (and, to use modern terminology, is thus both racial and racist).[77] Given the generalising nature of an ethnonym, this seems to imply a general condemnation of Welsh behavioural patterns as inappropriate or inadequate to the society described in the French romance, rather than a criticism of Perceval individually. If that is the case, it seems more logical to see the interpretation of the hero's silence in the French text as post-dating the act of silence itself. In other words, the possibility arises that faced with this act of silence, Chrétien introduced the need to ask a question and subsequent condemnation of the hero. This agrees with Richard Barber's interpretation of the Grail scene in Chrétien's text. Barber postulates that 'Perceval mistakes Gorneman's instructions not to be inquisitive as an absolute ban on the asking of questions', and that the function of the Grail procession in the narrative is to provide a scene where not only would questions need to be asked, but where the audience would wish for them to be asked.[78] If the instructions were a given in the original form of the narrative, the introduction of the condemnation of the hero's silence, following (new) audience expectations, formed without awareness of the Welsh laws that had conditioned the original instructions, makes sense. This also requires fewer conditionals than the supposition that, faced with a story of a Welshman's silence judged inappropriate in a French context and which would also have no explanation in a Welsh one, a Welsh redactor responsible for the earliest version of Peredur removed the condemnation, replaced the 'Grail' with a head to justify the silence, and then proceeded to introduce a large number of other episodes where the hero also encounters strange things and also asks for no explanation. The relationship between the Welsh and French texts, and the relative distance between them, depends on which version of the Welsh text we take. We therefore seem to be back to the supposition that there would have been an original Welsh Peredur story, similar in form to Episode I of the Short Version preserved in Peniarth 7, which then made its way to France, and subsequently came back with Chrétien's additions, to be added to the whole set of *Peredur* episodes (Episodes I–III) and thus influence in its turn the longer version of the Welsh tale that we now have in the White Book and the Red Book. This may not provide an answer to the chicken-or-egg problem of the *Mabinogionfrage*, but it does reinforce the need to account for the fact that the Grail story 'chicken', before it crossed the Channel into Wales, may also have hatched from a Welsh egg, and that the egg may have been something along the lines of what now survives as Episode I.

Notes
1 Goetinck (ed.), *Historia Peredur*, p. 20; Davies (trans.), *Mabinogion*, p. 73; Chrétien de Troyes, *Le Conte du Graal*, ll. 3128–275, ed. by Méla, pp. 1035–40; Kibler (trans.), *The Story of the Grail*, pp. 420–2.
2 Lloyd-Morgan, '*Historia Peredur*', p. 145.

3 See pp. 36 and 40 of this book for the summary.
4 This episode has attracted somewhat more attention than the second. See Goetinck, *Peredur*, pp. 75–6; Lloyd-Morgan, 'Historia Peredur', pp. 147–8, 150.
5 See, for example, Goetinck, *Peredur*, pp. 259, 290–2. For an overview of the developments of the topos of the unasked questions see Barber, *The Holy Grail*, pp. 44, 78, and especially pp. 93 and 108–12. See also the recent discussion of the importance of the questions in the German version of the tale in Michael Stolz, 'Wolfram von Eschenbach's *Parzival*: Searching for the Grail', in Leah Tether and Johnny McFadyen, with Keith Busby and Ad Putter (eds), *A Handbook of Arthurian Romance: King Arthur's Court in Medieval European Literature* (Berlin: De Gruyter, 2017), pp. 443–59 (p. 450).
6 Chrétien de Troyes, *Le Conte du Graal*, l. 3236, ed. by Méla, p. 1039; Kibler (trans.), *The Story of the Grail*, p. 421.
7 *DMF* s.v. *convenir* III, *www.atilf.fr/dmf/definition/convenir* (last accessed 22 May 2020). See also Barber, *The Holy Grail*, pp. 108–12.
8 The Perceval heroes' silence has been the subject of a large number of discussions. See, for instance, Harry F. Williams, 'The Unasked Questions in the *Conte del Graal*', *Medieval Perspectives*, 3 (1988), 292–302; L. P. Johnson, 'The Grail-Question in Wolfram and Elsewhere', in D. H. Green et al. (eds), *From Wolfram and Petrarch to Goethe and Grass: Studies in Literature in Honour of Leonard Forster* (Baden-Baden: Koerner, 1982), pp. 83–102; Stefanie A. Goyette, 'Milk or Blood? Generation and Speech in Chrétien de Troyes' *Perceval, ou le Conte du Graal*', *Arthuriana*, 26 (2016), 130–51; and discussion and further references in William Sayers, 'An Archaic Tale-Type Determinant of Chrétien's Fisher King and Grail', *Arthuriana*, 22 (2012), 85–101 (86, 91–3, 96).
9 See p. 118 of this book.
10 See particularly A. Joseph McMullen, 'The Communication of Culture: Speech and the "Grail" Procession in *Historia Peredur vab Efrawc*', *Arthuriana*, 23 (2013), 26–44. For the French, see Goyette, 'Milk or Blood?', 136–7, 139. Goyette's argument for the French hero's inability to engage in the knightly society through language links this to the absence of the father figure and, crucially, patronym. Note that for Peredur vab Efrawc the patronym is intact.
11 Even in the French tale, as Sayers notes, we might be left to wonder whether 'in courtly social terms a young guest might venture such questions as are expected from him here'. See Sayers, 'An Archaic Tale-Type', 92. I propose that for the Welsh tale the answer to this is in the negative and is dictated by social (though not courtly) convention.
12 For the various versions and the manuscripts that contain them, see p. 3 of this book.

13 A similar approach has been applied to this text, with different conclusions, in McMullen, 'The Communication of Culture'. See pp. 124–5 of this book, where I engage with McMullen's arguments.
14 For a parallel argument, see Evan J. Bibbee, 'Reticent Romans: Silence and Writing in *La Vie de Saint Alexis, Le Conte du Graal,* and *Le Roman de Silence*' (unpublished doctoral thesis, Louisiana State University, 2003), p. 74, *https://digitalcommons.lsu.edu/gradschool_dissertations/3768* (last accessed 22 May 2020).
15 Erich Poppe, '*Owein, Ystorya Bown*, and the Problem of "Relative Distance"'; Thomson (ed.), *Owein*, pp. xxviii–xxix.
16 Goetinck (ed.), *Historia Peredur*, p. 18.
17 Davies (trans.), *The Mabinogion*, p. 72.
18 Goetinck (ed.), *Historia Peredur*, p. 163.
19 Goetinck (ed.), *Historia Peredur*, p. 186; Vitt, '*Peredur*', pp. 119–20.
20 Goetinck (ed.), *Historia Peredur*, p. 186; my translation; according to Vitt, '*Peredur*', p. 120 n., *an* is deleted in the MS; for Vitt's translation, see Vitt, '*Peredur*', p. 121.
21 The uncle's instructions are not mentioned, for instance, by McMullen in the overview of silence and speech moments in the tale. See McMullen, 'The Communication of Culture', 27.
22 McMullen, 'The Communication of Culture', 30, 31.
23 Goetinck (ed.), *Historia Peredur*, p. 164; Vitt, '*Peredur*', pp. 140–1. Permission to depart is also received in the longer versions of the Welsh text; Goetinck (ed.), *Historia Peredur*, p. 20; Davies (trans.), *Mabinogion*, p. 73. It is a fairly standard procedure in medieval Welsh tales; cf. for instance Ian Hughes (ed.), *Math uab Mathonwy* (Dublin: DIAS, 2013), p. 2; Davies (trans.), *Mabinogion*, p. 48.
24 According to Charles-Edwards, the Peniarth 14 version occupies an intermediate position between the short early version of Peniarth 7 and the later, longer version preserved in the White Book and Red Book; 'The Textual Tradition', p. 27.
25 See pp. 36–41 of this book.
26 Noted, but not emphasised, by McMullen, 'The Communication of Culture', 32.
27 Goetinck (ed.), *Historia Peredur*, p. 21; Davies (trans.), *Mabinogion*, p. 73. The reference to this character as Peredur's foster sister is another indication of the importance of cultural conventions surrounding kinship structures within this text, as fosterage was an important form of artificial kinship in medieval Welsh society. For discussion, see, for instance, Thomas Charles-Edwards, *Wales and the Britons, 350–1064* (Oxford: Oxford University Press, 2012), pp. 298–300.

28　The article on which this chapter is based was inspired by reading Paul Russell's 'Three Notes'. For more on the head in *Canu Urien*, see pp. 109–10 of this book.

29　Quoted and discussed in Russell, 'Three Notes', 50. Sara Elin Roberts (ed. and trans.), *The Legal Triads of Medieval Wales* (Cardiff: University of Wales Press, 2007), triad *X71*, pp. 78–9. The reading quoted is of the triad preserved in British Library, Cotton Cleopatra B.v (s. xiv); versions also survive in other manuscripts; see Roberts, *The Legal Triads of Medieval Wales*, pp. 142–3 and discussion on p. 277.

30　Russell, 'Three Notes', 50. The remark in brackets is Russell's.

31　Dafydd Jenkins, 'Medieval Welsh Idea of Law', *Tijdschrift voor Rechtsgeschiedenis/Legal History Review*, 49/3–4 (1981), 323–48 (327, 329); and specifically in the context of discussions on kinship, Charles-Edwards, *Early Irish and Welsh Kinship*, pp. 182–200. Ben Guy points out that the prominence of genealogy in medieval Wales is connected to these legal practices; *Medieval Welsh Genealogy*, pp. 7–9.

32　See Goetinck (ed.), *Historia Peredur*, p. 46, and comments on p. 101; Davies (trans.), *The Mabinogion*, p. 88 and comments on p. 248. Both Goetinck and Davies note similarities to the Cauldron of Rebirth in *Branwen*. For a summary and discussion of this section of Episode III, see pp. 30 and 70 of this book.

33　See pp. 28 and 68 of this book.

34　For discussions, see Michael Cichon, 'Insult and Redress in Cyfaith Hywel Dda and Welsh Arthurian Romance', *Arthuriana*, 10 (2000), 27–43 (29–31) and 'Mishandled Vessels: Heaving Drinks and Hurling Insults in Medieval Welsh Literature and Law', *Canadian Journal of History*, 43 (2008), 227–40; Kirsten Lee Over, *Kingship, Conquest, and Patria: Literary and Cultural Identities in Medieval French and Welsh Arthurian Romance* (New York: Routledge, 2005), p. 141; John K. Bollard, 'The Structure of the Four Branches of the Mabinogi', p. 266, n. 32. Other discussions linking medieval Welsh literary texts with the legal tradition include Robin Chapman Stacey, 'Law and Literature in Medieval Ireland and Wales', in Helen Fulton (ed.), *Medieval Celtic Literature and Society* (Dublin: Four Courts Press, 2005), pp. 65–82; and Stacey, *Law and the Imagination*, especially p. 21; Paul Russell, 'From Plates and Rods to Royal Drink-Stands in *Branwen* and Medieval Welsh Law', *North American Journal of Celtic Studies*, 1 (2017), 1–26.

35　Cichon, 'Insult and Redress', 31.

36　It is worth noting that, as Robin Chapman Stacey argues, the relationship between laws and narrative texts may be symbiotic; see, for instance, Stacey, *Law and the Imagination*, pp. 20–6 (esp. pp. 23–4).

37　Lloyd-Morgan, 'Narrative Structure in *Peredur*', 227. The context is provided once again by the *Blegywryd* recension of the Welsh laws; Williams and

Powell (eds), *Cyfreithiau Hywel Dda*, p. 111. 29–30. See also p. 94, n. 11 of this book.

38 Goetinck (ed.), *Historia Peredur*, p. 57.
39 Davies (trans.), *The Mabinogion*, p. 94.
40 See, for instance, Davies (trans.), *The Mabinogion*, p. 249, note; Lloyd-Morgan, '*Historia Peredur*', pp. 147–8; Roberts, '*Peredur Son of Efrawg*', 65. Note that McMullen's discussion contains an error at this point: in the text there are two lads carrying the spear, not three: 'The Communication of Culture', 33.
41 Lloyd-Morgan, '*Historia Peredur*', p. 148.
42 Goetinck (ed.), *Historia Peredur*, p. 58; Davies (trans.), *The Mabinogion*, p. 95.
43 Goetinck (ed.), *Historia Peredur*, p. 58; Davies (trans.), *The Mabinogion*, p. 95.
44 For a detailed discussion of episodes that are unique to the Welsh text of *Peredur*, see the discussion in Chapter 1.
45 There are a number of examples in *Owain*, including the second countess whose magic balsam cures the hero's madness who might be construed as a maiden in distress; Lunet, imprisoned towards the end of the same narrative; and the twenty-four damsels of the 'Du Traws' episode, but each of these episodes have a French equivalent in Chrétien's *Chevalier au lion*. For the countess, see Thomson (ed.), *Owein*, pp. 21–4; Davies (trans.), *The Mabinogion*, pp. 131–3; Chrétien de Troyes, *Le Chevalier au Lion*, ll. 2887–3326, ed. by Méla, pp. 806–20; Kibler (trans.), *The Knight with the Lion*, pp. 331–6. I am grateful to the anonymous reviewer for pointing out the second and third examples. For a discussion and the suggestion that the different position of the 'Du Traws episode' in the Welsh narrative, compared to its location in the French, is dictated by the needs of the Welsh tale, see Luciana Cordo Russo, 'Modulaciones de la materia artúrica: el episodio de la *Pesme Aventure* en *Yvain* y *Owein*', *Hermēneus: Revista de traducción e interpretación*, 21 (2019), 75–105.
46 This may be a coincidence, but *Branwen* also contains the only instance of *llonyd* used with the negative outside of *Peredur* that I can find in the prose tales: 'A nachaf y dygyuor yn Iwerdon hyt nat oed lonyd idaw ony chaei dial y sarhaet'; Thomson (ed.), *Branwen*, l. 217; 'And there was such an uproar in Ireland that there was no peace for Matholwch until he avenged the insult' (Davies (trans.), *The Mabinogion*, p. 27). Disquiet (translated by Davies as 'no peace') here is associated with insult ('*sarhaed*') that requires redress. Insult, whether the maiden's to Peredur or his own earlier avoidance of inappropriate question to avoid insult, is, I would argue, also the dominant theme in these episodes of *Peredur*. The only other example of the word, in a positive sense this time, is in *Pwyll*: 'Y'r llys y doethant, a threulaw y nos honno a orugant drwy gerdeu a chyuedach, ual y bu llonyd ganthunt'; R. L. Thomson (ed.), *Pwyll*, ll. 258–61. 'They came to the court, and spent that night singing and

carousing, until they were contented'; Davies (trans.), *The Mabinogion*, p. 10. There are a number of further instances of the word in translated texts, in *Cynghorau Catwn*, the Welsh translation of *Disticha Catonis* in Peniarth 3ii (*c.*1275–1325), f. 39, but a full discussion is beyond the scope of the present discussion. For the transcript of the manuscript, and other instances of *llonyd* in medieval Welsh prose (all, apart from those discussed here, from translated texts), see Diana Luft et al. (eds), *Rhyddiaith Gymraeg*, 1300–1425 (2013), *www.rhyddiaithganoloesol.caerdydd.ac.uk* (last accessed 1 November 2020).

47 For a discussion of the terminology, see, for instance, Brynley F. Roberts, 'Ystoria', *Bulletin of the Board of Celtic Studies*, 26 (1974), 13–20; and Pierre-Yves Lambert, '*Style de traduction*: Les traductions celtiques de textes historiques', *Revue d'Histoire des Textes*, 24 (1994), 375–91, esp. 375–9.

48 *GPC* s.v. *ystyr*.

49 Chrétien de Troyes, *Le Conte du Graal*, ll. 4658–70, ed. by Méla, p. 1080; Kibler (trans.), *The Story of the Grail*, p. 439.

50 See discussion of this episode in the summary of the text on p. 37 of this book.

51 Erich Poppe and Regine Reck (eds), *Selections from* Ystorya Bown o Hamtwn (Cardiff: University of Wales Press, 2009), pp. xii–xiii, 43; Erich Poppe and R. Reck, 'A French Romance in Wales: *Ystorya Bown o Hamtwn*: Processes of Medieval Translations. Part I', *Zeitschrift für celtische Philologie*, 55 (2006), 122–80 (145–50); Petrovskaia (ed.), *Delw y Byd*, pp. 7, 11, 18–23.

52 Charles-Edwards, 'The Textual Tradition', p. 31.

53 Charles-Edwards, 'The Textual Tradition', p. 31.

54 Goetinck (ed.), *Historia Peredur*, p. 69; Davies (trans.), *The Mabinogion*, p. 102.

55 Stacey, *Law and the Imagination*, p. 23.

56 See p. 118 of this book. McMullen, 'The Communication of Culture', 35. The purpose here is not to argue against McMullen's interpretation of the story, but to suggest the possibility of a different, complementary, reading. *Peredur* has received analysis from the postcolonial perspective in a number of recent studies. See, for instance, Over, 'Transcultural Change: Romance to *rhamant*'; and Aronstein, 'Becoming Welsh'.

57 McMullen, 'The Communication of Culture', 35–6; with reference to Ngũgĩ wa Thiong'o, *Decolonizing the Mind: The Politics of Language in African Literature* (Portsmouth: Heinemann Educational Books, 1986), pp. 15–16.

58 The term I use here is from Gayatri Chakravorty Spivak's influential 1988 essay 'Can the Subaltern Speak?', in Cary Nelson and Lawrence Grossberg (eds), *Marxism and the Interpretation of Culture* (Urbana IL and Chicago IL: University of Illinois Press, 1988), pp. 271–313. For a brief overview of Subaltern Studies, see Dipesh Chakrabarty, *Provincializing Europe: Postcolonial*

Thought and Historical Difference (Princeton NJ and Oxford: Princeton University Press, 2000), pp. 11–16.
59 McMullen, 'The Communication of Culture', 36, particularly in comments about the Welsh manuscript production of the period.
60 McMullen, 'The Communication of Culture', 37.
61 I use the term 'sovereignty' here in the conventional sense, without the implications of the 'Sovereignty Theory'; for a discussion of its applicability to *Peredur*, see Petrovskaia, 'Dating *Peredur*', 223–4.
62 Spivak, 'Can the Subaltern Speak?', pp. 281–2.
63 Spivak, 'Can the Subaltern Speak?', p. 297.
64 Spivak, 'Can the Subaltern Speak?', p. 297.
65 See discussions referred to in n. 34 of this chapter.
66 For classifications of different types of elite in the colonial reality, see Spivak, 'Can the Subaltern Speak?', pp. 283–5. The idea of the subaltern subject that 'cannot speak' is relevant to medieval studies, as most of what we know about medieval culture is mediated through texts produced by dominant elites; the idea was voiced, among others, in a publication contemporary to Spivak's foundational work, in the analysis of medieval popular culture in Aaron Gurevich, *Medieval Popular Culture: Problems of Belief and Perceptions*, trans. by János M. Bak and Paul A. Hollingsworth (Cambridge: Cambridge University Press, 1988), originally published in Russian as *Проблемы средневековой народной культуры* (Moscow: Искусство, 1981). For a reading of Gurevich in the context of subaltern studies, see Chakrabarty, *Provincializing Europe*, p. 109.
67 Spivak, 'Can the Subaltern Speak?', p. 285. Spivak's emphasis.
68 The term 'silent majority', which I have previously rendered as 'silent multitude' is in the subtitle of the Russian edition of the book: *культура безмолствующего большинства* ('culture of the silent majority') (translation mine). А. Я. Гуревич, Средневековый *Мир. Культура безмолствующего большинства* ('Medieval world. Culture of the silent majority') (Moscow: Искусство, 1990); cf. Petrovskaia, '*Peredur* and the Problem of Inappropriate Questions', p. 19 n. 72.
69 The arguments proposed here support Bollard's assertion that throughout the narrative Peredur 'consistently does the best he can with the information he has available'; Bollard, 'Theme and Meaning', p. 88.
70 Examples of this include the empress episode, and the episode of the valley of changing sheep. For a discussion of the former, see Petrovskaia, 'Dating *Peredur*'; for the latter, see Calis, 'Peredur and the Valley of Changing Sheep'. Note, however, that the Welsh Continuation also contains unexplained elements that have no parallel in the French text; see pp. 39–43 of this book.
71 See, for instance, discussion in Lloyd-Morgan, '*Historia Peredur*', pp. 151–2.

72 This might be called a postcolonial reading of the tale; cf. discussion in McMullen, 'Communication of Culture', p. 34.
73 For discussion of the text's structure, see Chapter 1.
74 Examples include the three sets of trade practised by the heroes in *Manawydan*, the Third Branch of the Mabinogi, and the three journeys to the fountain undertaken by Cynon, Owein and Arthur in *Owein*. For *Manawydan*, see discussion in Hughes, 'Tripartite Structure in *Manawydan Uab Llyr*'. See also Thomson (ed.), *Owein*, pp. 2, 24 and 21; Davies (trans.), *The Mabinogion*, pp. 117, 133 and 131; and discussion in Petrovskaia, 'Où va-t-on pour son aventure?', pp. 163–6.
75 The distinction between Wales, England and the March is particularly important in terms of the application of law; see Sara Elin Roberts, '"By the Authority of the Devil": The Operation of Welsh and English Law in Medieval Wales', in by Ruth Kennedy and Simon Meecham-Jones (eds), *Authority and Subjugation in Writing of Medieval Wales* (Basingstoke: Palgrave Macmillan, 2008), pp. 85–97 (p. 91).
76 See discussion in Seán Duffy, 'Henry II and England's Insular Neighbours', in C. Harper-Bill and Nicholas Vincent (eds), *Henry II: New Interpretations* (Cambridge: Boydell & Brewer, 2007), pp. 129–53 (pp. 149–50). None of the murders discussed by Duffy took place in Gloucester itself, and may not provide any base for identification of the possible allusion in *Peredur*, but these events do provide a suggestive context. For further discussion of Gloucester in the geographical setting of *Peredur*, see pp. 59–60 and 142 of this book; for the witches of Gloucester and the possible historical allusions in the use of the place name, see p. 65 of this book.
77 See, for example, Goyette, 'Milk or Blood?', esp. 132, 141; Tony Davenport, 'Wales and Welshness in Middle English Romances', in *Authority and Subjugation*, pp. 137–58 (p. 141); Davenport refers to the more extensive discussion in Rupert T. Pickens, *The Welsh Knight: Paradoxicality in Chrétien's* Conte del Graal (Lexington KY: French Forum Publishers, 1977), pp. 113–17.
78 Barber, *The Holy Grail*, p. 93.

6

The Witches of Gloucester and Other Problematic Characters

As has been pointed out in Chapter 3, there is a proliferation of powerful female characters in *Peredur*.[1] Some of these may be explained with reference to contemporary social and legal changes, and the influence of the March, as with the laws on female inheritance already discussed in Chapter 3. Not all the characters or their features can be so explained, however, and some of these have been the subject of some discussion already. The witches of Gloucester, who train Peredur at the end of Episode I, and re-appear in the Chrétien-influenced Continuation, belong to this category.[2] Other characters have not been so closely examined, but also deserve attention. In Episode I, where Peredur encounters the witches of Gloucester it is worth noting, but not usually remarked on, that both the owner and the attackers of the castle in this adventure are female. The issue of the women holding power and ruling lands in Episodes I and III has already been discussed in Chapter 3. Yet the owner of the castle is also remarkable for another reason: described as 'gwreic vawr delediw' ('large, handsome woman'), she is not the standard maiden type.[3] *Telediw*, according to *GPC*, has the meaning of 'beautiful, fair, elegant, well-built; full of value, prime, physically perfect, in good condition, flawless, fit, apt'.[4] It is derived from *talu* ('to pay') and has a connection to value.[5] This imposing large woman of quality is the master of the house. Terminology such as *gwr vawr* in medieval Welsh texts tends to be read as an indication of giant nature. Thus, if we are to accept that the castle of this woman is being attacked by witches it is possible that she and her offspring are giants, and that Peredur is in the realm of the uncanny. However, given the fact, noted in Chapter 1, that other than the witches, there is no indication of anything supernatural in Episode I, one might suggest that in this case the text is telling us that the owner of the castle is a handsome middle-aged woman, possibly heavy-built, with the adjective *mawr* ('large') functioning merely as an attempt to distinguish her from a willowy maidenly figure of a young girl.[6] This reading is undermined by the description of the lad who opens the door for Peredur, who is clearly much larger than his age, which seems to point to a reading of these characters as giants. While it is possible to suggest that Peredur here visits a castle inhabited by benign giants, besieged by wicked witches, an alternative reading is possible. This alternative reading is based on the premise that since no downright magic or straightforward otherworldly features are present in Episode I, it may be worth trying to read this narrative from a realistic perspective. In this reading the large woman and her well-grown son are not giants, but simply particularly tall or heavily built humans. The witches (who, it must be noted, wield no magic in this episode) we shall return to later.

Without suggesting that medieval authors or audiences would necessarily have been aware of the relationship between body-build and living standards (particularly, though not exclusively, nutrition), it is worth delving into the question of how large is *mawr* in relation to normal human size. In other words, are these characters giants or are they simply large and well-built? The question has significant implications for our understanding of the episode: if these characters are found to be giants, it would not be unreasonable for the attackers to be witches. If these characters are merely well-nourished fully developed human beings, then the potential supernatural nature of the attackers would require even closer scrutiny. The matter might have further implications (which lie beyond the remit of the present study) for our understanding of other medieval Welsh texts, as it may suggest a need to re-evaluate what exactly is meant by qualifying a character with the adjective *mawr* in each instance.

Although it is difficult to argue from absence, it is worth pointing out that there is no indication that anything surrounding the large lady and the large lad is particularly oversized. Accepting for the moment the notion that these are simply human beings whose physical development was conditioned by a particularly benign environment, we might postulate that they are large compared to Peredur, who was brought up in an environment of a wasteland ('*diffeithwch*').[7] Although the land surrounding the house of Peredur's large hosts is also desolate, the lady tells Peredur that the land had been taken and laid waste by the witches ('diffeithaw y kyfoeth' ('laid waste the land')), which suggests that at an earlier point it was independent and fertile.[8] The concept of *diffeithwch* is worth dwelling on, since there has been some confusion about what precisely its implications are for Peredur's upbringing, and since it plays a role in our interpretation of the present episode.

The description of the voluntary exile chosen by Peredur's mother to protect her son should be taken in the context of other medieval Welsh prose texts. The limited description in the text offers association of desolation and wilderness: the hero's mother fled with her son 'y ynialwch a diffeithwch ac ymadaw a'r kyuanned' ('into a desert and a wilderness, and to quit inhabited parts').[9] The word *diffeithwch* also occurs in the Third Branch of the Mabinogi, also known as *Manawydan*, and there it seems to indicate uninhabited rather than desolate lands, and in that particular case does not mean infertile land incapable of supporting a self-sufficient existence.[10] It also occurs in *Owain*, where Cynon begins description of his adventure at the fountain by saying that he had travelled to 'eithauoed byt a diffeithwch' ('remote and uninhabited regions of the world').[11] It is presumably while in these uninhabited and desolate regions that Cynon comes across a beautiful plain with a castle. Presumably, the castle itself is not in the *diffeithwch* but is surrounded by them. The reference to 'remote and uninhabited regions' seems to emphasise distance from Cynon's own country and the Arthurian realm.[12] Further on in the tale, during the period of madness brought on by his wife's rejection of him, Owain himself wanders around 'eithaued byt a diffeith vynyded' ('remote regions of the world and desolate mountains') where he feeds with wild animals.[13] He does, however, eventually become so malnourished as to be unable to keep up with the animals, indicating that 'diffeith vynyded' ('desolate mountains') are not capable of adequately supporting (human) life. In both instances in *Owein*, the couplet distant-desolate seems to function in opposition to Arthur's court.[14]

A similar juxtaposition and contrast is visible in *Peredur*. The contrast implied between cultivated lands *kyfanhed* (= 'dwelling-place, habitation, abode; inhabited or cultivated place' GPC s.v. *cyfannedd*) and uncultivated lands *ynyalwch* (= 'desert, wilderness, uncultivated land' GPC s.v. *anialwh, ynialwch*) in the description of the horses that Peredur seeks out, may suggest a connection to the outside world.[15] The implication, even if the connection is external to the point of exile (which is probable), is presumably that Peredur's mother still holds lands beyond the location of their current habitation that are capable of supporting her household. Indeed, it may not be necessary to postulate such an external connection, and the packhorses may simply have been used to transfer goods from one point of their territory to another, because as Ian Hughes observes, *cyfannedd* seems to imply signs of human habitation and activity, including domestic animals.[16] The presence of humans, with goats, and the packhorses themselves, would suggest that Peredur was not brought up in the desert (with the connotations of lack of food or means of sustenance), but that uncultivated land was part of the new existence. Further, as the example of *Manawydan* demonstrates, such uncultivated land was not barren: once human activity starts in the *diffeithwch*, the land is perfectly capable of producing crops. However, and this is significant for the purposes of the present discussion, it seems, judging from the context in *Manawydan*, that although land that was *diffeithwch* was not barren, it required human effort to produce crops. This would make perfect sense for the episode of the witches because we can see their activity of 'laying waste' the land as removing the signs and results of human activity, including previous crops. The land, as we can see from *Owain* and *Manawydan*, which is in this state does not have to be completely incapable of supporting life, but it does seem to be associated with a lack of human intervention to make it fertile, and insufficiency (though not a complete absence of) nutritive capacity. Thus, land can become *diffeithwch* as a result of war, but it can also be *diffeithwch*, as the land where Peredur was brought up, as a starting point before people get there. There is no indication in the beginning of Episode I that the land remained in this state once Peredur's mother had settled there.

Returning to the witches episode, the fact that the land had been recently made *diffeithwch* by the witches implies that previously it had been rich. While I do not mean to suggest that medieval authors would have necessarily been thinking of the importance of nutrition to human development (and relationship to size), there are two points that deserve to be made here. The first point is that recent research has demonstrated that there was quite a sharp and visible distinction in the dimensions of individuals depending on their diet.[17] There is also some evidence for awareness of the importance of food to human health in the medieval period in general.[18] Perhaps it is not necessary to read a direct correspondence between well-being and size into the text, but an additional point can be made here: that the text at this point is equally susceptible to both an otherworldly and a real-world reading. The inhabitants of the castle could be giant or could be human. Their land could have been rendered waste by magic or by war.

What implications does this have for the passage describing the effect the *gwidonot* had on the land they had conquered? Let us return to the wording of the description, as given by the large handsome lady: 'Ac neur deryw udunt gwerescyn a diffeithaw y kyfoeth, onyt yr vn ty hwnn' ('And they have taken over and laid waste the land, except for this one house').[19] *Kyfoeth* means 'land', but the context, in terms of alternative translation, is 'power', 'country', 'domain', 'territory' or even 'people or subjects of a realm', rather than in the sense of arable land or ground.[20] Indeed, the primary senses of the word are 'wealth' and 'power'.[21] Thus, the *gwidonot* have taken over the territory or realm and have destroyed all buildings in it apart from the one manor. There is no specific reference to lack of food here (as there had been at the court of the first countess, at whose court Peredur was offered what food had been available at a nearby nunnery), but rather lack of man-made structures.[22] The house that is left is the last one standing, but given that the lady tells Peredur that they are in danger, it is also under threat.

Taking the passage in the context of *Manawydan* also raises the possibility that here is a similar scenario – magic-wielding individuals reducing land in south Wales to the status of land that is *diffeithwch*. However, in *Manawydan* there was no further physical attack on the last remaining buildings, as there is in *Peredur*. After Peredur stays in the threatened house overnight – like the good adventure-seeking knight he is – he is awoken by the screams of a guard who was being physically attacked by one of the *gwidonot*.[23] The association with physical attack, laying waste of land surrounding the manor, and the fact that the house/castle ambiguity reflects historical reality of Marcher territories in the period, suggests a possibility of reading this episode in light of contemporary cultural context, without any need for supposing the involvement of supernatural or magic elements, rather than as a parallel to *Manawydan*, with its vengeful wizard and magical mice.

The only apparently supernatural element in the episode is the *gwidonot*, who are, perhaps, one of the most perplexing aspects of this perplexing text, and it is time to give them some of our attention. Because these characters appear in only two episodes of the text – Episode I and the Continuation – they have a degree of significance within the longer version of the narrative, and Glenys Goetinck defines them as 'Peredur's principal enemies'.[24] This conclusion is drawn on the basis of the Continuation alone, since it is only there that the *gwidonot* are blamed for most of the misfortunes of Peredur's relations. Goetinck reads *gwiddon* here to mean 'witch or sorceress, the level to which pagan priestesses were reduced by the Christians', and suggests that around the Severn Basin there may have been memories of nine pagan priestesses that would have given rise to a legend, but also suggests that this might have combined with the 'tradition of the Celtic warrior woman, trainer of heroes in feats of arms and magic', and could have been used as an oblique reference to 'the representatives of the Norman church' subjugating the Welsh church.[25] She points out that the location of the witches at Gloucester seems to support the idea of Norman associations.[26] This introduces three possible threads that will require some unravelling.

The geographical association with the Severn Basin places the episode within the cultural remit of the March and, as we have seen, the castle/manor ambiguity fits in quite well with that context. The possibility of the association of the *gwydonot* of Gloucester with the Normans also seems reasonable, given that Gloucester was a (Norman) royal castle, held by a constable for the king.[27]

As far as the suggestion that these represent 'pagan priestesses' is concerned, the immediate objection is that it is difficult to imagine memories of pagan priestesses surviving for more than 1,000 years in twelfth or thirteenth-century Wales. Furthermore, it is unlikely that if such a tradition were to have existed it would have necessarily been tied to the area around Gloucester. One wonders whether it is a coincidence that the poem *Pa wr yw'r Porthor* ('What man is the porter'), preserved in the earliest Welsh vernacular manuscript, the Black Book of Carmarthen (mid-thirteenth century), also mentions nine witches (who are in the poem killed by Kei).[28] As Oliver Padel notes, however, the number of witches is simply three times three.[29] Thus, while the correspondence of the number of witches in these texts can be significant, it may also be mere coincidence due to a predilection for triadic structures.

The notion that the 'witches' are not 'sorceresses' but rather a representation of female warriors invites closer consideration, since the witches of Gloucester provide Peredur with the third part of his education as a warrior.[30] There has been a recent surge in interest in medieval warrior women, which mostly shows that these women were perceived as subversive to the normal order of things.[31] While it is difficult to reconstruct the full range of associations and implications of the medieval term in its original cultural context, it seems worth asking whether the implications of ugliness inherent in the translation terms 'hag' and 'witch' are not a function of modern discomfort with the concept of the older warrior woman in these texts, rather than a function of medieval discomfort with the same concept. I will return to the point of the terminology after discussing the warrior-women reading of the witches.

There have also been investigations of the possibility that warrior-women existed, specifically in medieval Scandinavia, but also on the Continent.[32] There is also, and this of more immediate interest for our purposes, evidence in Irish literature for a tradition of the warrior woman teaching the hero to fight. The relevance of this for the analysis of Welsh material rests on the consideration that Irish tradition has exerted a great deal of influence on the Welsh, as has been demonstrated by Patrick Sims-Williams.[33] Thus, since there are few female warrior figures in the medieval Welsh literary corpus, we may examine parallels in the medieval Irish material.

Lisa M. Bitel nicely summarises the presentation of such women in Irish literature:

> Images of hostile and powerful women were commonplace in all genres of the literature of this society, which otherwise cast its women as physically flawed, legally subordinate, and spiritually inferior. Female fighters instructed male heroes of saga in the arts of war. Hags turned up to prophesy, and even bring about, the heroes' downfall. Vicious sorceresses battled the saints in the vitae.[34]

According to Bitel, in medieval Irish texts these characters fall into two types:

> Two kinds of powerful females invaded the texts, both of whom drew strength from the uncontrolled sexuality so frightening and fascinating to the early Irish: militant women and magic-making women. Differences between the two were crucial, even if the literati did not always carefully distinguish between bloodthirsty females and those who cast spells, for goddesses of war were also sometimes fighters or spell casters, and the sorceresses of saints' lives sometimes resembled the prophesizing hags of secular tales.[35]

The limitations of the comparison with the examples examined by Bitel lie in the complete absence of the sexual element present in the example she discusses from Peredur's interaction with the *gwidon*.[36] Nevertheless, it is worth taking a closer look at the 'militant women' category examined by Bitel. These are women whose function in the narratives within which they feature appears to parallel that of Peredur's 'witches'.

The most striking parallels to the *gwidonot* of *Peredur* are offered by the characters of Scáthach and her daughters in *Tochmarc Emire*.[37] Just as Peredur learns skill with weapons from the witches, so does Cú Chulainn learn from Scáthach. According to Mark Williams, both these characters, and the *gwidonot* of *Peredur*, are examples of a 'warrior witch' figure. Mark Williams offers a brief prolegomenon to an analysis of these characters in both Welsh and Irish tales, with reference to the witches of the Black Book of Carmarthen poem, pointing out that the common modern English translation of the word might not reflect accurately the actual meaning of the term in its medieval context, 'for these women appear to be Amazons rather than workers of spells'.[38] This follows the interpretation of these characters as 'Amazons' by Sir John Rhŷs.[39] In *Peredur*, when the 'witch' first appears in the scene we are discussing, she is helmeted and is attacking a guard.[40] Peredur's attack flattens her helmet. The question then is whether these 'witches' have anything to do with witchcraft at all (in the sense that the English term implies). We are therefore back to the question of what the term *gwidonot* means. Like Scáthach, the witch offers to teach Peredur the use of weapons, and like Cú Chulainn, he stays with her and her sisters until his training is complete. Rhŷs also points out that in medieval Ireland, at least until the seventh century, there actually were female warriors.[41] This would give ample context for the figure of Scáthach, and she, in turn, for the masculine women training Peredur.[42] In Rhŷs's words, 'there need be nothing essentially non-historical in the whole incident where the witches of Gloucester figure except the predictions'.[43] The only indication of anything supernatural in the Welsh passage is the reference to the fact that it was 'tyghetuen a gweledigath' ('fated and foretold') that the witch would give Peredur his horse and weapons (i.e., arm him).[44] Rhŷs noted that the prophecy reference here is ambiguous: the agent is unclear and there is no particular reason to think that it was the witches.[45] The witches in *Peredur* thus have weapons but no magic.

The remaining question is, consequently, whether 'witch' is an accurate translation of the term, *gwiddon*. The range of meanings that the *GPC* gives for this term is as follows: 'giantess, female monster; hag, witch, sorceress, sometimes fig.; (latterly) giant, monster; wizard sorcerer; (dict.)

one of the woodland deities, satyr, nymph.'[46] The terms seems to convey a more general sense of a female person outside of societal norms. Given the internal evidence of the texts themselves, which do not refer to magic directly, it seems possible that it may rather mean skill, or knowledge, not of magic but of weaponry.

In the first translation of the text into English, Charlotte Guest rendered the word as 'sorceress', while the word *gwrach* by which Peredur addresses the first of these female characters when he encounters her as she is about to dispatch a castle guard, is rendered by Guest as 'hag'.[47] I would argue that this translation has coloured our interpretation of these characters since. Furthermore, the analysis of the witches of Gloucester as 'witches' appears to be influenced by a combination of Guest's interpretation of *gwiddon* as 'sorceress' (for which 'witch' is a synonym) together with Peredur's address to her. But what Peredur calls her does not necessarily reflect what she is, merely how he perceives her. Arguably, he is simply being rude, given the predominantly negative connotations of the word *gwrach*.[48]

One does wonder, however, if it might not be possible to subject this scene to a completely different reading. Although, as Sara Elin Roberts observes, the word does not occur in modern Welsh without negative connotations, and very rarely does so in medieval Welsh, it is possible to translate it as 'elderly woman' or even 'mother'.[49] Roberts herself in her analysis of the terminology for women of different ages in the poetry of Dafydd ap Gwilym allows her translation to be coloured by Dafydd's attitudes:

> He uses *morwyn* (with the *sangiad* (aside) that this is his preferred brand of woman) for virgin, *merch fach* for a little girl, a child; *gwrach* for an older woman or a hag – this word is rare in his work but he uses it to refer to old women and he is not fond of that group; and finally the word *gwraig*.[50]

Of these terms, only *gwrach* can be applied to an older woman and thus is the only term at hand to designate a woman past child-bearing age. This type of woman might not be the poet's preferred age group, as it is unsuited to his amorous intentions, but there is no reason to assume that the word invariably means 'old woman' or 'hag' rather than, for instance, 'elderly lady' or 'grandma'. Our interpretative problem might lie with the limited range of synonyms for 'older person of the female gender' that had not been endowed with negative connotations in modern English.[51] One thinks for instance, of 'beldam', which is quite apposite for rendering *gwrach* if taken without the later, acquired, negative connotations, which happen to include 'witch'.[52] My objective here is not to engage in a diatribe against the misogyny of modern language, but merely to suggest that this inherent misogyny in our terminology might be forcing us to read these medieval characters in a way that they were neither intended to be read or perceived by medieval audiences. It may, for argument's sake, be worth taking the supposedly rare positive medieval meaning of *gwrach* and seeing if it works in this scene.

Peredur, in addressing this woman, says 'Paham y gwdosti, wrach, mae Peredur wyf i?'.[53] The conventional reading is 'How do you know, witch, that I am Peredur?'.[54] But what if he is asking, 'How do you know, mother [= ma'am/(older) lady], that I am Peredur?'. Given the pattern that Peredur has for addressing unfamiliar young women as *chwaer* ('sister'), this suggestion might not be so outlandish as it might at first appear. For example, when he greets Angharad Law Eurog, he says 'Myn vyg cret, vy chwaer ... morwyn hygar gaueid wyt. A mi allwn arnaf dy garu yn uwyhaf gwreic, pei da genhyt' ('By my faith, sister ... you are a dear, lovely girl. And I could love you best of all women if you wished').[55] What he is offering Angharad is not brotherly love, so 'sister' is certainly merely an appellation. If this is the way that he addresses younger women, then is it not conceivable that an older woman would also be addressed by a corresponding term? The appropriate corresponding term for an older woman would be 'mother'.[56] It is differentiated from the term used by Peredur to address his own mother, whom he addresses as *mam* ('mother').[57] As Sarah Elin Roberts observes, there is no terminology in medieval Welsh for a middle-aged older women other than *gwraig* and *hen wraig*, respectively.[58] It may be that the appellations were already negative in connotation, since Peredur does not use any appellation at all for the large woman who is his host – and she is clearly older than he is, since she has sons who are old enough to respond to guests at the front door.

Given that after extracting the witch's promise not to do further harm to the lands of the countess, Peredur goes with her to the 'llys y gwidonot' ('witches' court') and learns horse riding and the use of weapons, a neutral reading of his address might make a little more sense than a rude one.[59] Furthermore, in medieval Welsh tales, heroes appear to address their enemies politely as a rule, and the only instances of rude address in *Peredur* texts are found in the Continuation.[60]

The crucial question of the woman's age remains. To interpret the term *gwrach* as a greeting appropriate to an older female (rather than as an insult), would imply that this woman is much older than Peredur himself, old enough to be his mother. Given the active nature of the warrior-*gwrach* in this scene, she cannot be too old (assuming that the narrative has internal logic). Further, Peredur's hostess had mentioned that the *gwidonot* were based in Gloucester with their father and mother. Given the generally extremely youthful age of medieval heroes, this question of relative ages is easy to solve. If Peredur is in his late teens or even early twenties, a woman in her late thirties to early forties would easily be his mother's age.

If the reasoning is sufficient to remove the 'hag' interpretation of Peredur's greeting, the second leg is knocked out from under the 'witch' argument for *gwidon*. We have already seen that they are not magic-wielding women. They are also not necessarily, in Episode I, perceived by the protagonist as anything other than opponents. This supports Mark Williams's suggestion that although modern English translations render them as 'witches', they appear rather to be warrior-women. The use of negative terminology – 'witch' and 'hag' – may ultimately stem from Lady Guest's Victorian discomfort at the concept of warrior women. It is possible that the discomfort was already there in the medieval period. If we read the word *gwidonot* as carrying negative connotations, then it could be argued that the representation of the warrior-women in *Peredur* may fit with twelfth-century attitudes towards women taking up arms. This attitude is found in the writings of Wace and Benoît de Sainte-Maure, who described women fighting against the English in Coutances in extremely negative terms, including as 'savages'.[61] It is almost impossible, based on the available data, to ascertain whether the negative connotations were already attached to these terms at the point of composition, or even at the point at which our manuscripts were written down. However, the question of whether 'witch' with its connotations of (dark/ominous) magic use, or even 'hag' with its connotations of age and ugliness, are appropriate translations for these terms in the Welsh context is worth asking. At the very least, one cannot help but agree with Glenys Goetinck's observation that 'the women who make their appearance in *Peredur* are not all the delicate, fearful creatures of the continental romances'.[62] Countesses, sometimes portly, rule their own lands, and women train knights to fight. The present book has attempted to read these figures in their contemporary medieval context, seeking to understand the text which introduces them on its own terms.

Notes

1. See p. 83 of this book.
2. Previous discussions include Sir John Rhŷs, 'The Nine Witches of Gloucester', in *Anthropological Essays presented to Edward Burnett Tylor in Honour of his 75th Birthday, Oct. 2, 1907*, ed. by contributors (Oxford: Clarendon Press, 1908) pp. 285–93; Goetinck, 'Peredur ... Upon Reflection'.
3. Goetinck (ed.), *Historia Peredur*, p. 29; Davies (trans.), *Mabinogion*, p. 78.
4. *GPC* s.v. *telediw*.
5. *GPC* s.v. *telediw*; s.v. *talaf: talu*. The term *telediw* is also used for animals in prime condition; I am grateful to Paul Russell for this information.
6. For use of *gwreic* in middle Welsh to designate middle-aged women, see Sara Elin Roberts, 'Seeking the Middle-Aged Woman in Medieval Wales', in Sue Niebrzydowski (ed.), *Middle-Aged Women in the Middle Ages* (Cambridge: Boydell and Brewer, 2011), pp. 25–36.
7. Goetinck (ed.), *Historia Peredur*, p. 7; Davies (trans.), *The Mabinogion*, p. 65.
8. Goetinck (ed.), *Historia Peredur*, p. 29; Davies (trans.), *The Mabinogion*, p. 78.
9. Goetinck (ed.), *Historia Peredur*, p. 7; translated in Jones and Jones, *The Mabinogion*, p. 153. The terms are translated as 'wasteland and wilderness' and 'inhabited regions' by Sioned Davies, in Davies (trans.), *The Mabinogion*, p. 65.
10. See the discussion in Hughes, 'Tripartite Structure', pp. 102–3; and also in Andrew Welsh, '*Manawydan fab Llŷr*: Wales, England, and the "new man"', in C. J. Byrne et al. (eds), *Celtic Languages and Celtic Peoples: Proceedings of the Second North American Congress of Celtic Studies* (Halifax NS: Saint Mary's University, 1992), pp. 369–83, reprinted in C. W. Sullivan (ed.), *The Mabinogi: a Book of Essays* (New York: Garland Press, 1996), pp. 121–41; the discussion of the term can be found in the latter version at p. 135.
11. Thomson (ed.), *Owain*, p. 2; Davies (trans.), *Mabinogion*, p. 117.
12. 'A gwedy daruot im goruot ar bob camhwri o'r a oed yn vn wlat a mi, ymgywe[i]raw a wneuthum a cherded eithauoed byt a diffeithwch' ('And when I had overcome every challenge in my own country, I got ready and travelled to the remote and uninhabited regions of the world'); Thomson (ed.), *Owain*, p. 2; Davies (trans.), *Mabinogion*, p. 117.
13. Thomson (ed.), *Owain*, p. 21; Davies (trans.), *Mabinogion*, p. 31.
14. In the latter case this is made explicit: 'nyt llys Arthur a gyrchwys namyn eithaued by a diffeith vynyded' ('did not make for Arthur's court but for the remote regions of the world and desolate mountains'); Thomson (ed.), *Owain*, p. 21; Davies (trans.), *Mabinogion*, p. 31.
15. Goetinck (ed.), *Historia Peredur*, p. 9; cf. discussion of the term in Hughes, 'Tripartite Structure', pp. 102–3.
16. Hughes, 'Tripartite Structure', p. 103.

17 For an investigation of human remains from a comparable period in medieval England, showing a range of height, weight, and body mass index measurements correlating to social status and living standards, see Marianne Schweich and Christopher Knüsel, 'Bio-Cultural Effects in Medieval Populations', *Economics & Human Biology*, 1 (2003), 367–77; for a discussion of the influence of environmental factors (including nutrition and disease or health during the formative years of childhood) on human development and height, see Phyllis B. Eveleth and James M. Tanner, *Worldwide Variation in Human Growth*, 2nd edn (Cambridge: Cambridge University Press, 1990), pp. 191–207.

18 For discussions see, for instance, Melitta Weiss Adamson, *Food in Medieval Times* (Westport and London: Greenwood Press, 2004); Theresa A. Vaughan, *Women, Food, and Diet in the Middle Ages: Balancing the Humours* (Amsterdam: Amsterdam University Press, 2020), esp. Chapter 2.

19 Goetinck (ed.), *Historia Peredur*, p. 29; S. Davies (trans.), *Mabinogion*, p. 78.

20 *GPC* s.v. *cyfoeth* (c).

21 *GPC* s.v. *cyfoeth*, (a) and (b).

22 For the discussion of the food provided by the nunnery, see pp. 61–2 of this book.

23 Goetinck (ed.), *Historia Peredur*, p. 29; Davies (trans.), *Mabinogion*, pp. 78–9.

24 Goetinck, '*Peredur* … Upon Reflection', 228.

25 Goetinck, '*Peredur* … Upon reflection', 228.

26 Goetinck, '*Peredur* … Upon reflection', 228.

27 See, for instance, discussions in R. Allen Brown, 'Royal Castle-Building in England, 1154–1216', *The English Historical Review*, 70 (1955), 353–98. During the Anarchy, this constable was Miles of Gloucester; Hanley, *Matilda*, pp. 123–4; Patterson, *The Earl*, pp. 71, 143. According to Hanley, Miles had 'seven or eight children', point illustrating that though by modern standards the number (nine) of sister *gwydonot* might seem large, it would not be so unusual for medieval noble families (certainly if one counts illegitimate children); Hanley, *Matilda*, p. 119.

28 For an edition and discussion of the poem, see Brynley F. Roberts, 'Rhai o gerddi ymddiddan Llyfr Du Caerfyrddin', in Rachel Bromwich and R. Brinley Jones (eds), *Astudiaethau ar yr Hengerdd/Studies in Old Welsh Poetry, Cyflwyneg I Syr Idris Foster* (Cardiff: University of Wales Press, 1978), pp. 281–325; and discussions in Padel, *Arthur in Medieval Welsh Literature* (Chapter 3); and Sims-Williams, 'The Early Welsh Arthurian Poems', pp. 38–46 (esp. p. 45 for a discussion of the witches).

29 Padel, *Arthur in Medieval Welsh Literature*, p. 22.

30 See the summary in Chapter 1.

31 See, for example, Megan McLaughlin, 'The Woman Warrior: Gender, Warfare and Society in Medieval Europe', *Women's Studies: An Interdisciplinary*

Journal, 17 (1990), 193–209; Lisa M. Bitel, *Women in Early Medieval Europe, 400–1100* (Cambridge: Cambridge University Press, 2002), pp. 73–80.
32 See, for instance, Leszek Gardeła, 'Amazons of the North? Armed Females in Viking Archaeology and Medieval Literature', in Alessia Bauer and Alexandra Pesch (eds), *Hvanndalir – Beiträge zur europäischen Altertumskunde und mediävistischen Literaturwissenschaft: Festschrift für Wilhelm Heizmann*, Reallexikon der germanischen Altertumskunde – Ergänzungsbände 106 (Berlin: De Gruyter, 2018), pp. 391–428.
33 Patrick Sims-Williams, *Irish Influence on Welsh Literature* (Oxford: Oxford University Press, 2011).
34 Lisa M. Bitel, *Land of Women: Tales of Sex and Gender from Early Ireland* (Ithaca NY: Cornell University Press, 1996), p. 204.
35 Bitel, *Land of Women*, p. 205.
36 Compare Bitel's discussion, *Land of Women*, p. 211.
37 Goetinck, *Peredur*, pp. 226–7; Kuno Meyer (ed. and trans.), 'The oldest version of *Tochmarc Emire*', *Revue Celtique*, 11 (1890), 433–57 (446–53); Bitel, *Land of Women*, p. 214.
38 Mark Williams, 'Magic and Marvels', in Geraint Evans and Helen Fulton (eds), *The Cambridge History of Welsh Literature* (Cambridge: Cambridge University Press, 2019), pp. 52–72 (p. 58).
39 Sir John Rhŷs, 'The Nine Witches of Gloucester', in *Anthropological Essays presented to Edward Burnett Tylor in Honour of his 75th Birthday, Oct. 2, 1907*, ed. by contributors (Oxford: Clarendon Press, 1908), pp. 285–93 (p. 288).
40 Goetinck (ed.), *Hisotria Peredur*, p. 29; Davies trans.), *Mabinogion*, p. 78.
41 Rhŷs, 'The Nine Witches of Gloucester', p. 287.
42 Rhŷs suggests Irish presence in Wales as the possible inspiration, but given Sims-Williams's recent discussion of the influence of Irish literature on the Welsh, historical presence of warrior-women in Wales is not a necessary condition here; Rhŷs, 'The Nine Witches of Gloucester', pp. 289–93; Sims-Williams, *Irish Influence on Welsh Literature*.
43 Rhŷs, 'The Nine Witches of Gloucester', p. 289.
44 Goetinck (ed.), *Historia Peredur*, p. 30; Davies, *Mabinogion*, p. 79.
45 Rhŷs, 'The Nine Witches of Gloucester', p. 287.
46 *GPC* s.v. *gwiddon*.
47 Goetinck (ed.), *Historia Peredur*, pp. 29–30; Charlotte Guest (trans.), *Mabinogion* (London and New York, 1906), p. 191.
48 *GPC* s.v. *gwrach* (a); in Welsh the first definition given is '*hen wraig*' ('old woman'), but the English translation gives only the following terms: 'ugly old woman, crone, hag, witch, sorceress; also transf. of anything that is old, ugly, loathsome, &c.'
49 Roberts, 'Seeking the Middle-Aged Woman in Medieval Wales', p. 27; with ref. to *GPC* s.v. *gwrach*.

50 Roberts, 'Seeking the Middle-Aged Woman in Medieval Wales', p. 28.
51 For observations regarding the influence of modern perceptions on our analysis of medieval women, see, for instance, John H. Van Enghen, 'Epilogue: Positioning Women in Medieval Society, Culture, and Religion', in Kathryn Kerby-Fulton, Katie Ann-Marie Bugyis and John Van Engen (eds), *Women Intellectuals and Leaders in the Middle Ages* (Cambridge: Boydell and Brewer, 2020) pp. 397–401 (pp. 398–9).
52 See discussion in Bożena Kochman-Haładyj, 'Low Wenches and Slatternly Queans: On Derogation of Women Terms', in *Studia Anglica Resoviensia*, 4 (2007), 206–28 (220) with reference to the foundational study by Muriel R. Schulz, 'The Semantic Derogation of Women', in Barrie Thorne and Nancy Henley (eds), *Language and Sex* (Rowley: Newbury House, 1975), pp. 64–75.
53 Goetinck (ed.), *Historia Peredur*, p. 30.
54 Davies (trans.), *Mabinogion*, p. 79.
55 Goetinck (ed.), *Historia Peredur*, p. 35; Davies (trans.), *Mabinogion*, p. 82.
56 Given the occurrence of the terms 'aunt' and 'mother' in the context of similar use of kinship terms for strangers in other cultures, it is tempting to suggest that *gwrach* might have such a meaning in medieval Welsh. Examples include Russian, Yoruba and Hindi, among others. In Russian, *тётя* [*tyotya*] can be used to address an aunt, in polite use to address more remote older relatives (such as a great aunt), and as a very informal and not very polite to neutral designation for a woman outside the kin group who is estimated to be of middle age or above; for discussion of Yoruba, see, for instance, Solomon Oluwọle Oyetade, 'A Sociolinguistic Analysis of Address Forms in Yoruba', *Language in Society*, 24 (1995), 515–35; for Hindi, see R. R. Mehrotra, 'Fluidity in Kinship Terms of Address in Hindi', *Anthropological Linguistics*, 19 (1977), 123–5, esp. 123 for further references to use of kinship terms for strangers in other societies.
57 Goetinck (ed.), *Historia Peredur*, pp. 8–9.
58 Roberts, 'Seeking the Middle-Aged Woman in Medieval Wales', p. 27.
59 Goetinck (ed.), *Historia Peredur*, p. 30; Davies (trans.), *Mabinogion*, p. 79.
60 Neither are used by Peredur; see discussion in Chapter 1.
61 See discussion in Duby, 'Women and Power', pp. 73–4.
62 Goetinck, *Peredur*, p. 22.

Conclusion

In 1959 Idris Llewelyn Foster wrote the following words regarding the then current state of the question of the relationship between Chrétien's tales and their Welsh equivalents: 'While the ... contention that Chrétien's poems were derived from the corresponding Welsh versions has now no advocates, the problem of the relationship has yet to be definitively resolved.'[1] More than sixty years later, the problem remains unresolved. Indeed, current scholarship now acknowledges that there is not one but three distinct problems – one for each pair of narratives. The present book makes no claim to elucidate the problems of *Gereint* and *Owein*, but I do step forward as the advocate for *Peredur*. The text we have, especially in its Long Version, is undeniably influenced by Chrétien's *Perceval*. The Short Version, however, is an entirely different matter. As I have aimed to show in Chapter 1, there is ample reason to believe that its three episodes can be treated as three independent compositions. Episode I may derive from a French source, although it seems more reasonable to assume the influence is the other way around, given the contrast between its use of fractal structures and the utter absence of such structure in the French-inspired Welsh Continuation. Episodes II and III, however, are a different matter. They have no Continental equivalents. Their fractal structure is particularly suited to memorisation and oral recital. Clinging to the notion that they represent mere interpolations badly fitted into a narrative borrowed from a French source, rather than stand-alone native Welsh tales, in the face of all the available evidence to contrary, and the complete lack of supporting evidence, would be illogical.

The present book began with the following theses:

- *Peredur* is not a Grail romance.
- *Peredur* is not a romance.

The following theses may be added to the list, as a conclusion to the present study:

- *Peredur* is not a single narrative.
- *Peredur* Episodes I to III not only show no trace of stylistic incompetence, but they do demonstrate structural virtuosity.
- *Peredur* Episodes I to III are anchored in Welsh historical, literary, legal and cultural context.
- *Peredur* Episodes I to III originated in Wales.

The identification of fractal structure in Episodes I to III has provided additional support to the view that the Short Version of *Peredur* was Welsh in origin. It is also apparent from the discussion of both the plot of the episodes and their geographical settings (see Chapter 2), that they represent separate, independent narratives. In Episode I Peredur stays close to home, where everyone he meets knows him and many belong to his kin group. He behaves according to rules of behaviour dictated by Welsh law, as we have seen in Chapter 5. He falls in love with a besieged young countess, whose court is sparsely fed by a destitute nunnery, which appears to be a reflection of real-world problems of female monastic houses in Wales and the March. Receiving training at the houses of two uncles and with the warrior-women of Gloucester (whose designation in modern translations as 'witches' might not be accurate), he returns to Arthur's court a proper warrior, capable of casually and almost accidentally avenging the insult that he had received from Cai.

In Episode II he travels far away, to lands where he is unknown, and possibly to the East. He keeps his oath not to speak to any Christian throughout, converts some non-Christians on the way, and ultimately returns to Arthur's court where he is not recognised. Angharad's greeting to him, deploring his mute state, once again echoes Welsh law.

Episode III is the only story in the Short Version to have otherworldly, supernatural elements, with its proliferation of monsters and unexplained marvels. It is even more striking, therefore, that some of the landscapes in it can be given Welsh prototypes: the cairn, as well as the windmills and watermills. The Empress of Constantinople (whose identity is explored in Chapter 3) may well provide another anchor to Welsh and Marcher reality of the twelfth century, if she is, indeed, an allusion to Empress Matilda, heir of Henry I.

CONCLUSION

As mentioned in the Introduction, it is not the objective of *This is Not a Grail Romance* to provide a full-scale companion to *Historia Peredur vab Efrawc*, nor to explain every aspect of the text, as we have it, which might cause difficulties of interpretation for a modern reader. Rather, it aims to re-open some questions and offer some solutions to perceived problems in the text. The primary foundation on which the arguments here have been built is that the text should not be read in light of the Continental Grail tradition. This book is intended as a starting point for reading *Peredur* on its own merits, in its own cultural, literary and historical context. I hope that I have succeeded in showing that when read that way, the text makes much more sense. The result is that understanding *Peredur* seems to presuppose a willingness to take it as a native Welsh creation, influenced by Anglo-Norman French cultural or literary conventions only insofar as general cultural influence from the Norman world would have seeped into Wales in the twelfth and thirteenth centuries. Episodes I to III of *Peredur* are therefore Welsh, or at best, Marcher, and there seems to be a certain poetic symmetry to the narratives of *Peredur* and of Peredur. After a rather lengthy sojourn on the Continent as a presumed Continental creation, *Peredur* appears to have finally returned to Wales – if not quite as its eponymous hero does at the conclusion of each series of adventures – to Arthur's court at Caerleon.

Note

[1] Foster, '*Gereint*, *Owein*, and *Peredur*', p. 192.

Bibliography

Manuscripts
Aberystwyth, NLW, Peniarth 1 (Black Book of Carmarthen, c.1250)
Aberystwyth, NLW, Peniarth 3ii (c.1275–1325)
Aberystwyth, NLW, Peniarth 4–5 (White Book of Rhydderch, c.1350)
Aberystwyth, NLW, Peniarth 7 (s. xiii^2)
Aberystwyth, NLW, Peniarth 8 (s. xiii/xiv)
Aberystwyth, NLW, Peniarth 10 (s. $xiv^{med.}$)
Aberystwyth, NLW, Peniarth 14ii (s. xiv^1)
Aberystwyth, NLW, Peniarth 15 (s. xiv/xv)
Aberystwyth, NLW, Peniarth 50 (Glamorgan, s. $xv^{med.}$)
Oxford, Jesus College, MS 111 (Red Book of Hergest, c.1382×1400)
Oxford, Jesus College MS 119 (Book of the Anchorite, 1346)
London, British Library, Cotton Cleopatra B.v (s. xiv)

Primary Sources
Benson, Larry D. (ed.), *King Arthur's Death: The Middle English Stanzaic Morte Arthur and Alliterative Morte Arthure*, revised by E. E. Foster, Middle English Texts (Kalamazoo: Medieval Institute Publications, Western Michigan University, for TEAMS, in association with the University of Rochester, 1994).
Blum, Owen J. (trans.), *Peter Damian: Letters*, 6 vols (Washington WA: Catholic University of America Press, 1989–2005).
Bromwich, Rachel (ed.), *Trioedd Ynys Prydein*, 2nd edn (Cardiff: University of Wales Press, 1978).
Bromwich, Rachel, and D. Simon Evans (eds), *Culhwch and Olwen: An Edition and Study of the Oldest Arthurian Tale* (Cardiff: University of Wales Press, 1992).
Bryant, Nigel (trans.), *The Complete Story of the Grail: Chrétien de Troyes' Perceval and its Continuations* (Cambridge: D. S. Brewer, 2015), pp. 79–235.
Chrétien de Troyes, *The Story of the Grail (Li Contes del Graal) or Perceval*, ed. by R. T. Pickens, trans. by W. W. Kibler (New York and London: Garland, 1990).

Chrétien de Troyes, *Arthurian Romances*, trans. by W. K. Kibler (London: Penguin Books, 1991).
Chrétien de Troyes, *Le Chevalier au Lion (Yvain)*, in C. Méla (ed.), *Chrétien de Troyes: Romans* (Paris: Livre de Poche, 1994).
Chrétien de Troyes, *Le Conte du Graal*, in C. Méla (ed.), *Chrétien de Troyes. Romans* (Paris: Livre de Poche, 1994).
Dafydd ap Gwilym project website, Swansea University, *www.dafyddapgwilym.net* (last accessed 3 February 2023).
Davies, Sioned (trans.), *The Mabinogion* (Oxford: Oxford University Press, 2007).
Digitaal Wetenschapshistorisch Centrum/Digital Web Centre for the History of Science in the Low Countries (Koninklijke Nederlandse Akademie van Wetenschappen), *www.dwc.knaw.nl* (last accessed 3 February 2023).
Ford, P. K. (ed.), *Manawydan uab Lyr* (Belmont: Ford & Bailie, 2000).
Gantz, Jeoffrey (trans.), *The Mabinogion* (Harmondsworth and New York: Penguin, 1976).
Geiriadur Prifysgol Cymru Online: A Dictionary of the Welsh Language (Aberystwyth: University of Wales Centre for Advanced Welsh and Celtic Studies, 2020), *https://geiriadur.ac.uk/gpc/gpc.html* (last accessed 3 February 2023).
Geoffrey of Monmouth, *Vita Merlini*, ed. and trans by Basil Clarke, *Life of Merlin* (Cardiff: University of Wales Press, 1973).
Geoffrey of Monmouth, *The History of the Kings of Britain*, ed. by Michael D. Reeve and trans. by Neil Wright (Woodbridge, 2007).
Goetinck, Glenys Witchard (ed.), *Historia Peredur vab Efrawc* (Cardiff: University of Wales Press, 1976).
Gwaith Cynddelw Brydydd Mawr, I, ed. by Nerys Ann Jones and Ann Parry Owen, Cyfres Beirdd y Tywysogion III (Cardiff: University of Wales Press, 1991).
Hughes, Ian (ed.), *Manawydan Uab Llyr: Trydedd Gainc y Mabinogi* (Cardiff: University of Wales Press, 2007).
Jones, Gwyn, and Thomas Jones (trans.), *The Mabinogion*, (London: Everyman [1949], 1993).
Jones, Thomas (ed.), *Ystoryaeu Seint Greal, Rhan I: Y Keis* (Cardiff: Gwasg Prifysgol Cymru, 1992).
Lewis, Charleton T., and Charles Short, *A Latin Dictionary* (Oxford: Oxford University Press, 1879).
Lewis, Henry, and P. Diverres (ed.), *Delw y Byd (Imago Mundi)* (Cardiff: University of Wales Press, 1928).
Luft, Diana, Peter Wynn Thomas and D. Mark Smith (eds), *Rhyddiaith Gymraeg 1300–1425* (2013), *www.rhyddiaithganoloesol.caerdydd.ac.uk* (last accessed 3 February 2023).
Malory, Sir Thomas, *La Morte d'Arthur*, ed. by P. J. C. Field, 2 vols (Cambridge: D. S. Brewer, 2013).
Meyer, Kuno (ed.), *Peredur ab Efrawc* (Leipzig: S. Hirzel, 1887).

Meyer, Kuno (ed. and trans.), 'The oldest version of *Tochmarc Emire*', *Revue Celtique*, 11 (1890), 433–57.

NLW, *www.library.wales* (last accessed 3 February 2023).

Petrovskaia, Natalia I. (ed.), *Delw y Byd: A Medieval Welsh Encyclopedia* (London: MHRA, 2020).

Poppe, Erich, and Regine Reck (ed.), *Selections from Ystorya Bown o Hamtwn* (Cardiff: University of Wales Press, 2009).

Rejhon, Annalee C. (ed. and trans.), *Cân Rolant: The Medieval Welsh Version of the Song of Roland*, University of California Publications in Modern Philology CXIII (Berkeley CA: University of California Press, 1984).

Reindel, K. (ed.), *Die Briefe des Petrus Damiani*, Monumenta Germaniae Historica: Briefe der deutschen Kaiserzeit IV, 4 vols (Munich: Monumenta Germaniae Historica, 1983–93).

Rhŷs, John, and J. Gwenogvryn Evans (ed.), *The Text of the Mabinogion and Other Welsh Tales from the Red Book of Hergest* (Oxford: Clarendon Press, 1887).

Roach, William (ed.), *The Continuations of the Old French Perceval of Chrétien de Troyes. Volume 1: The First Continuation* (Philadelphia PA: University of Pennsylvania Press, 1949).

Roberts, Brynley F. (ed.), *Breudwyt Maxen Wledic* (Dublin: DIAS, 2005).

Roberts, Sara Elin (ed. and trans.), *The Legal Triads of Medieval Wales* (Cardiff: University of Wales Press, 2007).

Rowland, Jenny (ed. and trans.), *Early Welsh Saga Poetry: A Study and Edition of the Englynion* (Cambridge: D. S. Brewer, 1990).

Thomas, Peter Wynn (ed.), *Peredur: Golygiad Lleiafol* (Cardiff: Cardiff University, 2000).

Thomson, Derick S. (ed.), *Branwen uerch Lyr* (Dublin: DIAS, 1961).

Thomson, Robert Leith (ed.), *Owein or, Chwedyl Iarlles y Ffynnawn* (Dublin: DIAS, 1968).

Thomson, Robert Leith (ed.), *Ystoria Gereint uab Erbin* (Dublin: DIAS, 1997).

Vitt, Anthony M., '*Peredur vab Efrawc*: Edited Texts and Translations of the MSS Peniarth 7 and 14 Versions' (MPhil thesis, University of Aberystwyth, 2010).

Williams, Robert (ed.), *Y Seint Greal: Selections from the Hengwrt MSS*, vol. 1 (London: Richards, 1876).

Williams, Robert (trans.), 'The History of Charlemagne: A Translation of "Ystorya de Carolo Magno", With a Historical and Critical Introduction', *Y Cymmrodor*, 20 (1907).

Williams, Stephen J. (ed.), *Ystoria de Carolo Magno o Lyfr Coch Hergest* (Cardiff: University of Wales Press, 1930).

Williams, Stephen J., and John Enoch Powell (ed.), *Cyfreithiau Hywel Dda yn ôl Llyfr Blegywryd (Dull Dyfed)*, 2nd edn (Cardiff: University of Wales Press, 1961).

Wright, Thomas (ed.), *The Book of the Knight of La Tour-Landry*, Early English Texts Society o.s. 33 (London: EETS, 1903).

Secondary Sources

Adamson, Melitta Weiss, *Food in Medieval Times* (Westport CT and London: Greenwood Press, 2004).

Akbari, Suzanne Conklin, *Idols in the East: European Representations of Islam and the Orient, 1100–1450* (Ithaca NY and London: Cornell University Press, 2009).

Armstrong, Harry, 'Giant Minds: A Study of the Emotions, Rational Thought and Self-Awareness of Giants in Middle High German and Middle Welsh Literature' (RMA thesis, Utrecht University, 2020).

Aronstein, Susan, 'Becoming Welsh: Counter-Colonialism and the Negotiation of Native Identity in *Peredur vab Efrawc*', *Exemplaria*, 17 (2005), 135–68.

Ashinof, Brandon K., and Ahmad AbuAkel, 'Hyperfocus: the Forgotten Frontier of Attention', *Psychological Research*, 85 (2021), 1–19.

Auerbach, Erich, *Mimesis: dargestellte Wirklichkeit in der abendländischen Literatur*, 5th edn (Bern: Dalp, 1971).

Bakhtin, Mikhail M., 'Forms of Time and of the Chronotope in the Novel: Notes toward a Historical Poetics', in Michael Holquist (eds), *The Dialogic Imagination: Four Essays by M. M. Bakhtin*, trans. by Caryl Emerson and Michael Holquist, University of Texas Press Slavic Series 1 (Austin TX: University of Texas Press, 1981), pp. 84–258.

Barber, Richard, *The Holy Grail: Imagination and Belief* (Cambridge MA: Harvard University Press, 2004).

Beem, Charles, and Miles Taylor (eds), *The Man Behind the Queen: Male Consorts in History* (New York: Palgrave Macmillan, 2014).

Bibbee, Evan J., 'Reticent Romans: Silence and Writing in *La Vie de Saint Alexis*, *Le Conte du Graal*, and *Le Roman de Silence*' (unpublished doctoral thesis, Louisiana State University, 2003), https://digitalcommons.lsu.edu/gradschool_dissertations/3768 (last accessed 22 May 2020).

Birkhan, Helmut, 'The Unholy Grail in Britain: A Remarkable Example of Secondary Paganisation', in Susanne Friede (ed.), *Autour du graal: Questions d'approche(s)* (Paris: Classiques Garnier, 2020), pp. 117–41.

Bitel, Lisa M., *Land of Women: Tales of Sex and Gender from Early Ireland* (Ithaca NY: Cornell University Press, 1996).

Bitel, Lisa M., *Women in Early Medieval Europe, 400–1100* (Cambridge: Cambridge University Press, 2002).

Blackburn, Stuart H., 'Oral Performance: Narrative and Ritual in a Tamil Tradition', *The Journal of American Folklore*, 94 (1981), 207–27.

Bollard, John K., 'The Structure of the Four Branches of the Mabinogi', *Transactions of the Honourable Society of Cymmrodorion 1974–75*, (1974–5), 250–76.

Bollard, John K., 'Theme and Meaning in *Peredur*', *Arthuriana*, 10 (2000), 73–92.
Brandsma, Frank, *The Interlace Structure of the Third Part of the Prose Lancelot* (Cambridge: D. S. Brewer, 2010).
Breeze, Andrew, 'Did a Woman Write the Four Branches of the Mabinogi', *Studi Medievali*, 38 (1997), 679–705.
Breeze, Andrew, '*Peredur son of Efrawg* and Windmills', *Celtica*, 24 (2003), 58–64.
Brodeur, A. G., 'The Grateful Lion: A Study in the Development of Medieval Narrative', *Publications of the Modern Language Association of America*, 39 (1924), 485–524.
Bromwich, Rachel, 'The Mabinogion and Lady Charlotte Guest', *Transactions of the Honourable Society of Cymmrodorion 1986*, (1986), 127–41.
Bruckner, Matilda Tomaryn, *Chrétien Continued: A Study of the* Conte du Graal *and its Verse Continuations* (Oxford: Oxford University Press, 2009).
Calis, Kiki, 'Peredur and the Valley of Changing Sheep' (unpublished RMA thesis, Utrecht University, 2018).
Carey, John, 'Time, Space, and the Otherworld', *Proceedings of the Harvard Celtic Colloquium*, 7 (1987), 1–27.
Carey, John, *Ireland and the Grail* (Aberystwyth: Celtic Studies Publications, 2007).
Carruthers, Mary, *The Book of Memory: A Study of Memory in Medieval Culture*, 2nd edn (Cambridge: Cambridge University Press, 2008).
Carruthers, Mary, and Ziolkowski, J. (ed.), *The Medieval Craft of Memory: An Anthology of Texts and Pictures* (Philadelphia PA: University of Pennsylvania Press, 2002).
Cartwright, Jane, 'The Desire to Corrupt: Convent and Community in Medieval Wales', in Diane Watt (ed.), *Medieval Women and their Communities* (Toronto: University of Toronto Press, 1997), pp. 20–48.
Cartwright, Jane, *Feminine Sanctity and Spirituality in Medieval Wales* (Cardiff: University of Wales Press, 2008).
Chakrabarty, Dipesh, *Provincializing Europe: Postcolonial Thought and Historical Difference* (Princeton NJ and Oxford: Princeton University Press, 2000).
Charles-Edwards, Thomas, *Early Irish and Welsh Kinship* (Oxford: Oxford University Press, 1993).
Charles-Edwards, Thomas, 'The Textual Tradition of Medieval Welsh Prose Tales and the Problem of Dating', in B. Maier and S. Zimmer (eds), *150 Jahre 'Mabinogion' – deutsch-walisische Kulturbeziehungen* (Tübingen: Max Niemeyer, 2001), pp. 23–39.
Charles-Edwards, Thomas, *Wales and the Britons, 350–1064* (Oxford: Oxford University Press, 2012).
Chibnall, Marjorie, *The Empress Matilda: Queen Consort, Queen Mother, and Lady of the English* (Oxford: Blackwell, 1991).

Cichon, Michael, 'Insult and Redress in Cyfaith Hywel Dda and Welsh Arthurian Romance', *Arthuriana* 10 (2000), 27–43.

Cichon, Michael, 'Mishandled Vessels: Heaving Drinks and Hurling Insults in Medieval Welsh Literature and Law', *Canadian Journal of History*, 43 (2008), 227–40.

Clanchy, Michael T., *England and Its Rulers, 1066–1307*, 4th edn (Malden, Oxford and Chichester: Wiley Blackwell, 2014).

Cooper, Helen, *The English Romance in Time: Transforming Motifs from Geoffrey of Monmouth to the Death of Shakespeare* (Oxford: Oxford University Press, 2004).

Cordo Russo, Luciana, 'Modulaciones de la materia artúrica: el episodio de la *Pesme Aventure* en *Yvain* y *Owein*', *Hermēneus. Revista de traducción e interpretación*, 21 (2019), 75–105.

Daniel, Glynn E., *The Prehistoric Chamber Tombs of England and Wales* (Cambridge: Cambridge University Press, 1950).

Davenport, Tony, 'Wales and Welshness in Middle English Romances', in *Authority and Subjugation in Writing of Medieval Wales* (Basingstoke: Palgrave Macmillan, 2008), pp. 137–58.

Davies, R. R., *The Age of Conquest: Wales, 1063–1415* (Oxford: Oxford University Press, 1987).

Davies, Sioned, 'Storytelling in Medieval Wales', *Oral Tradition*, 7/2 (1992), 231–57.

Davies, Sioned, *The Four Branches of the Mabinogi: Pedeir Keinc y Mabinogi* (Llandysul: Gomer Press, 1993).

Davies, Sioned, *Crefft y Cyfarwydd* (Cardiff: University of Wales Press, 1995).

Davies, Sioned, 'Written Text as Performance: the Implications for Middle Welsh Prose Narratives', in Huw Pryce (ed.), *Literacy in Medieval Celtic Societies* (Cambridge: Cambridge University Press, 1998), pp. 133–48.

Davies, Sioned, 'Cynnyd Peredur vab Efrawc', in Sioned Davies and Peter Wynn Thomas (eds), *Canhwyll Marchogyon: Cyd-destunoli Peredur* (Cardiff: University of Wales Press, 2000), pp. 65–90.

Davies, Sioned, 'A Charming Guest: Translating the Mabinogion', *Studia Celtica*, 38 (2004), 157–78.

Davies, Sioned, 'Performing *Culhwch ac Olwen*', in Ceridwen Lloyd-Morgan (ed.), *Arthurian Literature XXI: Celtic Arthurian Material* (Cambridge: Boydell & Brewer, 2012), pp. 29–52.

Davies, Sioned, and Peter Wynn Thomas (eds), *Canhwyll Marchogyon: Cyd-destunoli Peredur* (Cardiff: University of Wales Press, 2000).

Donaldson, E. Talbot, 'Malory and the Stanzaic *Le Morte Arthur*', *Studies in Philology*, 47 (1950), 460–72.

Draak, Maartje, 'Review Roger Sherman Loomis, *The Grail from Celtic Myth to Christian Symbol* (Cardiff: University of Wales Press, 1963)', *Medium Aevum*, 35 (1966), 260–4.

Duby, Georges, 'Women and Power', in Thomas N. Bisson (ed.), *Cultures of Power: Lordship, Status, and Process in Twelfth-Century Europe* (Philadelphia PA: University of Pennsylvania Press, 1995), pp. 69–85.

Duffy, Seán, 'Henry II and England's Insular Neighbours', in C. Harper-Bill and Nicholas Vincent (eds), *Henry II: New Interpretations* (Cambridge: Boydell & Brewer, 2007), pp. 129–53.

Edel, Doris, 'The "Mabinogionfrage": Arthurian Literature between Orality and Literacy', in Hildegard L. C. Tristram (ed.), *(Re)Oralisierung* (Tübingen: Gunter Narr, 1996), pp. 311–33.

Edel, Doris, 'Medb of Crúachain and the Empress Matilda: literature and politics in 12th-century Leinster', *Zeitschrift für celtische Philologie*, 64 (2017), 19–58.

Ehrmantraut, Brigid, 'Of Mice and Mounds: Prehistoric Monuments in the Literature of Medieval Wales', *Cambrian Medieval Celtic Studies*, 81 (2021), 93–111.

Emery, Anthony, *Discovering Medieval Houses* (Oxford: Shire Publications, 2011).

Evans, D. Simon, *A Grammar of Middle Welsh* (Dublin: DIAS, 1964).

Eveleth, Phyllis B., and James M. Tanner, *Worldwide Variation in Human Growth*, 2nd edn (Cambridge: Cambridge University Press, 1990).

Fischer, Christina, 'Innensicht und Außensicht: Zur Figurenpsychologie in *Chwedyl Iarlles y Ffynnawn (Owein)*', in Cora Dietl Christoph Schanze, Friedrich Wolfzettel and Lena Zudrell (eds), *Emotion und Handlung im Artusroman* (Berlin/Boston: Walter de Gruyter 2017), pp. 99–115.

Foster, Idris Llewelyn, '*Gereint, Owein*, and *Peredur*', in Roger Sherman Loomis (ed.), *Arthurian Literature in the Middle Ages: A Collaborative History* (Oxford: Clarendon Press, 1959), pp. 192–205.

Foucault, Michel, *Ceci n'est pas une pipe* (Montpellier: Fata Morgana, [1973] 2010).

Foucault, Michel, 'Ceci n'est pas une pipe', trans. by R. Howard, *October*, 1 (1976), 6–21.

Fößel, Amalie, 'The Political Tradition of Female Rulership in Late Medieval Europe', in Judith M. Bennett and Ruth Mazo Karras (eds), *The Oxford Handbook of Women and Gender in Medieval Europe* (Oxford: Oxford University Press, 2013), pp. 68–83.

Fulton, Helen, 'The Encomium Urbis in Medieval Welsh Poetry', *Proceedings of the Harvard Celtic Colloquium*, 26/27 (2006–7), 54–72.

Fulton, Helen, 'Gender and Jealousy in *Gereint uab Erbin* and *Le Roman de Silence*', *Arthuriana*, 24 (2014), 43–70.

Fulton, Helen, 'The Geography of Welsh Literary Production in Late Medieval Glamorgan', *Journal of Medieval History*, 41 (2015), 325–40.

Furtado, Antonio L., 'Geoffrey of Monmouth: A Source of the Grail Stories', *Quondam et Futurus*, 1 (1991), 1–14.

Gardeła, Leszek, 'Amazons of the North? Armed Females in Viking Archaeology and Medieval Literature', in Alessia Bauer and Alexandra Pesch (eds),

Hvanndalir – Beiträge zur europäischen Altertumskunde und mediävistischen Literaturwissenschaft. Festschrift für Wilhelm Heizmann, Reallexikon der germanischen Altertumskunde – Ergänzungsbände 106 (Berlin: De Gruyter, 2018), pp. 391–428.

Gelly, Christophe 'Sir Arthur Conan Doyle's Sherlock Holmes Stories: Crime and Mystery from the Text to the Illustrations', *Cahiers victoriens et édouardiens*, 73 (Spring 2011), 93–106, *https://doi.org/10.4000/cve.2188* (last accessed 3 February 2023).

de Gendt, Anne-Marie, *L'Art d'éduquer les nobles damoiselles: Le Livre du Chevalier de la Tour Landry* (Paris: Champion, 2003).

Gimpel, Jean, *La révolution industrielle du Moyen Âge* (Paris: Editions du Seuil, 1975).

Goetinck, Glenys Witchard, 'The Female Characters in *Peredur*', *Transactions of the Honourable Society of Cymmrodorion*, (1966), 378–86.

Goetinck, Glenys Witchard, *Peredur: a Study of Welsh Tradition in the Grail Legends* (Cardiff: University of Wales Press, 1975).

Goetinck, Glenys Witchard, '*Peredur* … Upon Reflection', *Études Celtiques*, 25 (1988), 221–32, *https://doi.org/10.3406/ecelt.1988.1881* (last accessed 3 February 2023).

Google Maps, *www.google.com/maps* (last accessed 3 February 2023).

Goyette, Stefanie A., 'Milk or Blood? Generation and Speech in Chrétien de Troyes' *Perceval, ou le Conte du Graal*', *Arthuriana*, 26 (2016), 130–51.

Grant, Michael, *Constantine the Great: The Man and His Times* (New York: Barnes & Noble, 1993).

Grigsby, John L., 'A New Source of the *Livre du Chevalier de La Tour Landry*', *Romania*, 84 (1963), 171–208.

Grooms, Chris, *The Giants of Wales: Cewri Cymru* (Lewiston NY: Edwin Mellen Press, 1993).

Гуревич, А. Я. [Gurevich, Aaron], *Проблемы средневековой народной культуры* ('Problems of medieval popular culture') (Moscow: Искусство, 1981).

Gurevich, Aaron, *Medieval Popular Culture: Problems of Belief and Perceptions*, trans. by János M. Bak and Paul A. Hollingsworth (Cambridge: Cambridge University Press, 1988).

Гуревич, А. Я. [Gurevich, Aaron], *Средневековый Мир. Культура безмолствующего большинства* ('Medieval world: Culture of the silent multitude/majority') (Moscow: Искусство, 1990).

Guy, Ben, *Medieval Welsh Genealogy: An Introduction and Textual Study* (Woodbridge: Boydell Press, 2020).

Haist, Margaret, 'The Lion, Bloodline, and Kingship', in Debra Hassig (ed.), *The Mark of the Beast: The Medieval Bestiary in Art, Life, and Literature* (New York: Routledge, 2013; originally published by Garland Publishing, 1999), pp. 3–21.

Hamp, E. P., 'Mabinogi and Archaism', *Celtica*, 23 (1999), 96–110.

Hanley, Catherine, *Matilda: Empress, Queen, Warrior* (New Haven CT and London: Yale University Press, 2019).
Harfield, C. G., 'A Hand-List of Castles Recorded in the Domesday Book', *The English Historical Review*, 106 (1991) pp. 371–92.
Harris, Julian, 'The Rôle of the Lion in Chrétien de Troyes' *Yvain*', *PMLA*, 64/5 (1949), 1143–63.
Hemming, J., 'Ancient tradition or Authorial Invention? The "mythological" Names in the Four Branches', in J. F. Nagy (ed.), *Myth in Celtic Literatures* (Dublin: Four Courts Press, 2007), pp. 83–104.
Heng, Geraldine, *Empire of Magic: Medieval Romance and the Politics of Cultural Fantasy* (New York: Columbia University Press, 2003).
Henley, Georgia, and Joshua Byron Smith (ed.), *A Companion to Geoffrey of Monmouth*, Brill's Companions to European History 22 (Leiden: Brill, 2020).
Herlihy, David, 'Land, Family, and Women in Continental Europe, 701–1200', in Susan Mosher Stuard (ed.), *Women in Medieval Society* (Philadelphia PA: University of Pennsylvania Press, 1976), pp. 13–45.
Hinton, Thomas, *The* Conte du Graal *Cycle: Chrétien de Troyes's* Perceval*, the Continuations, and French Arthurian Romance* (Cambridge: D. S. Brewer, 2012).
Hodges, Kenneth, 'Haunting Pieties: Malory's Use of Chivalric Christian "Exempla" after the Grail', *Arthuriana*, 17 (2007), 28–48.
Hoffman Berman, Constance, 'Agriculture and Economies', in Mette Birkedal Bruun (ed.), *The Cambridge Companion to the Cistercian Order* (Cambridge: Cambridge University Press, 2012), pp. 112–24.
Horgan, A. D., 'The Grail in Wolfram's *Parzival*', *Medieval Studies*, 36 (1974), 354–81.
Hughes, Ian, 'Tripartite Structure in *Manawydan Uab Llyr*', in Mícheál Ó Flaithearta (ed.), *Proceedings of the Seventh Symposium of Societas Celtologica Nordica* (Uppsala: Uppsala Universitet, 2007), pp. 99–109.
Hunt, Tony, 'Some Observations on the Textual Relationship of *Li Chevaliers au Lion* and *Iarlles y Ffynnawn*', *Zeitschrift für Celtische Philologie*, 33/1 (1974), 93–113.
Hunt, Tony, 'The Lion and Yvain', in P. B. Grout et al. (eds), *The Legend of Arthur in the Middle Ages: Studies Presented to A. H. Diverres by Colleagues, Pupils and Friends* (Cambridge: D. S. Brewer, 1983), pp. 86–98.
Hunter, J., 'Dead Pigs, Place Names, and Sir John Rhŷs: Reconsidering the Onomastic Elements of *Kulhwch ac Olwen*', *Proceedings of the Harvard Celtic Colloquium*, 11 (1991), 27–36.
Huot, Sylvia, *Outsiders: The Humanity and Inhumanity of Giants in Medieval French Prose Romance* (Notre Dame IN: University of Notre Dame Press, 2016).
Hurlock, Kathryn, *Wales and the Crusades, c. 1095–1291* (Cardiff: University of Wales Press, 2011).
Huws, Daniel, *Medieval Welsh Manuscripts* (Aberystwyth: University of Wales Press and National Library of Wales, 2000).

Huws, Daniel, 'Y Pedair Llawsgrif Canoloesol', in Sioned Davies and Peter Wynn Thomas (eds), *Canhwyll Marchogyon: Cyd-destunoli Peredur* (Cardiff: University of Wales Press, 2000), pp. 1–9.

Jamroziak, Emilia, 'Centres and Peripheries', in Mette Birkedal Bruun (ed.), *The Cambridge Companion to the Cistercian Order* (Cambridge: Cambridge University Press, 2012) pp. 65–79.

Jarman, A. O. H., 'The Merlin Legend and the Welsh Tradition of Prophecy', in Rachel Bromwich, A. O. H. Jarman and Brynley F. Roberts (eds), *The Arthur of the Welsh: The Arthurian Legend in Medieval Welsh Literature* (Cardiff: University of Wales Press, 1991), pp. 117–45.

Jenkins, Dafydd, 'Medieval Welsh Idea of Law', *Tijdschrift voor Rechtsgeschiedenis/ Legal History Review*, 49/3–4 (1981), 323–48.

Johnson, L. P., 'The Grail-Question in Wolfram and Elsewhere', in D. H. Green et al. (eds), *From Wolfram and Petrarch to Goethe and Grass: Studies in Literature in Honour of Leonard Forster* (Baden-Baden: Koerner, 1982), pp. 83–102.

Jones, Aled Llion, *Darogan: Prophecy, Lament and Absent Heroes in Medieval Welsh Literature* (Cardiff: University of Wales Press, 2013).

Jones, Leslie, 'Heads or Grails? A Reassessment of the Celtic Origin of the Grail Legend', *Proceedings of the Harvard Celtic Colloquium*, 14 (1994), 24–38.

Jones, R. M., 'Narrative Structure in Medieval Welsh Prose Tales', in Ellis D. Evans, John G. Griffith and E. M. Jope (eds), *Proceedings of the Seventh International Congress of Celtic Studies* (Oxford: D. E. Evans: Distributed by Oxbow Books, 1986), pp. 171–198.

Kapphahn, Krista, 'Celtic Heroines: The Contributions of Women Scholars to Arthurian Studies in the Celtic Languages', *Journal of the International Arthurian Society*, 7 (2019), 120–39.

Karras, Ruth Mazo, *From Boys to Men: Formations of Masculinity in Late Medieval Europe* (Philadelphia PA: University of Pennsylvania Press, 2003).

Kelly, Douglas, *The Art of Medieval French Romance* (Madison WI: University of Wisconsin Press, 1992), pp. 282–3.

Kelly, Patricia, 'The *Táin* as Literature', in James P. Mallory (ed.), *Aspects of the Táin* (Belfast: December Publications, 1992), pp. 69–102.

Kenyon, John R., *The Medieval Castles of Wales* (Cardiff: University of Wales Press, 2010).

Knowles, David, and Richard Neville Hadcock, *Medieval Religious Houses: England and Wales* (London: Longman, 1971).

Kochman-Haładyj, Bożena, 'Low Wenches and Slatternly Queans: On Derogation of Women Terms', *Studia Anglica Resoviensia*, 4 (2007), 206–28.

Lacy, Norris J. (trans.), *The Death of Arthur*, Lancelot-Grail. The Old French Arthurian Vulgate and Post-Vulgate in Translation 7 (Cambridge: D. S. Brewer, 2010)

Lambert, Pierre-Yves, '*Style de traduction*: Les traductions celtiques de textes historiques', *Revue d'Histoire des Textes*, 24 (1994), 375–91.

Langdon, John, 'Water-Mills and Windmills in the West Midlands, 1086–1500', *Economic History Review*, 44 (1991), 424–44.

Langdon John, and James Masschaele, 'Commercial Activity and Population Growth in Medieval England', *Past & Present*, 190 (2006), 35–82.

Lee, John S., 'Grain Shortages in Late Medieval Towns', in Ben Dodds and Christian D. Liddy (eds), *Commercial Activity, Markets and Entrepreneurs in the Middle Ages* (Woodbridge: Boydell Press, 2011), pp. 63–80.

Lieberman, Max, *The Medieval March of Wales: The Creation and Perception of a Frontier, 1066–1283* (Cambridge: Cambridge University Press, 2010).

Lloyd, Sir John Edward, *A History of Wales: From the Earliest Times to the Edwardian Conquest*, 2 vols, 3rd edn (London: Longmans, 1948).

Lloyd-Morgan, Ceridwen, 'A study of *Y Seint Greal* in relation to *La Queste del Saint Graal* and *Perlesvaus*' (unpublished PhD thesis, University of Oxford, 1978).

Lloyd-Morgan, Ceridwen, 'Narrative Structure in *Peredur*', *Zeitschrift für celtische Philologie*, 38 (1981), 187–231.

Lloyd-Morgan, Ceridwen, 'Perceval in Wales: Late Medieval Welsh Grail Traditions', in Alison Adams, Armel H. Diverres and Karen Stern (eds), *The Changing Face of Arthurian Romance: Essays on Arthurian Prose Romance in Memory of Cedric E. Pickford* (Cambridge: Boydell Press, 1986), pp. 78–91.

Lloyd-Morgan, Ceridwen, 'Triadic Structures in the Four Branches of the *Mabinogi*', *Shadow*, 5 (1988), 3–11.

Lloyd-Morgan, Ceridwen, 'Medieval Welsh Tales or Romances? Problems of Genre and Terminology', *Cambrian Medieval Celtic Studies*, 47 (2004), 41–58.

Lloyd-Morgan, Ceridwen, 'Migrating Narratives: Peredur, Owain and Geraint', in Helen Fulton (ed.), *A Companion to Arthurian Literature* (Oxford and Malden: Wiley-Blackwell, 2009), pp. 128–56.

Lloyd-Morgan, Ceridwen, '*Historia Peredur ab Efrawg*', in Ceridwen Lloyd-Morgan and Erich Popp (eds), *Arthur in the Celtic Languages: the Arthurian Legend in Celtic Literatures and Traditions*, Arthurian Literature in the Middle Ages 9 (Cardiff: University of Wales Press, 2019) pp. 145–57.

Lloyd-Morgan, Ceridwen, '*Y Seint Greal*', in Ceridwen Lloyd-Morgan and Erich Poppe (eds), *Arthur in the Celtic Languages: the Arthurian Legend in Celtic Literatures and Traditions*, Arthurian Literature in the Middle Ages 9 (Cardiff, University of Wales Press, 2019), pp. 129–37.

Lloyd-Morgan, Ceridwen, and Erich Poppe (eds), *Arthur in the Celtic Languages: the Arthurian Legend in Celtic Literatures and Traditions*, Arthurian Literature in the Middle Ages 9 (Cardiff, University of Wales Press, 2019).

Lloyd-Morgan, Ceridwen, and Erich Poppe, 'The First Adaptations from French: History and Context of a Debate', in Ceridwen Lloyd-Morgan and Erich

Poppe (eds), *Arthur in the Celtic Languages: the Arthurian Legend in Celtic Literatures and Traditions*, ed. by, Arthurian Literature in the Middle Ages 9 (Cardiff, University of Wales Press, 2019), pp. 97–101.

Loomis, Roger Sherman (ed.), *Arthurian Literature in the Middle Ages: A Collaborative History* (Oxford: Clarendon Press, 1959).

Loomis, Roger Sherman, *The Grail: From Celtic Myth to Christian Symbol* (Cardiff: University of Wales Press, 1963).

Lovecy, Ian C., 'The Celtic Sovereignty Theme and the Structure of *Peredur*', *Studia Celtica*, 12–13 (1977–8), 133–46.

Lovecy, Ian C., '*Historia Peredur ab Efrawg*', in Rachel Bromwich, A. O. H. Jarman and Brynley F. Roberts (eds), *Arthur of the Welsh: The Arthurian Legend in Medieval Welsh Literature* (Cardiff: University of Wales Press, 1991), pp. 171–82.

Lucas, Adam, *Ecclesiastical Lordship, Seigneurial Power and the Commercialization of Milling in Medieval England* (Farnham: Ashgate, 2014).

Luttrell, Claude, 'Le Conte del graal et d'autres sources françaises de l'*Historia Peredur*', *Neophilologus*, 87 (2003), 11–28.

Mac Cana, Proinsias, *Branwen Daughter of Llŷr: A Study of the Irish Affinities and of the Composition of the Second Branch of the Mabinogi* (Cardiff: University of Wales Press, 1958).

Mandelbrot, Benoît M., *The Fractal Geometry of Nature* (New York: Freeman, 1982).

Mandelbrot, Benoît M., 'A Geometry Able to Include Mountains and Clouds', in N. Lesmoir-Gordon (ed.), *The Colours of Infinity: The Beauty and Power of Fractals* (London: Springer, 2010), pp. 38–57.

Martina, Piero Andrea, 'Les aventures avec le lion: *Huon d'Auvergne*, *Yvain* (et les autres…)', *Reinardus: Yearbook of the International Reynard Society*, 26 (2014), 107–24.

Marx, Jean, *La légende arthurienne et le graal* (Paris: Presses universitaires de France, 1952; Geneva: Slatkine, 1996 reprint).

Marx, William, 'Middle English Texts and Welsh Contexts', in Ruth Kennedy and Simon Meecham-Jones (eds), *Authority and Subjugation in Writing of Medieval Wales* (Basingstoke: Palgrave Macmillan, 2008), pp. 13–26.

Mayer, Hans Eberhard, 'Studies in the History of Queen Melisende of Jerusalem', *Dumbarton Oaks Papers*, 26 (1972), 93–182.

McLaughlin, Megan, 'The Woman Warrior: Gender, Warfare and Society in Medieval Europe', *Women's Studies: An Interdisciplinary Journal*, 17 (1990), 193–209.

McMullen, A. Joseph, 'Three Major Forts to Be Built for Her: Rewriting History through the Landscape in *Breuddwyd Maxen Wledig*', *Proceedings of the Harvard Celtic Colloquium*, 31 (2011), 225–41.

McMullen, A. Joseph, 'The Communication of Culture: Speech and the "Grail" Procession in *Historia Peredur vab Efrawc*', *Arthuriana*, 23 (2013), 26–44.

Mehrotra, R. R., 'Fluidity in Kinship Terms of Address in Hindi', *Anthropological Linguistics*, 19 (1977), 123–5.

Meredith-Jones, Cyril, 'The Conventional Saracen of the Songs of Geste', *Speculum*, 17 (1942), 201–25.

Middleton, R., 'Chwedl Gereint ab Erbin', in Rachel Bromwich, A. O. H. Jarman and Brynley F. Roberts (eds), *Arthur of the Welsh* (Cardiff: University of Wales Press, 1991), pp. 150–1.

Miles-Watson, Jonathan, *Welsh Mythology: A Neostructuralist Analysis* (Amherst NY: Cambria Press, 2010).

Morgans, Lowri, '*Peredur son of Efrawg*: The Question of Translation and/or Adaptation', in Leah Tether and Johnny McFadyen, with Keith Busby and Ad Putter (eds), *A Handbook of Arthurian Romance: King Arthur's Court in Medieval European Literature* (Berlin: De Gruyter, 2017), pp. 403–14.

Muckerheide, Ryan, 'The English Law of Treason in Malory's *Le Morte Darthur*', *Arthuriana*, 20 (2010), 48–77.

Murphy, G. Ronald, *Gemstone of Paradise: The Holy Grail in Wolfram's Parzival* (Oxford: Oxford University Press, 2006).

Ngũgĩ wa Thiong'o, *Decolonizing the Mind: The Politics of Language in African Literature* (Portsmouth: Heinemann Educational Books, 1986).

Niehues, Jan, 'All The King's Men? On Celtic Board-games and Their Identification', in Franziska Bock, Dagmar Bronner and Dagmar Schlüter (eds), *Allerlei Keltisches. Studien zu Ehren von Erich Poppe: Studies in Honour of Erich Poppe* (Berlin: curach bhán, 2011), pp. 45–60.

Nitze, William A., 'The Sister's Son and the *Conte del Graal*', *Modern Philology*, 9 (1912), 1–32.

Nitze, William A., 'Yvain and the Myth of the Fountain', *Speculum*, 30 (1955), 170–9.

Norris, Ralph, 'Malory and His Sources', in Megan G. Leitch and Cory James Rushton (eds), *A Companion to Malory* (Cambridge: D. S. Brewer, 2019), pp. 32–52.

O'Donnell, Thomas Charles, 'The Affect of Fosterage in Medieval Ireland' (unpublished PhD thesis, University College London, 2016).

Ó hUiginn, Ruairí, 'The Background and Development of *Táin Bó Cúailnge*', in James P. Mallory (ed.), *Aspects of the Táin* (Belfast: December Publications, 1992), pp. 29–67.

Ong, Walter J., *Orality and Literacy: The Technologizing of the Word* (London and New York: Methuen, 1982).

Over, Kirsten Lee, *Kingship, Conquest, and Patria: Literary and Cultural Identities in Medieval French and Welsh Arthurian Romance* (New York: Routledge, 2005).

Over, Kirsten Lee, 'Transcultural Change: Romance to *Rhamant*', in Helen Fulton (ed.), *Medieval Celtic Literature and Society* (Dublin and Portland OR: Four Courts Press, 2005), pp. 183–204.

Oyetade, Solomon Oluwọle, 'A Sociolinguistic Analysis of Address Forms in Yoruba', *Language in Society*, 24 (1995), 515–35.

Padel, Oliver J., *Arthur in Medieval Welsh Literature* (Cardiff: University of Wales Press, 2013).

Parins, Marylyn (ed.), *Sir Thomas Malory: The Critical Heritage* (London and New York: Routledge, 1987).

Patterson, Robert B., *The Earl, The Kings and the Chronicler: Robert Earl of Gloucester and the Reigns of Henry I and Stephen* (Oxford: Oxford University Press, 2019).

Petrovskaia, Natalia I., 'Dating *Peredur*: New Light on Old Problems', *Proceedings of the Harvard Celtic Colloquium*, 29 (2009), 223–43.

Petrovskaia, Natalia I., 'Oaths, Pagans and Lions: Arguments for a Crusade Sub-Narrative in *Historia Peredur fab Efrawc*', *Poetica*, 77 (2012), 1–26.

Petrovskaia, Natalia I., *Medieval Welsh Perceptions of the Orient* (Turnhout: Brepols, 2015).

Petrovskaia, Natalia I., 'Cross-legged Gods and One-legged Foresters', in Franca Ela Consolino, Lucilla Spetia and Francesco Marzella (eds), *Aspetti del meraviglioso nelle letterature medievali. Aspects du merveilleux dans les littératures médiévales – Medioevo latino, romanzo, germanico e celtico* (Turnhout: Brepols, 2016), pp. 357–69.

Petrovskaia, Natalia I., 'Les Cisterciens transmetteurs de littérature vernaculaire. Le cas gallois', in Anne-Marie Turcan-Verkerk, Dominique Stutzmann, Thomas Falmagne and Pierre Gandil (eds), *Les Cisterciens et la transmission des textes (XIIe–XVIIIe siècles)* (Turnhout: Brepols, 2018), pp. 355–79.

Petrovskaia, Natalia I., 'Où va-t-on pour son aventure? Mondes connus et mondes inconnus dans le roman chevaleresque au Moyen Âge', in Danielle Buschinger, Mathieu Olivier, Till Kuhnle, Florent Gabaude, Marie-Geneviève Grossel and Pierre Levron (eds), *Ce qui advient … les déclinaisons de l'aventure – Actes du Colloque international des 14, 15 et 16 mars 2018 (Maison de la Culture d'Amiens)* (Amiens: Presses du Centre d'Etudes Médiévales de Picardie, 2018) pp. 160–9.

Petrovskaia, Natalia I., 'Real and Imaginary Towns in Medieval Wales', in Marie-Françoise Alamichel (ed.), *Les villes au Moyen Âge en Europe occidentale – (ou comment demain peut apprendre d'hier)* (Paris: LISAA Editeur, 2018), pp. 355–70.

Petrovskaia, Natalia I., 'Die Identität des Riesen in Owein – Die Herrin der Quelle', in Ronny F. Schulz and Silke Winst (eds), *Riesen: Entwürfe und Deutungen des Ausser/Menschlichen in mittelalterlicher Literatur* (Vienna: Fassbaender, 2020), pp. 419–38.

Petrovskaia, Natalia I., 'Peredur and the Problem of Inappropriate Questions', *Journal of the International Arthurian Society*, 9 (2021), 3–23, https://doi.org/10.1515/jias-2021-0002 (last accessed 3 February 2023).

Pickens, Rupert T., *The Welsh Knight: Paradoxicality in Chrétien's* Conte del Graal (Lexington KY: French Forum Publishers, 1977).

Poppe, Erich, '*Owein, Ystorya Bown*, and the problem of "relative distance": some methodological considerations and speculations', in Ceridwen Lloyd-Morgan (ed.), *Arthurian Literature XXI: Celtic Arthurian Material* (Woodbridge: Boydell & Brewer, 2004).

Poppe, Erich, 'Charlemagne in Wales and Ireland: Some Preliminaries on Transfer and Transmission', in Jürg Glauser and Susanne Kramarz-Bein (eds), *Rittersagas: Übersetzung, Überlieferung, Transmission*, Beiträge zur nordischen Philologie 45 (Tübingen: A. Francke, 2014) pp. 169–90.

Poppe, Erich, 'Ystorya Geraint fab Erbin', in Ceridwen Lloyd-Morgan and Erich Poppe (eds), *Arthur in the Celtic Languages: the Arthurian Legend in Celtic Literatures and Traditions*, Arthurian Literature in the Middle Ages 9 (Cardiff: University of Wales Press, 2019), pp. 132–44.

Poppe, Erich, 'Love, Sadness and Other Mental States in the Middle Welsh *Owain* (and Related Texts)', *Journal of the International Arthurian Society*, 8 (2020), 38–60.

Poppe, Erich, 'Ystoryaeu Seint Greal', in R. Rouse, S. Echard, H. Fulton, G. Rector and J.A. Fay (eds), *The Encyclopedia of Medieval Literature in Britain*, Wiley Online Library (2017), *https://doi.org/10.1002/9781118396957.wbemlb436* (last accessed 3 February 2023).

Poppe, Erich, and R. Reck, 'A French romance in Wales: *Ystorya Bown o Hamtwn*: Processes of Medieval Translations. Part I', *Zeitschrift für celtische Philologie*, 55 (2006), 122–80.

Pounds, N. J. G., *The Medieval Castle in England and Wales: A Social and Political History* (Cambridge: Cambridge University Press, 1990).

Reck, Regine, '*Owain* or *Chwedyl Iarlles y Ffynnawn*', in Ceridwen Lloyd-Morgan and Erich Poppe (eds), *Arthur in the Celtic Languages: the Arthurian Legend in Celtic Literatures and Traditions*, Arthurian Literature in the Middle Ages 9 (Cardiff: University of Wales Press, 2019), pp. 117–31.

Reilly, Bernard F., *The Kingdom of León-Castilla Under King Alfonso VII 1126–1157* (Philadelphia PA: University of Pennsylvania Press, 1998).

Rejhon, Annalee C., 'The "Mute Knight" and the "Knight of the Lion": Implications of the Hidden Name Motif in the Welsh *Historia Peredur vab Efrawc* and Chrétien de Troyes's *Yvain ou le Chevalier au Lion*', *Studia Celtica*, 20 (1985–6), 110–22.

Rhŷs, Sir John, *Studies in the Arthurian Legend* (Oxford: Clarendon Press, 1891).

Rhŷs, Sir John, 'The Nine Witches of Gloucester', in *Anthropological Essays presented to Edward Burnett Tylor in Honour of his 75th Birthday, Oct. 2, 1907*, ed. by contributors (Oxford: Clarendon Press, 1908), pp. 285–93.

Roberts, Brynley F., 'Ystoria', *Bulletin of the Board of Celtic Studies*, 26 (1974), 13–20.

Roberts, Brynley F., 'Rhai o gerddi ymddiddan Llyfr Du Caerfyrddin', in Rachel Bromwich and R. Brinley Jones (eds), *Astudiaethau ar yr Hengerdd/Studies in*

Old Welsh Poetry, Cyflwyneg I Syr Idris Foster (Cardiff: University of Wales Press, 1978), pp. 281–325.

Roberts, Brynley F., 'Oral Tradition and Welsh Literature: A Description and Survey', *Oral Tradition*, 3/1–2 (1988), 61–87.

Roberts, Brynley F., 'The Idea of a Welsh Romance', in Brynley F. Roberts, *Studies on Middle Welsh Literature* (Lewiston NY: Edwin Mellen Press, 1992), pp. 133–46.

Roberts, Brynley F., 'Tales and Romances', in Brynley F. Roberts (ed.), *Studies on Middle Welsh Literature* (Lampeter: Edwin Mellen Press, 1992), pp. 41–79.

Roberts, Brynley F., '*Peredur Son of Efrawg*: A Text in Transition', *Arthuriana*, 10 (2000), 57–72.

Roberts, Helen A., 'Court and *cyuoeth*: Chrétien de Troyes' *Erec et Enide* and the Middle Welsh *Gereint*', *Arthurian Literature*, 21 (2004), 53–72.

Roberts, Sara Elin, '"By the Authority of the Devil": The Operation of Welsh and English Law in Medieval Wales', in Ruth Kennedy and Simon Meecham-Jones (eds), *Authority and Subjugation in Writing of Medieval Wales* (Basingstoke: Palgrave Macmillan, 2008), pp. 85–97.

Roberts, Sara Elin, 'Seeking the Middle-Aged Woman in Medieval Wales', in Sue Niebrzydowski (ed.), *Middle-Aged Women in the Middle Ages* (Cambridge: Boydell and Brewer, 2011), pp. 25–36.

Rockel, Martin, 'Fiktion und Wirklichkeit im *Breuddwyd Macsen*', in Hildegard L. C. Tristram (ed.), *Medialität und mittelalterliche insulare Literatur* (Tübingen: Gunter Narr, 1992), pp. 170–81.

Rodway, Simon, 'The Where, Who, When and Why of Medieval Welsh Prose Tales: Some Methodological Considerations', *Studia Celtica*, 41 (2007), 47–89.

Rodway, Simon, 'The Mabinogi and the Shadow of Celtic Mythology', *Studia Celtica*, 52 (2018), 67–85.

Russell, Paul, 'Texts in Contexts: Recent Work on the *Mabinogi*', *Cambrian Medieval Celtic Studies*, 45 (2003), 59–72.

Russell, Paul, 'From Plates and Rods to Royal Drink-Stands in *Branwen* and Medieval Welsh Law', *North American Journal of Celtic Studies*, 1 (2017), 1–26.

Russell, Paul, '"Go and Look at Latin Books": Latin and the Vernacular in Medieval Wales', in Richard Ashdowne and Carolinne White (eds), *Latin in Medieval Britain*, Proceedings of the British Academy 206 (Oxford: Oxford University Press and The British Academy, 2017), pp. 213–46.

Russell, Paul, 'Geoffrey of Monmouth's Classical and Biblical Inheritance', in Georgia Henley and Joshua Byron Smith (eds), *A Companion to Geoffrey of Monmouth*, Brill's Companions to European History 22 (Leiden: Brill, 2020), pp. 67–104.

Russell, Paul, 'Three Notes on *Canu Urien*', *North American Journal of Celtic Studies*, 4/1 (2020), 48–78.

Russell, Thomas, *Byzantium and the Bosporus: A Historical Study, From the Seventh Century BC until the Foundation of Constantinople* (Oxford: Oxford University Press, 2017).

Sala, Nicoletta, 'Fractal Geometry in the Arts: An Overview Across the Different Cultures', in Miroslav M. Novak (ed.), *Thinking in Patterns: Fractals and Related Phenomena in Nature* (New Jersey, London: World Scientific, 2004), pp. 177–88.

Salmon, John, 'The Windmill in English Medieval Art', *Journal of the British Archaeological Association*, 3rd series, 6 (1941), 88–102.

Saunders, Corinne J., *The Forest of Medieval Romance: Avernus, Broceliande, Arden* (Cambridge: D. S. Brewer, 1993).

Sayers, William 'An Archaic Tale-Type Determinant of Chrétien's Fisher King and Grail', *Arthuriana*, 22 (2012), 85–101.

Scherb, Victor I., 'Assimilating Giants: The Appropriation of Gog and Magog in Medieval and Early Modern England', *Journal of Medieval and Early Modern Studies*, 32 (2002), 59–84.

Schulz, Muriel R., 'The Semantic Derogation of Women', in Barrie Thorne and Nancy Henley (eds), *Language and Sex* (Rowley: Newbury House, 1975), pp. 64–75.

Schweich, Marianne, and Christopher Knüsel, 'Bio-Cultural Effects in Medieval Populations', *Economics & Human Biology*, 1 (2003), 367–77.

Sims-Williams, Patrick, 'Some Functions of Origin Stories in Early Medieval Wales', in T. Nyberg et al. (eds), *History and Heroic Tale: A Symposium* (Odense: Odense University Press, 1985), pp. 97–131.

Sims-Williams, Patrick, 'The Irish Geography of *Culhwch ac Olwen*', in D. Ó Corráin et al. (eds), *Sages, Saints and Storytellers: Celtic Studies in Honour of James Carney* (Maynooth: An Sagart, 1989), pp. 412–26.

Sims Williams, Patrick, 'The Early Welsh Arthurian Poems', in Rachel Bromwich, A. O. H. Jarman and Brynley F. Roberts (eds), *The Arthur of the Welsh: The Arthurian Legend in Medieval Welsh Literature* (Cardiff: University of Wales Press, 1991), pp. 33–71.

Sims-Williams, Patrick, 'The Death of Urien', *Cambrian Medieval Celtic Studies*, 32 (1996), 25–56.

Sims-Williams, Patrick, *Irish Influence on Welsh Literature* (Oxford: Oxford University Press, 2011).

Sims-Williams, Patrick, 'Dating the poems of Aneirin and Taliesin', *Zeitschrift für celtische Philologie*, 63 (2016), 163–234.

Smith, Joshua Byron, '"Til þat he neȝed ful neghe into þe Norþe Walez": Gawain's Postcolonial Turn', *The Chaucer Review*, 51 (2016), 295–309.

Smith, Llinos Beverly, 'Fosterage, Adoption, and God-Parenthood: Ritual and Fictive Kinship in Medieval Wales', *Welsh History Review/Cylchgrawn hanes Cymrui*, 16 (1992), 1–35.

Spivak, Gayatri Chakravorty, 'Can the Subaltern Speak?', in Cary Nelson and Lawrence Grossberg (eds), *Marxism and the Interpretation of Culture* (Urbana IL and Chicago IL: University of Illinois Press, 1988), pp. 271–313.

Stacey, Robin Chapman, 'Law and Literature in Medieval Ireland and Wales', in Helen Fulton (eds), *Medieval Celtic Literature and Society* (Dublin: Four Courts Press, 2005), pp. 65–82.

Staccy, Robin Chapman, *Law and the Imagination in Medieval Wales* (Philadelphia PA: University of Pennsylvania Press, 2018).

Stacey, Robin Chapman, 'Gender and the Social Imaginary in Medieval Welsh Law', *Journal of the British Academy*, 8 (2020), 267–93.

Stalls, William Clay, 'Queenship and Royal Patrimony in Twelfth-Century Iberia: the Example of Petronilla of Aragon', in Theresa M. Vann (ed.), *Queens, Regents and Potentates* (Cambridge: Academia Press, 1993), pp. 49–61.

Stewart, Ian, 'The Nature of Fractal Geometry', in N. Lesmoir-Gordon (ed.), *The Colours of Infinity: The Beauty and Power of Fractals* (London: Springer, 2010), pp. 2–23.

Stolz, Michael, 'Wolfram von Eschenbach's *Parzival*: Searching for the Grail', in Leah Tether and Johnny McFadyen, with Keith Busby and Ad Putter (eds), *A Handbook of Arthurian Romance: King Arthur's Court in Medieval European Literature* (Berlin: De Gruyter, 2017), pp. 443–59.

Szkilnik, Michelle, 'Medieval Translations and Adaptations of Chrétien's Works', in Norris J. Lacy and Joan T. Grimbert (eds), *A Companion to Chrétien de Troyes*, Arthurian Studies LXIII (Cambridge: Brewer, 2005), pp. 203–13.

Theuerkauf, Marie-Louise, 'Dragon Slayers and Lion Friends: Intertextual Considerations in *Tochmarc Emire*', *Aigne*, 5 (2014), 80–94.

Thomas, Peter Wynn, 'Cydberthynas y Pedair Fersiwn Ganoloesol', in Sioned Davies and Peter Wynn Thomas (eds), *Canhwyll Marchogyon: Cyd-destunoli Peredur* (Cardiff: University of Wales Press, 2000), pp. 10–49.

Thurneysen, Rudolf, 'Review of Mary Rh. Williams, *Essai sur la composition do roman gallois de Peredur*, Paris, Champion, 1909', *Zeitschrift für celtische Philologie*, 8 (1912), 185–9.

Valade, Isabelle, Luciana Cordo Russo and Lee Raye, 'Uses of the Supernatural in the Middle Welsh *Chwedyl Iarlles y Ffynnawn*', *Mirabilia: electronic journal of antiquity and middle ages*, 23 (2016), 168–88, *www.raco.cat/index.php/Mirabilia/article/view/321023* (last accessed 4 February 2023).

Van Enghen, John, 'Epilogue: Positioning Women in Medieval Society, Culture, and Religion', in Kathryn Kerby-Fulton, Katie Ann-Marie Bugyis and John Van Engen (eds), *Women Intellectuals and Leaders in the Middle Ages* (Cambridge: Boydell and Brewer, 2020) pp. 397–401.

Vaughan, Theresa A., *Women, Food, and Diet in the Middle Ages: Balancing the Humours* (Amsterdam: Amsterdam University Press, 2020).

Whitaker, Muriel A., 'Otherworld Castles in Middle English Arthurian Romance', in Robert Liddiard (ed.), *Late Medieval Castles* (Woodbridge: Boydell & Brewer, 2017), pp. 393–408.

White, Donna R., 'The Crimes of Lady Charlotte Guest', *Proceedings of the Harvard Celtic Colloquium*, 15 (1995), 242–9.

Williams, David H., *The Welsh Cistercians* (Leominster: Gracewing, 1997).

Williams, Harry F., 'The Unasked Questions in the *Conte del Graal*', *Medieval Perspectives*, 3 (1988), 292–302.

Williams, Mark, 'Magic and Marvels', in Geraint Evans and Helen Fulton (eds), *The Cambridge History of Welsh Literature* (Cambridge: Cambridge University Press, 2019), pp. 52–72.

Williams, Mary Rh., *Essai sur la composition do roman gallois de Peredur* (Paris: Champion, 1909).

Withycombe, Susan Mary, '"O mihti meiden! O witti wummon!": the early English Katherine as a model of sanctity', *Parergon*, 9 (1991), 103–15.

Woodacre, Elena (ed.), *A Companion to Global Queenship* (Leeds: ARC Humanities Press, 2018).

Wright, John K., *Geographical Lore of the Time of the Crusades: A Study in the History of Medieval Science and Tradition in Western Europe*, American Geographical Research Series XV (New York: American Geographical Society, 1925).

Zimmermann, Claudia, 'Between me and God! Interjections in the Middle Welsh *Ystoryaeu Seint Graal* "Stories of the Holy Grail" and their French Source Texts', in Axel Harlos and Neele Harlos (eds), *Adapting Texts and Styles in a Celtic Context: Interdisciplinary Perspectives on Processes of Literary Transfer in the Middle Ages: Studies in Honour of Erich Poppe* (Münster: Nodus Publikationen, 2016), pp. 185–94.

Index

A
Abergavenny 62
Aconbury 61
Adam of Usk 62
adanc 30, 70
　see also monster
age
　Peredur's 29, 48, 51–2, 66, 147
　female characters' 48, 138, 142–3, 145–7
　other characters 63, 86, 138, 147
　see also fosterage; Peredur; women
Ailill 86
　see also Medb
Albertus Magnus 33–4
Alfonso VI, king of Léon-Castille 86
Amesbury 62
Anagni 25
Angharad Law Eurog 17, 19, 20, 27, 28, 30, 66, 146, 154
Anglo-Norman 42, 127, 142, 64, 65
　cultural influence 67–8, 84, 87, 88, 92, 94, 155
　see also Wales, March of
anonymity *see* recognition of the hero
apples 6, 97–104
　see also bread; feast; food; poison
Arawn, king of Annwn 69
　see also Otherworld
armour 28, 29, 31, 33, 37, 101, 109
　Peredur's lack of 28, 29, 69

Arthur 21, 22, 24, 27, 28, 29, 38, 40, 67–8, 108–9
　knights of 4–5, 16, 21, 24, 28, 60, 68, 97, 99–100, 127
　land of 67, 69, 139
　see also Britain; Caerleon; court
audience (medieval) 6, 7, 15, 25, 28, 43, 60, 61, 63, 65, 68, 73, 83, 85–6, 89, 91, 97, 104, 105, 109–10, 119–20, 124, 125, 126–9, 138, 146
aurality 36
　see also orality; performance

B
Baldwin, king of Jerusalem 87
battle 20, 21, 22, 23, 27, 28, 30, 38 40, 65, 66, 67, 83, 86, 98, 107, 109, 112, 141, 142, 143
Battle of Lincoln 92
Bendigeidfran *see* Bran
Benedictines 60
　see also Cistercians; monastery; Usk Priory
Benoît de Sainte-Maure 147
Berkeley Castle 64
Black Book of Carmarthen 142, 144
　see also manuscripts
Black Oppressor 19, 29, 30, 60, 69

Blancheflor 23, 122
  see also countess; damsel; love
Bort 4–5
Black Serpent of the Cairn *see* cairn, monster of
Bran 42, 107–10
Branwen 122
Branwen uerch Lyr 70, 107, 108, 110
Breudwyt Macsen Wledic 36, 84
Brangor, king 5
bread 61, 62, 75
  see also food; Miller; mills
Britain 22, 68, 72, 91, 107, 108
Brittany 59
Brut y Saeson 90
Brutus 68
Buchedd Catrin 90
Buckland 62

C

Caerleon 24, 27, 59–60, 64, 65, 69, 72, 73, 85, 155
  see also court, of Arthur
Caer Loyw *see* Gloucester
Cantor set 43
  see also fractals; Sierpiński gasket
castle 60, 62–3, 65, 86, 107, 116
  architecture 60, 64–5, 141–2
  process of building (destructive effects) 65, 140–1
  in *Peredur* 2, 21, 23, 27, 36–7, 39, 40, 59–60, 61, 62–4, 104, 118, 121, 137–8, 139, 140, 145
  Norman 62–3, 64–5, 141–2
  see also court; house (manor); Fortress of Wonders
Castle of Pride 36
Cai 19, 21, 27, 60, 99
Cairn 69–70, 154
  monster of 29, 69, 83
  see also Carn Llidi
Cân Rolant 41, 90

Canu Urien
Carn Llidi 69
Cauldron of Rebirth 70, 107
  see also Branwen uerch Lyr; Grail
chanson de geste 102
Charlemagne Cycle, Welsh 18, 41, 43, 67, 79, 89–90
Chepstow Castle 64
Chevalier au lion 67, 117
Chevalier de la charrette 41
Chrétien de Troyes 1, 3, 4, 16, 17, 18, 20, 21, 23, 36, 39, 41, 42, 43, 59, 67, 97, 105, 107, 115, 117, 118, 119, 121, 127, 128, 129, 137, 153
  see also Chevalier au lion; Chevalier de la charrette; Conte du graal
Christianity 27–8, 37, 38, 66–8, 73, 142, 154
  see also Cistercians; monastery; nuns
chronotope 63, 65, 83
Cistercians 5, 60, 72
  see also Benedictines; monastery, Cistercian; nuns
colonialism 67–8, 124–7
combat *see* battle
compensation 28, 40, 119, 122
  see also insult; law
Conte du graal 1–2, 3, 4, 16–18, 20, 21, 23, 36, 37–43 *passim*, 49, 110, 115–18 *passim*, 121, 122–4, 126, 127, 128–9, 153
  see also Chrétien de Troyes; Continuations, of *Conte du graal*; Grail; Perceval (character)
Constantine I, emperor 91
Constantinople 68, 88, 89, 91
  Empress of 2, 3, 5, 6, 19, 31, 70, 71, 88, 91, 154
  terms in Welsh texts 6, 88–91
Continuations 43
  of *Peredur see Historia Peredur vab Efrawc*

INDEX

of *Conte du graal* 3, 39, 40, 41, 43, 107
  see also Chrétien de Troyes; *Conte du graal*
convent 62
  in *Peredur* 61, 62
  historical sizes 60–2
  see also monastery; nuns
conversion (to Christianity) 28, 66, 67, 68, 154
  see also Christianity; homage; non-Christians
countess 87, 147
  Countess of the Feats 29, 30, 42, 83, 84
  of the manor attacked by witches 63–5, 128, 138, 141, 146
  oppressed countess (Peredur's love) 19, 23–4, 48, 49, 60–1, 83, 141, 154
  see also damsel in distress; lady; women
cousin
  explaining the procession in *Peredur* 40, 127
  of Perceval 23, 115
  head of 40, 123
  see also fosterage; Peredur (character), uncles
court
  of Arthur 2, 6, 17, 19, 20, 21–3, 24, 27, 28, 29, 35, 36, 59, 60, 64, 73, 85, 97–8, 101, 115–16, 120, 121, 139, 154, 155
  of Peredur's uncles 2, 3, 22, 104, 105, 107, 109, 110, 119, 120, 121, 122, 124, 126, 128, 154
  see also uncles
  of the Witches of Gloucester 60, 65, 142, 146
  see also witches
Cronicl Turpin 41
  see also Charlemagne Cycle
crusades 66, 91–2

Cú Chulainn 144
Culhwch ac Olwen 40, 98, 116
cyfarwydd 34
cyfarwyddyd 34–5
Cynddelw Brydydd Mawr 108
Cynon 51, 139

D

Dafydd ap Gwilym 49, 145
damsel in distress 23, 97, 112, 133
  see also countess; women; Ugly Damsel
Delw y Byd 89, 90, 123
desert 139–40
  see also waste; wilderness
distain 23
dwarfs 17, 21, 24, 48

E

Edlym Gleddyf Goch 30, 83
emotion 19, 23, 74–5, 118, 147
empress *see* Constantinople, empress of; Matilda, empress
England 69, 71, 83, 84, 128, 149
  see also Anglo-Norman; Middle English; Wales

F

feast
  at Peredur's uncle's court 36–7
  of the poisoned apples 98–9, 100–1
  see also food; poison
Fisher King 23, 42, 107, 109, 113
Fortress of Wonders 39, 40
  see also castle
food 21, 60–1, 62, 64, 71–2, 98, 140–1
  see also apples; bread; feast
fosterage 48, 52, 131
  Peredur's foster-sister 22, 23, 48, 116, 118, 120, 131

179

fractals
    definition in mathematics 24, 43
    examples in nature 24
    mnemonic function 26, 31, 32, 34, 35
    in medieval art 25
    in *Historia Peredur* 20, 24–6, 27–31, 33, 35, 40
    in other medieval Welsh narratives 35
    see also Cantor set; Sierpiński gasket; triadic narrative structures; triads
France 108, 129
    culture 4, 155
Fulk, king of Jerusalem 87, 91

G
Galahad 4
Gawain/Gauvain 37–8, 39, 67, 98, 100–1, 104
    see also Gwalchmai
Gereint (text) see *Ystoria Gereint vab Erbin*
Geoffrey of Anjou 87
Geoffrey of Monmouth 67–8, 92, 102, 104
genealogies 84, 110
geography 43, 59–73 *passim*, 88, 128
    see also castles; landscape; Severn (river)
giants 67, 107, 144
    Gog and Magog 68
    in *Historia regum Britanniae* 67–8
    in *Historia Peredur* 27–8, 67–8, 137–8, 140, 154
    see also Bran; Ysbaddaden
Glamorgan 4, 73
Gloucester 59, 60, 63, 64, 65, 73, 85, 128, 142, 147
    Castle 65, 142
    see also castles; Robert, Earl of Gloucester; witches

Gloucestershire 61, 64
Gornemant of Gohort 21, 23
Grail 1, 4, 5, 6, 88, 105, 107, 109, 115, 122, 129
    procession 1, 22, 39, 105–6, 115, 118, 121, 122, 129
    grail romance tradition 1, 2, 4, 5, 20, 22, 40, 41, 42, 104, 105, 107, 153, 155
    see also Conte du graal; *Y Seint Greal*; *Queste del Saint Graal*; *Perlesvaus*
Guinevere 98, 99, 104
Guinganbresil 37
Gutun Owain 99
Gwair son of Gwystyl 97
Gwalchmai 19, 21, 24, 29, 31, 33, 36, 37–8, 40, 74–5, 97–8, 100, 101–2, 121–2
    see also Gawain/Gauvain
Gwenhwyfar 2, 21
    see also Guinevere
gwidonot see witches
Gwlad Ieuan Vendigeid 90
Gwyddbwyll 29, 38, 39

H
head 107
    in procession scene in *Peredur* 1, 22, 36, 40, 104, 105–7, 109, 110, 115, 119, 121, 123–4, 128, 129
    of Bran 107–8, 109, 110
    of Urien Rheged 109–10
    see also Bran; *Canu Urien*; Urien Rheged
Henry I, king of England 83, 87, 92, 154
Henry V, emperor of the Holy Roman Empire 83
hermitage 38–9

Historia Peredur vab Efrawc 1, 5–6, 18, 34, 61, 63, 73, 100, 102, 103–4, 110, 118, 119, 125–6, 127, 137, 139, 144, 153, 155
   Continuation 2, 15, 18, 20, 21, 36–40, 41, 115–16, 119, 120–1, 122, 126–7, 137, 141, 146, 153–4
   Episodes 16–18, 19, 20, 24, 26, 32, 33, 35, 40, 41, 43, 59, 71, 73, 83, 97, 127, 129, 154
      Episode I 20, 21-4, 28, 33, 35, 36, 37, 41, 60, 68, 71, 73, 83, 85–6, 87, 88, 92–3, 98, 100, 104, 105–6, 109, 116, 118, 120, 122, 123, 126, 129, 137, 138, 141, 153
      Episode II 20, 27–9, 35–6, 42, 66, 68, 71, 73, 92–3, 153, 154
      Episode III 20, 29–31, 35–6, 41, 42, 60, 68–71, 73, 83–8, 92–3, 119, 120, 137, 153, 154
   Long Version 2, 3, 15, 18, 41, 42, 102, 106, 116, 117, 122, 123, 127
   manuscripts of *see* manuscripts
   relationship to French text 2, 3–4, 5, 20, 21, 23, 36–40, 41, 42–3, 49, 67, 92, 115, 117–18, 119, 121–2, 123–4, 126–7, 128–9, 137, 153, 155
   Short Version 2, 3, 15, 18, 25, 31, 32, 33, 36, 40, 43, 59, 105, 117, 118, 129, 154
   structure 4, 6, 15–44 *passim*, 123–4, 127, 153, 154
   unity 2, 15–18, 19, 41, 42–3, 44–5, 97, 123–4, 127, 154
Historia regum Britanniae 67, 68, 92
   see also Geoffrey of Monmouth
Holy Roman Empire 83
Hospitallers 61
house 27, 31
   manor 22, 24, 63–5, 83, 138, 141
   see also castle; court
hunting 17, 29, 30, 69
hyperfocus 19

I

Chwedl Iarlles y Ffynnawn 4, 38, 59, 67, 70, 117, 122, 139, 140, 153
India 30, 68, 70, 72, 125
inheritance 28, 84–7, 91, 137
insult 2, 17, 21, 133, 154
   in asking questions 107, 126
   legal aspects 28, 107, 119, 120, 122
   to Queen Gwenhwyfar 2, 21, 101
   to the Black Oppressor 19
   verbal 37–8, 57, 122, 147
interlace (narrative technique) 37
Ireland 107, 113, 133, 144
   Irish literature 49, 52, 69–70, 86, 143–4
Italy 25, 94

J

Jerusalem 66, 91
   Latin Kingdom of 87, 91–2
   kings of 86, 91
   see also Baldwin; Fulk; Melisende
Joseph of Arimathea 5

K

Kei *see* Cai
knighthood 2, 21, 22, 52, 109, 130
knights 2, 5, 16, 20, 21, 22, 27–8, 28, 31, 33, 37, 38, 60, 75, 86, 97–8, 99, 101, 104, 117, 120, 141, 147
   conquered by Peredur 21, 22, 28, 33, 42
   twenty-four knights of Arthur's court 24, 98, 99–100

L

lady 24, 37, 40, 61, 64, 69, 122
  see also countess; women
Lancelot (character) 4
Lancelot (text) 39, 41
landscape 59–73 *passim*, 83, 88, 154
law 2, 21, 28, 34, 35, 49, 65, 84, 85, 94, 107, 110, 115, 116, 119–20, 121, 122, 124, 127, 128, 129, 154
  Blegywryd recension 11, 132
  legal triads 34, 119–20, 124
  in literature 21, 65, 85, 107, 120, 124
  see also inheritance; insult; muteness
Limebrook Priory 61, 62
lion 67
  as gatekeeper in *Peredur* 66, 67, 68
  grateful lion in *Owain* 67
Llanllugan 60
Llanllŷr 60
Llewelyn ab Iorwerth 110
love 19, 21, 24, 28, 30, 31, 37, 47, 66, 83, 86, 100, 146, 154
  see also hyperfocus; marriage

M

Mabinogi, Four Branches of 85, 98, 108, 110
  see also Branwen uerch Lyr; Manawydan uab Lyr; Pwyll Pendeuic Dyuet
Mabinogionfrage 4, 129
magic 2, 39, 67, 69, 116, 117, 133, 138, 140, 141
  gold-generating stone 29, 30, 69, 85
  invisibility 30, 70, 1
  individuals 70, 116, 138, 141, 142, 143, 144–5, 147
  see also monster; supernatural; witches
Magnus Maximus 84
  see also Breudwyt Macsen Wledic

Malory, Sir Thomas *see Morte Darthur*
Manawydan uab Lyr 35, 51, 98, 136, 139, 140, 141
Mandelbrot, Benoît (mathematician) 43
  see also Cantor set; fractals; Sierpiński, Wacław (mathematician); Sierpiński gasket
manuscripts 5, 21, 22, 41, 89–90, 97–8, 108, 110, 122, 123–4, 129, 142
  layout 16–17, 36, 47, 55
  of *Peredur* 2–4, 31, 32–3, 35–6, 42–3, 71–2, 73, 88–91, 101–2, 106, 107, 110, 117, 118, 120, 123–4, 126, 127, 147
  see also Black Book of Carmarthen; Peniarth 7; Peniarth 14; Peniarth 50; Red Book of Hergest; White Book of Rhydderch
marriage 2–3, 17, 22, 23, 69, 83, 84, 87
  see also Constantinople, empress of; love
Matilda, empress 83–4, 86, 87, 91–2, 154
Matilda of Canossa 94
Medb 86, 87, 93
Melisende, queen of Jerusalem 86, 87, 91
memory 17, 18, 31–5, 153
  cultural memory 1, 142
  in medieval Europe 32–4
  techniques 5, 26, 31–4, 35, 43
  see also repetition
Merlin 102
  see also Vita Merlini
Middle English 5, 57, 100, 102, 103
miller 31, 69, 71–2
mills 31, 59, 70–3, 81, 83, 88, 92, 154
Minchinhampton Priory 61

INDEX

mnemonic techniques *see* memory, techniques
Mort Artu (French prose text) 100, 103–4
Morte Darthur (Malory) 40, 98–100, 104
Le Morte Arthur (Middle English stanzaic text)
monastery 60, 62, 63, 154
    Cistercian 5, 60
    see also Cistercians; convent; nuns
monster 27, 28, 29, 30, 60, 66, 69–70, 83, 85, 144, 154
    see also magic
mound 30, 60, 69–70, 83
    Mound of Mourning 30, 69
mountain 40, 63, 64, 67, 68, 69, 139
muteness 28, 66, 154
    see also silence
Mute Knight 28
    see also Peredur (character)

N

non-Christians *see* giants
nunnery *see* convent
nuns 60–3

O

oath 27, 28, 66, 73, 154
orality 17, 18, 31–3, 35–6, 38, 40, 42, 43, 53–4, 109, 153
    see also aurality; mnemonic techniques
Otherworld 69–70, 73, 85, 138, 140, 154
    see also Arawn, king of Annwn; magic; monster; supernatural
Owein (text) *see Chwedl Iarlles y Ffynnawn*
Owain son of Urien (character) 4, 21, 29, 31, 33, 51, 97–8, 101, 109–10, 136, 139

P

Patryse of Irlande, Sir 98–9
Peckham, Archbishop 62
Pedwar Marchog ar Hugain Llys Arthur 'Twenty-four knights of Arthur's Court' 99–100
Pembrokeshire 69, 73
Peniarth 7 2, 3, 8, 17, 21, 31, 33, 35, 43, 55, 62, 71, 72, 73, 75, 88, 89, 91, 101, 106–7, 108, 116, 117, 118, 126, 129, 131
Peniarth 14 3, 8, 10, 55, 97–8, 101, 117–18, 131
Peniarth 50 4, 5, 88
    see also manuscripts; Red Book of Hergest; White Book of Rhydderch
penteulu 'chief of household troops' 23
Perceval (text) *see Conte du graal*
Peredur (character) 19, 23, 24, 29, 33, 35, 37, 39, 41, 43, 60, 66, 69, 72, 84, 85, 86, 92, 97–8, 100, 101, 109–10, 116, 118–19, 121–2, 123, 124, 125, 126–8, 138–9, 144–6, 147, 154, 155
    adventures 2, 3, 17, 19, 21–4, 27–31, 34, 38–40, 61, 63–4, 65 6, 66–8, 70–1, 86–7, 97, 104, 105–7, 109, 119–20, 137, 141–2, 144
    association with the Grail 4–6, 92, 104–5, 129
    love interests *see* love; marriage
    uncles 2, 3, 20, 21, 22, 23, 24, 28, 36, 52, 104–5, 107, 109, 110, 117–24 *passim*, 154
    relatives 22, 68, 85, 118; *see also* fosterage
    training 17, 22, 24, 60, 117–18, 121, 123, 137, 142, 144
    upbringing 2, 17, 21, 28, 84–5, 116, 138–40

Peredur (text) *see Historia Peredur vab Efrawc*
Pererinnod Siarlymaen 41, 90
performance 17–18, 31–3, 34, 36, 42–3, 53, 54, 127
see also orality
Perlesvaus 4, 107
Petronilla, queen of Aragon 86–7
Pinel le Savage 98–9
see also apples; Malory, Sir Thomas
place name 59, 85, 88, 89, 91, 128
poison spear 70, 98, 100, 101, 102, 103–4, 107, 111–12
see also apples; feast; spear
postcolonialism 125–7
priest 37, 38
priestesses, pagan 142
see also witches
priory 60, 61, 62
procession scene 3, 104–5
in *Peredur* 1, 22, 36, 40, 104, 105–6, 109, 110, 115–16, 118–19, 120–3, 124, 126, 127, 129
in *Conte du graal* 22, 39, 105, 107, 109, 115–16, 118, 121, 122, 123–4, 127–8
see also Grail; head; spear
prophecy 5, 40, 143, 144
Proud One of the Clearing 19, 24
wife of 19, 23, 24
Pwyll (character) 69
Pwyll Pendeuic Dyuet 68–9, 133–4

Q
quest 38
Queste del Saint Graal 4
questions 6, 37, 60, 105, 107, 115, 117–29 *passim*
queenship 91–2

R
Ramiro II, king of Aragon 86–7

Ramon Berenguer, count of Barcelona 87
recognition of the hero 28–9, 37, 68, 154
Red Book of Hergest 2, 3, 21, 22, 31, 33, 35, 36, 42, 47, 72, 88, 89, 101, 106, 107, 108, 110, 118, 119, 120, 123, 127, 129
repetition 18, 24, 26, 32, 33, 40, 121, 127–8
see also memory
Robert, Earl of Gloucester 83–4, 92
Round Valley 27, 28, 66–7, 68
see also giants

S
Scáthach 144
serpent *see* monster
Severn 63, 64, 72–3, 88, 142
sheep 30, 70, 85
Sierpiński, Wacław (mathematician) 50
Sierpiński gasket 24–5, 26, 50
silence 105–6, 115–29 *passim*
see also muteness
Sons of the King of Suffering 29, 30, 70, 119
sovereignty 70, 83, 84, 87, 125
spear 63, 109
associated with Bran 70, 108
in the procession 1, 22, 37, 105–9, 121, 123
of the cave monster 30, 70
see also poison; sword
steward *see distain*
Strata Florida 60
Strata Marcella 60
see also Cistercians; monastery
supernatural 60, 68, 70, 73, 138, 141, 144, 154
see also magic; monster; Otherworld; witches
sword 22, 30, 56

T

Táin Bó Cúailnge 86, 87
Theodora, empress 91
tent maiden *see* Proud One of the Clearing, wife of
Tochmarc Emire 144
tournament 31
   see also battle
triadic narrative structures 16, 20, 23, 24–32 *passim*, 34, 40, 44, 127, 142
   see also fractals
triads 4–6, 34, 35, 43, 88, 98, 99, 103, 107–8, 110, 119–20, 124
   see also fractals

U

Ugly Damsel 17, 20, 36, 38, 115
Urraca, queen of Léon-Castille 86
Usk 60, 63
Üsküdar/Scutari 91

V

Vita Merlini 102, 103, 104
   see also Geoffrey of Monmouth; *Historia regum Britanniae*
Vulgate Cycle 100

W

Wace 147
Wales 4, 5, 31, 40, 60, 64, 65, 68, 69, 72, 73, 84, 85, 86, 87, 91–2, 103, 125, 128, 129, 141, 142, 154, 155
   March of 61–4, 65, 69, 72, 83–4, 85–6, 87, 88, 92, 128, 137, 141–2, 154, 155
waste (land) 22–3, 24, 63–5, 138–41
   see also wilderness

Welsh
   authors 25, 39, 127
   language 5, 68, 103, 109, 122, 137, 145, 146
   redactors 18, 38, 39, 42, 43
   texts 1–2, 3, 4, 5, 6, 17, 18, 28, 31, 32, 34, 35, 37, 40, 43, 67–8, 69, 70, 73, 84, 89, 98, 99, 100, 109, 110, 116, 122, 123, 124, 137, 138, 139, 143, 144, 146
   see also audience (medieval); *cyfarwydd*; *cyfarwyddyd*; law; Wales
White Book of Rhydderch 2, 3, 21, 22, 31, 35–6, 42, 47, 55, 72, 88, 89, 101, 106, 110, 118, 119, 120, 123, 127, 129, 131
wilderness 27, 139
   see also desert; waste (land); wilderness
windmills *see* mills
witches 141–2
   of Gloucester 17, 24, 37, 40, 60, 63–5, 83, 115, 128, 137, 141, 142, 144, 145, 147, 154
   see also Gloucester; women
Wolfram von Eschenbach 105
women 23, 24, 37, 47–8, 60, 61, 63–4, 83–7, 91–2, 102, 104, 116, 137–47 *passim*
   see also countess; Empress of Constantinople; nuns; queenship; witches; supernatural; queenship

Y

Ysbaddaden 40
Yspidinongyl 40
Y Seint Greal 4–6
Ystoria Bown o Hamtwn 123
Ystoria Gereint vab Erbin 4, 19, 38, 59, 153
Yvain (romance) *see Chevalier au lion*